# The Ethics of Capitalism

*An Introduction*

DANIEL HALLIDAY AND JOHN THRASHER

OXFORD
UNIVERSITY PRESS

**OXFORD**
UNIVERSITY PRESS

Oxford University Press is a department of the University of Oxford. It furthers the University's objective of excellence in research, scholarship, and education by publishing worldwide. Oxford is a registered trade mark of Oxford University Press in the UK and certain other countries.

Published in the United States of America by Oxford University Press
198 Madison Avenue, New York, NY 10016, United States of America.



Library of Congress Control Number: 2020936285
ISBN 978-0-19-009621-2 (pbk.)
ISBN 978-0-19-009620-5 (hbk.)

*For Molly and Jessie*

# Contents

# Preface for Students

We offer this book to you as a gateway drug: it'll give you a taste of what's available in scholarship in political economy, and (we hope) make you hungry to consume the "hard stuff," namely the material that your professors might be reluctant to assign. At first glance, much of it looks like hundreds of pages of dry prose. Often enough it's written by old, dead, white guys. If not, it's penned by professional scholars who, though alive and more diverse, write mainly for each other and not for students. How far this book will take you in developing an interest in political economy is, of course, dependent on what kind of person you are. If our book doesn't leave you hooked, then that's fine, so long as it's given you a chance to gain a first-hand acquaintance with the substance we're offering.

When we teach the material covered in this book, we're often approached by students who are unsure of how to approach political economy. On the one hand, there's the philosophy major who's wary of taking a class that's actually about the real world (as in, *real* real world, not just whether the world is real). On the other hand, there are majors from economics and the other empirical social sciences who want to get deeper into the moral significance of what they are studying, but aren't used to reading and writing about philosophical arguments.

Our response is that whatever one's background, we are all more or less in the same boat: virtually nobody has a complete handle on every aspect of political economy. The days of Adam Smith and David Ricardo, when one person could master virtually every aspect of the topic, are largely gone. This fact is one reason that political economy in the sense that we use it here is so exciting; there is still so much work to be done. Even though no one knows everything, most know something, and each perspective can inform the others and vice versa. As Adam Smith noted, it's a mark of humanity that "the most dissimilar geniuses are of use to one another." One of the nice things about studying and teaching political economy is to see this in action.

Here's another more detailed way of putting that last point. If you're old enough to be enrolled at university, then you already have some relevant experience as a participant in the economy. You've quite likely held a job, even if it's "merely" a temporary or casual one that you fit around school or college (and if so, this job probably taught you things about the economy that other jobs don't). You have a sense of how much things cost and how various institutions relevant to the economy actually work (if only educational institutions like schools and colleges). You also probably have some moralized intuitions about how the economy, and its regulation, ought to proceed. At any rate, you almost certainly care about wage inequality, leisure time, the environment, consumerism, and persistent poverty (at home and abroad). All of these are covered in this book, and we've yet to meet a student who's indifferent to all of them. Last but not least, you've probably been told a fair bit by the older generation (politicians, your parents, and so on) about the relative merits of capitalism and socialism. This book is your chance to ask whether what you've been told stands up—though the book will leave you free to make up your own mind.

# Preface for Instructors

This book was conceived in response to a problem that Halliday encountered when first teaching a midlevel class in political economy to undergraduates in Melbourne. There was no shortage of material—plenty of historically significant writings, and an ever-growing supply of article-length publications by current scholars. The difficulty was in finding material in a digestible form for undergraduates coming from a variety of backgrounds. The class went ahead and Halliday assigned both Smith's *Wealth of Nations* and Mill's *Principles of Political Economy* as primary texts (though students weren't asked to read these huge books in their entirety!), along with a selection of contemporary articles. To make things easier, long handouts were produced that guided students through the main points covered in each lecture. In the end, this meant something like ten pages of handouts for each week of the semester. This seemed needlessly inefficient. Better to just develop a textbook that makes the points more effectively than overly long handouts could and go from there. The two of us sat down and worked out how we might move forward, and this book is the eventual result.

We've tried to write this book for teachers in a similar position to that facing Halliday in 2016. In addition, philosophy departments are increasingly being asked to teach classes in political economy (perhaps described more loosely as "political philosophy applied to economics"), often as part of interdisciplinary undergraduate degree programs like PPE. While we think that there are good independent, intellectual reasons to want to teach this material to undergraduates in philosophy and elsewhere, we also recognize that philosophy instructors sometimes find themselves teaching PPE when perhaps they would not have chosen to, or at any rate when their formal training or research experience is not especially well suited to political economy. It is our aim in writing this book to help instructors in this position, as well as instructors for whom PPE is an area of specialization, but where there remains the problem of a mismatch between assignable material and the local expectations or capacities of students in the institution where you teach.

The book is structured so that the whole class can be structured with one chapter for (roughly) each week of the semester.

We are grateful for feedback from anyone (students and instructors) about this book at any time. The internet will give you our current email addresses.

*Supplementary material for the book and aids for instructors are available at* www.EthicsofCapitalism.com

# Acknowledgments

We're jointly grateful to Peter Momtchiloff and Peter Ohlin, both of Oxford University Press, for encouraging the project at the outset, and to Ohlin for handling it as editor through to completion. Thanks are also due to three anonymous readers for Oxford University Press, each of whom provided us with written reports that enabled a number of improvements.

A number of parties have helped us in the course of writing this textbook. Various individuals provided detailed written feedback, email exchanges, and useful conversations based on having read through our manuscript at various points. Here we would like to thank Jonny Anomaly, Jason Brennan, Mark Budolfson, Tom Dougherty, Gaurav Khanna, Keith Hankins, Mark Howard, Holly Lawford-Smith, Tom Mulligan, Martin, O'Neill, Knox Peden, and Chad van Schoelandt.

Especially important were two manuscript workshops on early versions of the book held at the University of Arizona and Georgetown University in September 2018. We would like to thank John Hasnas, Jason Brennan, Peter Jaworski, and the Georgetown Institute for the Study of Markets and Economics (GISME) for organizing and hosting the Georgetown workshop, as well as Tom Mulligan, Justin Tosi, Bill English, and others who commented and attended the workshop. At Arizona, we would like to thank David Schmidtz and the Freedom Center for organizing the workshop and Jerry Gaus, Cathleen Johnson, Mario Villareal-Diaz, and others who commented on the manuscript and participated in the workshop.

Versions of the manuscript were made available to (imposed upon?) several cohorts of undergraduates enrolled in PHIL 20044, "The Ethics of Capitalism," at Melbourne University between 2017 and 2019. We thank the students for their feedback and the various postgraduate tutors who helped: Nick Evans, Alastair James, Kai Tanter, Will Tuckwell, and Kieran McInerney. An unusual opportunity to try some of the material out on high school students came up when Halliday was invited to spend a week at Hale School in Perth, Western Australia, in May 2019, as part of their annual Philosopher in Residence program. Thanks here to Hale's full-time philosophy teaching staff, Dominic Hodnett and Jon Lamotte, and to a very mature and intellectually committed group of year-12 students.

We also want to express separate thanks as individuals. Halliday's work on the textbook was aided by some financial support from the Institute for Humane Studies, specifically the Hayek Fund, to visit California so as to continue collaborating after Thrasher's move from Monash to Chapman University in 2018. Completion of the manuscript was aided by sabbatical leave from Melbourne University in early 2019, most of which was spent as the Plumer Fellow at St Anne's College, Oxford. Halliday would like to thank the college for providing a supportive environment, and especially Umut Baysan, Roger Crisp, and Terry O'Shaughnessy for many conversations relating to the book's substance.

Thrasher did his writing on the manuscript directly before his son was born in June 2017, the patience and support of his wife, Molly, was crucial during this period, as well as when he needed to travel across the Pacific for two manuscript workshops immediately after. John would also like to thank Bill Glod and the Institute for Humane Studies for support over the years. Similarly, Halliday's daughter was born in September 2018, and he'd like to express heartfelt thanks to Jessie, his partner, not least for the extraordinary step of sacrificing an Australian summer for an Oxford winter while research leave and maternity leave overlapped.

# The Ethics of Capitalism

# 1
# Introduction
## What Is This Book about?

In this chapter, we lay out the basic question of this textbook: what do we mean by asking about the "ethics" of capitalism? And what makes this question so important that it gets its own book? We're going to get started by clarifying the intellectual discipline of *political economy*, emphasizing its philosophical and moralized content. This will help us draw your attention to the problem of economic justice. We'll then use this chapter to distinguish capitalism from alternative institutional systems before articulating the key questions about capitalism and justice that we will ask, and the methods we will use to consider various answers to them.

### 1. Everyone Hates Capitalism?

When you type a recognizable word or phrase into an internet search engine, you'll get presented with some extra words that you might use to narrow your search—we call these "autocompletes." Try doing this with the phrase "capitalism is." When we tried, the autocompletes were quite a dramatic bunch. They included "bad," "slavery," "failing," "exploitative," "a pyramid scheme," and even "the root of all evil." What's interesting about these autocompletion results is that they reflect frequent actual searches by human internet users. As such, they provide reasonably good evidence of how a large body of people actually feel about any given search terms. By this admittedly somewhat unscientific measure, capitalism has an image problem.

This is consistent with polling in the United States and elsewhere. In 2016, Harvard University asked 18- to 29-year-olds whether they "supported capitalism." Only 42% said that they did. In a similar poll conducted by YouGov in 2017, millennials in the United States were asked whether they would prefer

*The Ethics of Capitalism*. Daniel Halliday and John Thrasher, Oxford University Press (2020).

DOI: 10.1093/oso/9780190096205.001.0001

to live in a capitalist, socialist, communist, or fascist country—only 42% picked the capitalist option. Compare this to a poll taken in 2002 when 80% of Americans said capitalism is the best system to live under. In Europe and other parts of the world, the numbers are even starker. In France, for instance, only 6% of respondents "strongly" support capitalism, and overall support is only 30%. Capitalism's image around the world has rarely been worse, it seems.

Such an assessment is backed up by other, more localized evidence. If you're reading this book, you're probably a university student, or perhaps a recent graduate. Your campus probably has various groups that present themselves as being in some way opposed to capitalism. On and off university campuses, it's easy to find activist groups and various campaigns that seek to emphasize some sort of failing of capitalism or some injustice associated with it. And there is a good deal of popular writing—books and journalism—that blames various contemporary global problems or injustices on capitalism, in whole or in part. It is much harder to find genuine grassroots activist groups that seek to defend capitalism.

The various "anti-capitalist" groups on campus often stand up for concerns that are genuinely important. In Melbourne, Australia, where we lived when writing this book, student Marxist and socialist groups worked hard to highlight such urgent matters as the mistreatment of migrants in offshore detention facilities that the Australian government has created, but tried to keep hidden from public scrutiny. There are good grounds for regarding such practices as gravely unjust, and we give them some discussion later in this book (chapter 8, on trade and migration). In the past, socialist groups highlighted the injustice of segregation in the United States and apartheid in South Africa. It's good when activist groups draw attention to injustices. But does opposition to apartheid or racial segregation *require* any prior opposition to capitalism? That remains to be seen—indeed Nelson Mandela, perhaps the most famous opponent of apartheid, had relatively positive things to say about capitalism (see chapter 3). More generally, one of the goals of this book is to open up the possibility that highlighting an economic injustice is not the same as highlighting a *capitalist* injustice.

## 2. What Is Capitalism?

We might begin by asking, why is capitalism so widely disliked? But in a way, this is the wrong question. Instead, it is better to ask two other questions:

1. What is it that people actually dislike?
2. What kind of thing is capitalism?

The first question is easier. What people dislike are problems or injustices in the status quo with regard to economic matters and how governments approach them. But the status quo is not straightforwardly identical with capitalism. And it's not obvious that most aspects of the status quo are the way they are *because* of capitalism.

One can say this without even having a theory of what capitalism really is. This is due to the fact that, in most countries at most times, the way of regulating the economy never aligns completely with *any* theoretical view about how such regulation ought to be done. Typically, the status quo is a hodgepodge, whose laws and policies reflect a mixture of capitalist, socialist, and even feudalist elements, shaped not just by legal and economic forces but also by prevailing social norms and other environmental factors. For sure, countries tend to err toward one system rather than another. But very few societies represent a pure instantiation of any theoretical system. There may be *something* that is as bad as (according to the search engines) people think it is. This thing may be representative of major aspects of how society and the economy are currently organized. But that thing may not be capitalism—it could even turn out that capitalism is part of the remedy.

One aspect of the economic status quo that people typically find troubling is the persistence of poverty. Certainly, poverty is bad and results in all sorts of harms and problems. Poverty exists in all societies, rich or poor, including societies that tend toward a capitalist system of organization. The same is true of inequality, oppression, and other factors commonly seen as unjust, or at least bad. What we need to know is whether capitalism or its rivals are better or worse at alleviating poverty and other bad things. This is a *comparative* question. We compare the working of actual capitalist societies with plausible alternatives the best we can using the tools of economics, social science, history, and philosophy. We know at the outset that neither capitalism nor its rivals are perfect; the question is which is likely to be *better* along the dimensions we care about.

The second question is harder. The term "capitalism" was introduced and popularized by its opponents (most notably by Karl Marx), so looking at the actual usage and history of the term is likely to give a one-sided picture. There is a tendency by critics and friends of capitalism alike to identify capitalism with the "free market" or with markets in general and to view government as something that meddles with the free market and gets in its way. When speaking of "economic ills" in 1981, Ronald Reagan famously said that "government is not the solution to our problem; government is the problem."[1] Reagan is known for being among the first politicians to bring such talk into the mainstream, even though capitalism was around for at least a couple of centuries before he started using such slogans.

More important, markets have, to a certain extent, always existed. As we discuss in later chapters, exchange and trade are characteristically human endeavors and we find, albeit limited, trade in our earliest human ancestors. But this leaves room for much nuance as to what markets are good for and what their relationship should be to government and laws.

The idea that a proper defense of capitalism involves the worship of markets and a suspicion of governments is a mistake (one that we'll say more about in chapter 3). As we'll explain in chapter 4, markets aren't the sort of things that straightforwardly become more and more "free" as government "interferes" less. Talk of free markets in the sense of markets without rules may not even make strict sense. The economist Ha-Joon Chang has actually said that "there is no such thing as a free market."[2] Part of Chang's point is that markets don't work without a number of laws and norms that, by definition, restrict the freedom of people and companies. This is absolutely right and is partly why the popular term "free market" is one that we have chosen not to use often in this book. We would encourage you to talk of *market freedoms* instead. After all, it is not really markets that are free or unfree, but participants within them, namely individual people and organizations, like firms, who are in a position to possess (or be denied) the market freedoms (principally of property and contract).

In any case, the relationship between markets, government, and social norms is a complex one. For instance, social scientists have become increasingly interested in the question of trust in market societies. Societies with advanced markets tend to be very trusting societies, but one of the puzzles is whether trust is required to have well-developed market societies or whether well-developed markets generate trust. High-trust societies also tend to have better functioning governments with lower levels of corruption, but again

[1] From his Inaugural Address, that is, the speech Reagan gave upon being sworn in as President of the United States.

[2] Chang (2010). Similar points are made by the philosopher Debra Satz (Satz 2010, chap. 1).

the question of which came first is central. Increasingly, economists and political scientists see markets societies and democracy as arising together from a background set of institutions that create the conditions for openness and inclusivity.[3] Treating the relationship between markets and freedom as all or nothing tends to be a mistake of both the "purest" defenders and opponents of capitalism.

It is better, then, to think of capitalism as a certain approach to *harnessing* and *promoting* markets, in part with the help of government and civil society, not a deference to markets as such. We see market forces at work at all levels of society and throughout history. Even (especially) where trade is banned, for instance in socialist societies or with certain goods (e.g., drugs, sex, guns, etc.), we see market forces emerge in so-called black markets. Often, these markets are where we find the worst injustices and most distasteful practices. Black markets also provide a source for innovations that often get inserted later into the regulation of legal markets. One of the earliest employer pension schemes was pioneered by a successful 18th-century pirate called Bartholomew "Black Bart" Roberts.[4] With modifications, such schemes have become a familiar feature of legitimate labor markets (pirates still exist, too, but we've been unable to establish whether they still offer pension schemes).

Market forces are powerful and virtually impossible to eliminate. We find markets emerging in most intuitively unlikely of places, such as prisons.[5] But market forces at work where they don't belong can be extremely destructive. For instance, markets in political power where politicians sell their votes and services to the highest bidder are not only unjust but also inimical to the function of a market economy that benefits everyone in a capitalist society. Indeed, it is often in places with weak market institutions that political corruption is so prevalent.

Market forces and markets are ubiquitous, and yet the existence and promotion of markets alone are not the "essence" of capitalism. What, then, is? Maybe, we can think of capitalism as being an institutional structure that

[3] See the work of Daron Acemoglu and James Robinson, especially *Why Nations Fail* (2012), as well as the work of Douglass North, John Wallis, and Barry Weingast, especially *Violence and Social Orders* (2009).

[4] Piracy was encouraged by a mercantilist world order; see chapter 8. For a summary of the pirate's code, see https://en.wikipedia.org/wiki/Pirate_code; for an economic analysis of pirate codes and constitutions, see *The Invisible Hook*, by Pete Leeson (2009).

[5] The James Clavell novel (1962) and movie *King Rat* (1965) is a particularly good illustration of the power and importance of trade even in a Japanese prisoner-of-war camp during World War II.

seeks to align markets and market forces in certain ways—namely for mutually beneficial exchange. The philosopher John Rawls wrote that society is a "cooperative venture for mutual exchange."[6] He had much more to say on this, but his description is a pretty good slogan for capitalist society as well.

Perhaps it would be better to talk about "commercial society" rather than capitalism. Indeed, this is how the early political economists like Adam Smith described the society they were beginning to see emerge in their time. The emphasis on commerce is useful, even though we may be stuck with the term "capitalism." Commerce is trade, and capitalism is a system of institutions that creates and stabilizes the conditions of productive and peaceful trade. Capitalism, then, is defining and respecting people's market freedoms with the right set of rules and norms so that mutually productive and peaceful trade can flourish.

In many respects, no two capitalist societies are entirely alike, so there is limited value in generating an exhaustive, philosophically precise definition of capitalism. That said, any definition of capitalism can't be so broad that it includes too many societies that don't seem capitalist, nor so narrow that it excludes many existing societies that seem obviously capitalist. Especially in debates with socialists, there is a tendency to compare existing capitalist societies to idealized socialist societies. Sometimes defenders of capitalism do the opposite and compare "ideal" conceptions of the market, for example, ones in which everyone has complete information and competition is perfect, to existing socialist societies. Both approaches fail to make real progress. For a comparative approach to work, we need to compare apples to apples. While there is value in comparing idealized systems against each other, actual capitalist systems, with all their warts, need to be compared to actual socialist systems and other alternatives.

To do this, though, we need to make sure that any definition of capitalism, however flexible, at least captures most existing societies that are seen as more or less capitalist. One crude way to do this is to use a proxy measure like the Economic Freedom of the World Index, which is produced annually by the Fraser Institute. Their methodology measures size of government, legal system and security of property rights, sound money, freedom to trade internationally, and regulation. In the 2019 report, the top countries on their list were:

1. Hong Kong
2. Singapore

[6] This idea is developed at length in Rawls's *A Theory of Justice* (1999).

3. New Zealand
4. Switzerland
5. United States
6. Ireland
7. United Kingdom
8. Canada
9. Australia
10. Mauritius
11. Malta
12. Georgia

Some countries on the list are perhaps surprising, like Georgia or Mauritius, but maybe this just shows how different reputation can be from reality (note, though, that economic freedom is not all freedom—how a country governs with respect to other types of freedom doesn't directly affect this ranking—and at the time of writing, things are becoming steadily more uncertain as to the future of political freedom in Hong Kong). On the other hand, looking at the countries that are rated for the worst economic freedom largely includes countries not widely regarded as capitalist:[7]

150. Chad
151. Central African Rep.
152. Ginnea-Bissau
153. Iraq
154. Congo, Rep. of
155. Egypt
156. Syria
157. Congo, Dem. Rep. of
158. Angola
159. Algeria
160. Sudan
161. Libya
162. Venezuela

[7] It is worth noting that North Korea was not rated because basic data about the regime are unavailable. If rated, it would surely be number 163 on the list. Other countries not rated were Iraq, Afghanistan, Belarus, Sudan, Turkmenistan, Somalia, and Uzbekistan.

A country's economic freedom score is highly correlated with its per capita income.[8] Countries that are unfree, like Venezuela, have very low per capita incomes, while countries that are very free, like Hong Kong or Canada, have very high per capita incomes. The ranking on the list also correlates well with where people around the world are trying to enter as immigrants and from where they are trying to escape.

This gives us one way of arriving at an approximate and preliminary definition of capitalism. Although we will expand on this somewhat, we should think of capitalist societies as those that rank highly on most of the measures that the Economic Freedom of the World Index highlights. In particular, capitalist societies will have:

A. Strong legal protections for private property
B. Wide dispersion of private property across their population
C. Extensive international trade
D. Consumer sovereignty (including competition in the provision of goods and services)
E. Diversity of employment contracts

Existing capitalist countries will have these features to greater or lesser degrees, but without at least meeting these (admittedly broad) conditions, it is unlikely that we would consider the society in question capitalist.

The first two conditions are important since private property ownership and the rights protecting private property are necessary for trade. By "private property" we mean a wide range of things—basically, anything that is typically bought and sold. Of course, there are important ethical and philosophical questions about exactly what should count as property, and whether all property should be fully tradable—you own your body, surely, but can you sell (or rent) it? These are questions that we take up in chapter 12 but that we leave aside for now. It is also important that basically anyone can, and most people do, own private property of some sort. It is also difficult to imagine a capitalist society that doesn't permit extensive international trade, though most nations have some protections for domestic industry, often by way of taxes (tariffs) on imports.

[8] Per capita income is a measure of gross domestic product (GDP) adjusted for purchasing power parity (PPP). Basically, it is a measure of how much the average person can afford to buy in their society corrected for differences between currency and quality. Despite some problems, this is the best measure of how rich a society is and a defensible proxy for the level of general welfare in the society.

Consumer sovereignty means, in this context, that decisions about who produces what and to what extent are primarily driven by consumer demand. What Robert Nozick called "capitalist acts between consenting adults" tend to be neither forced nor blocked in capitalist societies.[9] If consumers really demand a good, the market will deliver it. If they don't want it, no one is forced to produce it. At the same time, nobody is prevented from being able to produce something new if they think consumers might be willing to pay for it. Similarly, a producer who has enjoyed some period of time being able to sell some good or service should not be able to suppress the activities of anyone seeking to compete with them. There are some special cases here, including what are called "public goods," but we talk about those in more detail in later chapters.

The final point is about labor and employment contracts. In capitalist societies, there are many types of labor contracts. Questions about whom to hire, for how long, and at what price are determined largely by the labor market and not by the state or other entity. Although "at-will" employment, whereby an employer can fire a worker for any reason, may seem to be the most "capitalist" form of labor contract, it might not be the most appropriate in every industry or for every employer and, hence, it is likely that there will be other types of labor contracts. It is here, perhaps, that we see the most variety in and between different capitalist societies.

## 3. What Are the Alternatives to Capitalism?

Given the definition of capitalism that we defended in the last section, it is worth asking what the possible alternatives to capitalism are. For simplicity, we can think of two different competitors. The first is the political economic system that existed throughout the world in one form or another before the rise of capitalism and still exists in a number of places. We call it *feudalism*. If you have any intuitive sense of feudalism, you probably associate it with conditions in medieval Europe or in the various fictional worlds resembling it, like *Game of Thrones*.

In these societies, there existed peasants and their lords and not much in between. More generally, feudalism is really any hierarchical political

[9] Robert Nozick offers a view of the market based on strong rights to noninterference and property in his *Anarchy, State, and Utopia* (1974).

and economic system that restricts property ownership, employment, and trade significantly in the service of maintaining explicit legal and social distinctions of rank. Rank or status in feudalism is usually conferred through hereditary succession. Protection for property may not be a right in the traditional sense at all, but rather a privilege that depends on the continued goodwill of the reigning authority, who is likely to demand loyalty and sacrifice in return. Feudal societies tended to maintain their structure through very violent means of enforcement, which is perhaps why they make for popular television adaptations.

In addition, private personal property may be widely owned in a feudal society, but productive property and financial assets will be controlled by a small elite. Property of the *productive* sort is much more widely dispersed in capitalist societies. Currently, around two out of three Americans own stocks in publicly traded companies. Of course, this doesn't mean that they directly control the companies, and their investments are very often indirect, for example, via a pension scheme. But nevertheless these Americans have (or will come to have) a source of income through ownership of capital (i.e., productive property), rather than just the sale of their labor. Perhaps more surprising is the fact that in 2017, there were 28 million small businesses in the United States that were individually owned, most with only one or two employees. Approximately 120 million Americans are employed by small businesses—that's a group of people six times the size of Australia or twice the size of the United Kingdom. In hierarchical societies, however, trade, both internal and external, tends to be severely restricted. In feudal societies of the past, for instance, sumptuary codes regulated who could wear what kind of clothes in public. Consumer sovereignty in general is not a major force in feudal or hierarchical societies.

The most important distinction, however, between capitalist and feudal societies concerns employment. Employment in feudal societies is typically not contractual and tends to be based heavily on one's status within the society. At the extreme, there is slavery, or serfdom, where workers are tied to the land and may not move or change jobs (which is almost slavery). In capitalist societies, workers may often have limited options as to what work is available, but they can always, in principle, move somewhere else or attempt to acquire additional skills. Feudal societies block these options to one degree or another.[10]

[10] Feudalism in this, general, sense is the most common way to organize states in human history, a specification of Douglass North, John Wallis, and Barry Weingast (2009) call the "Natural State."

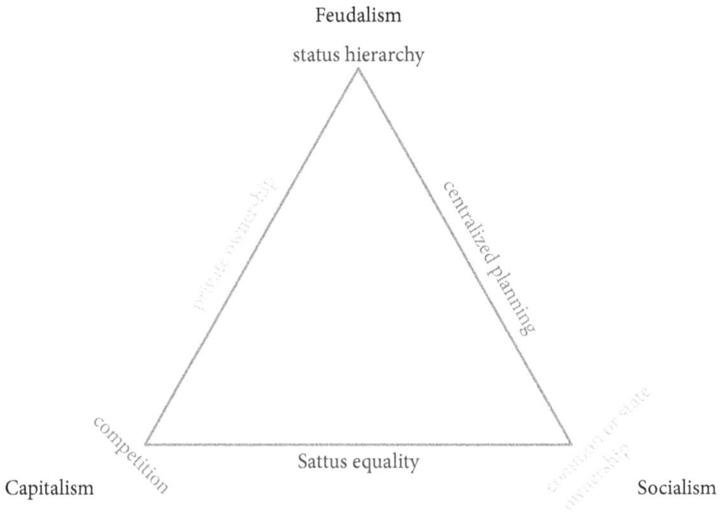


**Figure 1.1** Political Economy Triangle

Perhaps the most important thing to say about feudalism is that it still exists. It is not merely the stuff of history and fictional TV shows. Some current societies, like North Korea and Saudi Arabia, approximate feudalism far more closely than either capitalism or socialism. This may sound like a strange claim, particularly as North Korea brands itself as communist and the Gulf States have quite sophisticated infrastructure. But were it not for nonfeudal societies from which these countries can import certain goods and expertise, they might resemble medieval Europe much more closely than they in fact do. Apart from that, Saudi Arabia and North Korea are very much alike in that much of the workforce suffers conditions of near slavery, while the few who enjoy power, status, and wealth have had it conferred on them via hereditary privilege (the Kim dynasty in North Korea is really a hereditary monarchy not unlike the Saudi royal family).

So how should we distinguish these different economic systems? Figure 1.1 represents a way of "mapping logical space," that is, getting a sense of how different economic systems relate to each other, for the purposes of doing political economy. The shaded descriptions identify mutually opposing concepts, helping us jointly distinguish two systems from one of the others. For instance, a planned economy, with strict rules about who can't or must perform what sort of work, is a shared feature of feudalism and socialism, contrasting both with capitalism, in which production and distribution rely primarily on competition and markets where consumers, rather than producers or planners, reign.

The triangle does two things for us. First, it helps define in a more comparative way what we mean by "capitalism" and what we mean by "socialism" and "feudalism." As we have said, in this book we define "pure" capitalism as the economic arrangement in which power is decentralized, property is widespread, and employment options are diverse. What this means is that nobody has any exclusive or protected ownership or control of "the means of production" (to use the old-fashioned term), and people generally have economic freedoms in the ways necessary to facilitate competition among them and the companies that might employ them (companies are typically legal "persons," in that they can own property and participate in contracts). This is, in fact, a fairly orthodox definition of capitalism, at least by contemporary standards in the political economy literature, and it fits with what we said in the opening sections.[11] Our emphasis is not on persuading you to accept any sort of unorthodox definition, but just to get a sense of how the definition of capitalism doesn't just serve to distinguish it from socialism but—just as important—from feudalism as well.

Second, the triangle helps us map the *range* of possibilities when it comes to the organization of an economic system. This enables us to identify both where we are and where we might aim to go. It does this while allowing for the important fact that conformity to any political economic system is a matter of degree. As we've said, real-world economies typically embody some combination of capitalist, feudalist, and socialist elements: they occupy some "point" inside the triangle rather than sit tightly into any of the corners. The ultimate question of economic justice—the question of which sort of economy is most just—approximates the question of which point within this space an economy ought to be. This may not be one of the corners either, though it may be much closer to one corner than to the others. There will be some point within the triangle (or perhaps several points, or a "zone") that represents which combination of the economic systems is the one that is the "best" given some conception of economic justice. Identifying where this point lies is the *moral*, philosophical objective of political economy. And this book is about trying to help *you* do that, by familiarizing you with

[11] Our definition is very similar to that used by Samuel Freeman (2001) and James Otteson (2014, 12).

the questions you need to grapple with, as well as with some of the answers defended so far by others.

The labels attached to the triangle's side might refer to slightly different things, depending on how close we are to the corners. For example, "planning" in a feudal economy will differ from planning in a socialist economy. Feudal planning involves coercion of the working masses to serve an elite. Socialist planning will also involve coercion, but the planning can take many different forms. The state will make decisions as to which industries and jobs should exist, but workers may (or may not) have quite extensive freedom to choose which job suits them and work in industries that are designed to serve everyone. Capitalism is an opposite to both of these systems at the same time, just because planning of either sort is largely absent.

Socialism makes plenty of room for things not usually found in feudal societies, like paid holiday, and free education and healthcare. In this way, socialism can aim at status equality, perhaps of a sort different from whatever status equality is achievable in capitalism. In contrast, feudalism was very much built on status *inequality*. As we've said, only a privileged few could own substantial property in land, which inheritance prevented from dispersing around the population. Women typically couldn't own substantial property of any sort, and most feudal societies contained some form of slavery. In this way, though the status equality associated with capitalism and socialism is not the same, there is a strong sense in which they are both opposite to the hierarchy of feudalism.

Similarly, "private ownership" in a feudal society may simply mean that the means of production are owned by private individuals. In capitalism, private ownership involves a wide dispersion of property rights, and certain requirements about how easy it is to exercise these rights along with other economic rights, like freedom of contract. Though these systems of private ownership differ from each other, they are both very different to the state ownership associated with socialism.

There are, frankly, no good arguments for feudalism, or at least not arguments that are seriously seeking to show that feudalism promotes justice. The point of having that triangle we showed you earlier is not to take feudalism seriously as an alternative for where we should *go*, but as an alternative when thinking about where we might *currently be*. This makes it easier to identify unjust economic arrangements as something other than versions of capitalism or socialism. As we'll argue in chapter 3, a number of status quo injustices are not accurately blamed on capitalism but may be remnants or resurgences of feudalism.

Remember, though, that graphic illustrations like the one earlier are just *heuristics*: they are simplifications to help get us get started and to avoid some mistakes early on. A picture of a triangle with some labels is hardly a complete theory or methodology. You're entitled to think for yourselves about how to expand on definitions of the various economic systems, and of the relations between them. Just don't think of capitalism and socialism as binary, absolute alternatives that exhaust the set of possibilities on offer. In particular, if you perceive some aspect of the status quo that you think might be unjust, consider whether it might be an aspect of capitalism, socialism, or a leftover influence of feudalism. It could, in principle, be any of these three things, even if the system overall tends toward another one of the three extremes. Unfortunately, popular discourse often oversimplifies, particularly with the use of labels like "left wing" and "right wing," which promote precisely the sort of one-dimensional picture of logical space that the triangle helps us avoid.

And please remember another thing: though this book will evaluate capitalism in ways that start by looking at the thoroughly *moral* arguments first given in its favor, we will not try to persuade you of the right answer. That is not what this book is for. Instead, to repeat, it is to *help* you think of what makes a better or worse political/economic system—where in the triangle we should aim at.

## 4. The "Ethics of Capitalism": An Oxymoron?

We have said that it's hard, nowadays, to find *heartfelt* support for capitalism. But it is relatively easy to find a reluctant, perhaps begrudging, endorsement of what passes for capitalist ways of running contemporary societies. Thus, it is sometimes said that socialism is a utopian but unrealistic body of ideas—one that simply assumes that people would be willing to work hard for the common good. Socialist theories, it is often said, simply go about describing how nice things would be if this were so.

Of course, the begrudging defense of capitalism goes, such optimistic assumptions about human nature are false. The reality is that humans are selfish creatures, who seek to advance their own good over that of society, perhaps only seeking to help close family and a few friends. To get people to be productive in ways that benefit everyone, we need to set up society with the right incentives. This inevitably results in things like economic inequality, high levels of consumption, and pretty harsh enforcement of laws that protect private property. This state of affairs may be less desirable than a socialist utopia, but it's the best we can hope for. After all, feudalism as a third alternative is horrible.

Those who advance such an argument see it as an *effective* defense of capitalism—and it may be—but it's not typically sold as an *ethical* defense. On this approach, capitalism simply has no "ethics," in terms of having moral foundations. Instead, it's a sort of remedial way of organizing the economy, one that tries to save us from ourselves and from each other, without aspiring to any higher moral goal or justification. On this view, capitalism is, at best, second best. Socialism may have moral foundations, but it's utopian—capitalism, on the other hand, is *realistic*.[12] Or so this defense goes.

Once upon a time, things were different. The philosophical defense of capitalism was once a good deal more aspirational than the reluctant defense often voiced today. Capitalism was not seen as the best of a bad bunch of options. Instead, it was seen as a force for justice as well as prosperity. As we've said, the word *capitalism* did not enter widespread usage until late in the 19th century. Its early proponents talked of "commercial society," or "the system of private property." But capitalism, properly understood, was very much what they had in mind. A capitalist economy, they argued, was one that would see less material poverty, less domination of workers by bosses, increased leisure time, more peace and less war between countries, reduced levels of arbitrary privilege, greater potential for the spread of education, democracy, and other values associated with a rise of the middle class, and the erosion of a society dominated by a wealthy and largely hereditary political elite. Moreover, these early thinkers were right—capitalism did lead (eventually) to less poverty, domination, peace, freedom, education, the erosion of privilege, and democracy. All of these things seem not only like material advances but also *moral* advances.

Starting in the 18th century, most notably in Adam Smith's *The Wealth of Nations* (1776), various philosophical accounts emerged of how capitalism

[12] You can find slightly longer summaries of what we're calling the "reluctant" defense of capitalism, and how it contrasts with the supposedly more moralistic case for socialism, elsewhere. See Jason Brennan (2014) and James Otteson (2014).

could achieve all or nearly all of these things.[13] Now, the 18th century was a long time ago. It's fair to say that the current status quo was not what the early standard bearers of capitalism were hoping for. But many contemporary economic injustices are actually quite old, too. The world's most economically developed countries all exhibit some combination of overly expensive housing, inherited wealth on a large scale (but concentrated into a small portion of the population), government willingness to use taxpayers' money to pay for failures in financial industries, some degree of material poverty alongside great wealth, failure to grant workers freedom of movement, massive corporations that sometimes dominate their employees and exercise disproportionate political influence, and draconian punishments that the state imposes on private citizens for buying and selling certain things.

There is reasonable disagreement about how bad these problems have become and what ought to be done about them. But it's worth noting that all, or nearly all, of these injustices were running riot at the time when capitalism was a new idea. Capitalism was supposed to fix these problems, not make them more entrenched. A popular answer is that these trends are all various symptoms of the way in which capitalism is unjust. Another view, one worth taking seriously, is that they mark ways in which capitalism has remained absent, or represent consequences that could be made to disappear without rejecting capitalism altogether.

In short, here's the "hook" for this book: if we want to figure out whether capitalism is just or unjust, we can start by asking why people were inclined to defend it (on thoroughly moral grounds) in the first place. And once we've identified the essence of the moral foundations for capitalism, we can ask whether capitalism's supporters would have been happy with how things have turned out since. The short answer (we think) is that, in large part, those who saw capitalism as a route to a more just society would have been pretty disappointed with many aspects of the status quo in the 21st century. In short, a theory of *why* capitalism is a force for good will allow us to come to a more sophisticated perspective on what's wrong with the economic aspects of contemporary society and what ought to be done about them.

[13] Throughout we use the Liberty Fund editions of Adam Smith with the *Wealth of Nations* (Smith 1982) abbreviated as WN and *Theory of Moral Sentiments* (Smith 1976) as TMS.

This task is what will occupy us over the twelve chapters in this book. We'll begin with a brief history of how the moralized evaluation of economic systems got going. This will give a sense of how the philosophical defense of capitalism emerged and also of why it has become somewhat suppressed by the way in which the study of economic matters has become distanced from the study of morality and justice.

## Conclusions

*This chapter has shown that the foundations of a capitalist system are moral foundations. It has also shown that defending capitalism is not the same thing as defending the economic status quo. Instead, working out how to identify conditions of economic justice is very much about comparing against not one but two alternatives, which we've identified as socialism and feudalism. In reality, the distinction between capitalism is neither binary nor absolute—it is more accurate to think of economic justice as a "region" of the logical space that lies between extremes of very pure (perhaps unattainable) extremes of these three systems. The task of providing moral foundations for capitalism lies in arguing that economic justice is closer to the capitalist extreme than the other two, noting that this leaves much room for alternative ways of refining a capitalist economic system.*

## Study Questions

- How often do you find yourself arguing with people, or being presented with arguments, that treat the current economic status quo and capitalism as the *same thing*? How much do you think this has influenced the way you think about economic justice?
- Can you think of an aspect of your country's status quo that resembles feudalism, even if it is not typically represented as such?
- We've suggested that people often treat socialism as utopian and idealistic while seeing capitalism as more realistic and concessive to "facts" about human nature. Do you think it's especially difficulty to be both

realistic and morally aspirational? And do you think it's harder for capitalism to be both of these things than socialism?

- How distinctive is economic justice from other sorts of justice? For example, do you think that a society exhibiting injustice along (say) racial or religious lines is more likely to exhibit economic injustice? Why would you think this?

# 2

# Capitalism Seemed Like a Good Idea at the Time

## The Rise and Fall (and Resurrection?) of Political Economy

In this chapter, we will give you a sense of how political economy is an attempt to unify what are now recognized as the distinct disciplines of economics and political philosophy. We will do this largely by giving you a historical narrative, one that details the rise of political economy and the authors behind it, such as Adam Smith and John Stuart Mill, before providing some reasons for its decline in the 20th century as academia underwent increased specialization and fragmentation. This will provide some background for appreciating the comeback that political economy is now enjoying, as another golden age is perhaps approaching.

### 1. 1770–1868: The "Golden Age" of Political Economy

Economics and political philosophy are different academic disciplines. They're taught in different parts of the university, by different people with different training, and students don't always get the chance to study both. Research in these disciplines is also siloed, perhaps even more than teaching. With some exceptions, philosophers and economists steer clear of each other and don't really speak the same language. To a large extent, economists distance themselves from questions about morality and justice and identify as scientists. They see themselves as developing theories that can explain the causes of economic phenomena. Their goal is to *predict* the workings of the economy, not evaluate whether it's just or unjust. On the whole, philosophers

*The Ethics of Capitalism*. Daniel Halliday and John Thrasher, Oxford University Press (2020).

DOI: 10.1093/oso/9780190096205.001.0001

generally do the opposite—they develop ideas about what *ought* to be the case and make little professional effort to predict anything or understand its causes.

Although the division between "economics" and "philosophy" is real, it is a rather recent development that only fully took hold in the 20th century. While there are some reasons behind it, it's basically an artificial distinction—one that's emerged thanks to the sociological forces driving academia, rather than anything particularly intellectual, or essential to the subject matter of studying the economy (see section 4).

The discipline of economics is a descendant of the more inclusive and comprehensive academic discipline that we first spoke of in the last chapter, known as *political economy*. This discipline gained momentum and prominence in Western Europe in the mid-18th century. This is where the bulk of our narrative starts. Political economy seeks to combine the study of morality and justice (where economic matters are concerned) with sensitivity to facts about economic causation and feasibility. While it contains strong elements of what would now be recognized as economics and political philosophy, there are also elements of what would now be regarded as sociology, political science, and legal theory.

The 18th century witnessed the beginnings of a revolution in the study of political economy—what we're calling its "golden age," We do not mean to say that no one engaged in economic thinking before the dawn of this age, however. Economic exchange and cooperation are central parts of human life and always have been. Despite this, early social and economic life was, until very recently, characterized more by conflict and scarcity than by cooperation. It should be no surprise, then, that most of the early attempts at political economy were motivated by political questions of security and, hence, tended to focus on the dangers rather than the benefits of trade.

In Plato's *Republic*, written in early 4th-century BCE Athens, Socrates describes the city based on commerce and trade as a "city of pigs." He argues that increased economic activity—especially trade with foreigners—will inevitably lead to conflict and war. It is possible that Plato adapted this view of commerce from the notoriously xenophobic and anti-trade Spartans, who used iron for their coins instead of gold to reduce the attraction of wealth accumulation. Spartans were meant to spend their time preparing for war and other supposedly more noble activities instead of trade.

Aristotle (384–322 BCE), though worldlier than his teacher in many ways, did not differ from this essentially zero-sum view of economic exchange.[1] It is in his teachings that we find the origin of the idea of the "just price" that was so influential in the Middle Ages as filtered through the work of Thomas Aquinas (1225–1274). The basic idea is intuitive enough: the price of goods should not exceed their value. To charge more than a good is worth is to swindle and exploit the buyer. This idea is still with us in common-sense notions of exploitation and "price gouging" but is open to the objection that it relies on a mistake about value—an objection that took until the 19th century to work out fully.

The just price is premised on the idea that goods have objective and relatively fixed values. This value may be the result of the cost of production of the good or the value of its ultimate use. The key point is that the value of a good is, on this view, independent of how much someone values it. The medieval view of just price held that economic *value* and economic *valuing* are distinct: something's price might or might not reflect the actual value of the good. This disconnect between value and price led to serious puzzles in economic thought. One that appears again and again is the "diamond-water paradox." The puzzle is how water, which is necessary for survival and, hence, of very high value, cannot command as high of a price as diamonds, which are a mere frippery. This problem led Adam Smith (1723–1790) to later divide value into two types: *value in use* and *value in exchange*. Water, he claimed, was valuable in its use, while diamonds were valuable in exchange. Smith presents the puzzle thus:

> The things which have the greatest value in use have frequently little or no value in exchange; and on the contrary, those which have the greatest value in exchange have frequently little or no value in use. Nothing is more useful than water: but it will purchase scarce any thing; scarce any thing can be had in exchange for it. A diamond, on the contrary, has scarce any value in use; but a very great quantity of other goods may frequently be had in exchange for it. (WN I.4.13)

[1] "Zero-sum" means that for someone to gain from an exchange or encounter, someone else has to lose. Many competitive games like football or poker are zero-sum. Market exchanges are typically positive sum—both parties are able to benefit (but see chapter 9).

One popular solution to this problem was to think that value in use could only really arise from labor: things become more valuable as we add our labor to them. Raw lumber has some value, but if that lumber is shaped into a beautiful and useful chair through hours of work, it is reasonable to think that the chair is now worth more than the lumber precisely because of the work that went into it. This idea developed, during the 17th and 18th centuries, into what became called the "labor theory of value." It was endorsed by all the great political economists of the golden age of political economy until the "marginal revolution" of the late 19th century.

Although the labor theory of value is false (we'll explain in chapters 5 and 6), it was nevertheless a dramatic improvement over any alternative around at the time. The most influential competitor to the labor theory was mercantilism. You might have read *The Hobbit* (1937) by J. R. R. Tolkein or seen the film adaptation. If so, you already have a good sense of mercantilism thanks to the character Smaug the dragon. Smaug had one ambition in life, namely to accumulate gold. He was willing to kill any number of humans (elves, dwarves, etc.) in order to acquire it, and contented himself by sleeping on a big pile of the stuff, having no other use for it.

Real-world mercantilism represents more or less this outlook, as a view about national prosperity. The chief theorist of the mercantilists, Thomas Mun (1571–1641), argued that the key to enriching the nation is to focus the domestic economy for export. The basic idea was that trade can either bring in finished goods or currency. Finished goods can, for the most part, be made domestically, so there is no point in importing them. Further, ships bearing imports will return to their home nations with valuable currency that should be kept at home. The secret to increasing the currency at home, then, is to focus on producing exports and to hoard gold at home. Trade, on this view, is a basically zero-sum interaction. One "wins" at trade by having more exports than imports. Mimicking Smaug, a nation's ambition should be to find ways to get gold off other nations and then hang on to it. The mercantilists argued that economic value came from holding hard currency like gold or, more precisely, value came from a positive balance of trade in the manner just described.

From the point of view of the nation as a whole, this idea is ludicrous. After all, finished goods can be used or consumed, but bars of gold cannot. But, from the point of view of a state constantly expecting war, having substantial liquid currency available to finance warfare, while simultaneously depleting your potential enemies of their currency, is a plausible strategy. Mercantilism was, therefore, an economic theory of the state for the purpose of warfare. Smaug, who could breathe fire and fight his own battles without raising an army, is the purer mercantilist, since he really did love gold for its own sake. In the history of the real world, mercantilism suited self-aggrandizing monarchs who were paranoid about foreign invasion. The dominance of mercantilism may also be explained, however, by its intuitiveness. Although we are not quite as obsessed with gold as were the Spanish imperialists in the preindustrial era, there is still a concern about exporting more than we import. We still see this kind of thinking in modern political economy from time to time, sometimes under the name of "economic nationalism." We'll come back to this in chapter 8.

Adam Smith largely wrote *The Wealth of Nations* as an extended demolition of every mercantilist argument. Smith showed persuasively that when economies focus on more efficient production through the division of labor and trade, they will become substantially richer than their gold-hoarding, export-obsessed mercantilist counterparts. This argument spoke to the interests of the rulers as well as to the average person. By doing so, Smith turned the focus of political economy away from the public finance of monarchs to the question of how to improve the welfare of the average person in society. To this day, economic doctrines are judged by how they will affect the average man and woman. The entire science of economics is, then, largely built on this important and unstated moral premise introduced by Smith.

It is hard to overestimate the importance of the shift in the focus of political economy that occurred as a result of Smith's work. Economic ideas and policy were now expected to improve the status of the commonwealth as a whole, rather than just the rulers or the upper classes. The great "classical" economists that followed Smith were all dedicated political and social reformers, and these reforms were largely backed by their economic theories. David Ricardo (1772–1823), for instance, developed a powerful defense of free trade, while also showing how the existing land ownership system in Britain was both inefficient and unjust because it allowed landowners to reap benefits off their land without contributing value to the rest of society. Thomas Malthus (1766–1834) was an ardent, though perhaps misguided, advocate in favor of changing the English poor laws, which basically imprisoned the poor in workhouses when they could no longer support themselves independently.

The culmination, both theoretically and socially, of this movement during the "classical" era of political economy is found in the work of John Stuart Mill (1806–1873). Mill's utilitarianism fully develops the transition that began with Smith that the average person is the source of moral interest into a full-fledged moral theory. His *On Liberty* (1859) defends the fundamental aspects of a free society that are both the result of and the necessary preconditions for a free economy. His work on women's rights and contraception (with his eventual wife Harriet Taylor) were in line with the expanding egalitarian social change that economic change wrought.

Mill's much longer *Principles of Political Economy* (1848) was another great work of this era of political economy.[2] In it, Mill took all the insight of the political economists who had come before him and drew new implications from their theories. Many of Mill's innovations involve subtle applications of his utilitarianism to economic theory. He argues that inherited wealth, excessive rents to landlords, and certain methods of production cannot be fully justified if they do not really contribute to the economic life of the society as a whole. His most important and influential idea, however, was that the economic science of production can—at least in principle—be distinguished from decisions of distribution. In the 20th century, this separation of production and distribution would go far beyond what Mill described, often with dire consequences.

The golden age of political economy wasn't only about defending capitalism against mercantilism and feudalism, however. Far from it, in fact. The other stalwart of this era, and perhaps still the best known, was Karl Marx (1818–1883). Marx didn't like capitalism. Unlike Smith and Mill, who were both to some degree optimists, Marx was a staunch pessimist. He accepted that capitalism was an inevitable stage in the development of society, but he argued it was not the final stage. Though better than feudalism, Marx argued that capitalism would give way to a more desirable and harmonious phase of human existence—communism (see chapter 5).

Marx is in some ways hard to work with. This is not to degrade his contribution one bit, but rather to say something about his style of writing and how it contrasts with his peers from the golden age. Though he certainly developed philosophical ideas, at times Marx explicitly denounced philosophy as a distraction. For instance, he argued that there is no point explaining why

[2] It was reissued several times—we'll be quoting from the seventh and final edition, which appeared in 1871.

capitalism is unjust since it is doomed anyway. Questions of justice or welfare were, for Marx and Marxists, simply fetishes or "bourgeois" moralism. This contrasts with other political economists, who either strongly identified as philosophers or had nothing against doing it. Marx was unlike Smith in another way, in that he often (though not always) wrote in the mode of an activist. This often gave his work a somewhat fiery rhetorical character. Much of his writing, aside from the three volumes of *Das Kapital*, involves attacks on now obscure rival socialists or theorists. This appeals to some readers and irritates others.

Special care is required when reconstructing and representing Marx's views. Fiery writers often attract fiery followers. As professional philosophers, we regularly attend conferences where professionals like us gather to present ideas to each other. Anecdotally, we can report that whenever someone gives a talk about Marx, very likely someone in the audience will accuse the speaker of having totally misunderstood what Marx is about. Conferences that we attend frequently contain talks about Smith, Mill, and others. The audiences in these talks usually remain fairly calm, even though there is disagreement about how best to reconstruct the ideas of these other philosophers, too. Marx wasn't the only activist, either: John Stuart Mill was certainly politically *active*—he distributed pamphlets arguing for contraception while still a teenager, which got him arrested. He later spent time as a member of parliament. All in all, Mill was a counterexample to Marx's famous slogan that "philosophers have only interpreted the world . . . the point is to change it." That being said, Mill's work has a very consistent scholarly tone, even when written for a more popular audience. It is perhaps not a coincidence that Mill was reportedly quite dull as a public speaker.

For Marx, capitalism could never deliver economic justice. It had exploitation, class struggle, and oppression baked into its very core. Injustice is the essence of capitalism, like sweat is the essence of exercise, pouring out of us until we finally come to our senses and bring on a revolution.[3]

Marx continues to be a source of misgivings about capitalism, though his ideas need to be modified if we're to make the most of their applicability to contemporary questions about economic justice. Marxist ideas remain powerful, and we'll make much use of them in what follows. Marx will be left out of the early chapters, but only because these chapters aim to lay out the arguments that led some people to endorse capitalism and Marx was not one

[3] That's our attempt at Marx-style rhetoric. We're not great at it, but you get the idea.

of these people. The specter of Marx will return to haunt later chapters, particularly those on inequality, labor markets, and exploitation.

Smith, Marx, and Mill are the superstars from the golden age who play the leading roles in this book. There's a good reason for this: these three members of the golden age were most preoccupied with the *ethics* of capitalism: they studied political economy in ways that were particularly attentive to questions of social justice with respect to the core elements of economic life, such as wages, taxation, economic inequality, workers' conditions, and so on. Other writers from the golden age sought to study the economy in a less moralized way. Partly because of this, their works were often shorter, and sometimes more technical. Ricardo is something of a co-star, as he had important things to say specifically about the rise of machines and the nature of what has since become called globalization. Malthus and some others (such as Thomas Paine and the Utopian Socialists) will also make cameos.

## 2. The "Fragmented Age:" Economics and Political Philosophy in the 20th Century

The golden age ended as a casualty of hyperspecialization in academia. Over the years since Mill died in 1873, it became steadily harder to be good at political economy and comparatively easier to attain narrower academic expertise. So people stopped trying to do political economy and started doing economics or philosophy instead. In the 20th century, economics increasingly used sophisticated mathematical tools and addressed more specialized questions than those addressed in the golden age.

The fragmentation of economics also coincided with an important split in the study of economics between "micro" and "macro" economics. Macroeconomic is that study of the economies of nations and the world as a whole. Do high tax rates reduce growth? Is free trade good for the poor? What causes inflation? All of these are questions of macroeconomics. When noneconomists think of "economics," macroeconomics is typically what they think of.

Microeconomics, on the other hand, is the study of how individuals and firms (and any other "rational" chooser) make choices in relation to prices and scarcity. That may sound pretty abstract and that is because it is. Microeconomics is fundamentally the study of rational choice that relies on considerable abstraction. An important axiom of microeconomics, for instance, is the "Law of Demand," which states that "all things being equal" individuals will tend to consume more of a good as the price decreases. Once you know what "consume," "price," and "rationality" mean to the economist, the law of demand follows logically. In this sense, the trend in microeconomics since the early 20th century has been to understand microeconomics as the study of rational maximization under constraints or, increasingly, as strategic choice.

The paradox, in economics, is that while microeconomics has a rock-solid logical and mathematical foundation (notwithstanding some important philosophical questions), macroeconomics has no such foundation in microeconomics. Perhaps even more troubling, while basically all academic economists agree on the central tenets of microeconomics, though often disagreeing about many of the implications, there is considerable disagreement about pretty much every aspect of macroeconomics.

Depressions and recessions hobble economies, cause substantial misery, and promote political upheaval. It is no surprise then that a central question of macroeconomics would be why and how depressions and recessions occur and what might prevent or mitigate them. Despite the wealth of attention paid to this question, however, there is no generally accepted theory of the business cycle (what economists also call the cycle of boom and bust). Some believe that the problem is related to excess supply in the economy or overproduction. Others believe that booms and busts are a result of the money supply expanding or contracting in unpredictable ways. Still others believe that it has to do with lags in the structure of production and the way that capital is allocated in the economy. All of these ideas are internally coherent, and all match the data in some cases but not all. Given that public policy depends on the truth of one of these views (or others), it is an important question which is right. Although there is no shortage of defenders of each of these views, it is telling that unlike, say, the theory of evolution or even microeconomics, there is no general agreement between experts on this and many more crucially important questions.

The split between micro and macroeconomics illustrates an important point about the fragmentation of economic thought in the 20th century. As economics has focused on rigor and certainty in the realm of microeconomics, many of the more moralized questions that animated political economists of the golden age were ignored or sidelined.

Along with the fragmentation of economics into specialized subfields with less emphasis on the big questions of political economy, philosophy took a similar turn. Political philosophy in the 20th century was largely about the abstract analysis of political concepts, like freedom, equality, and fairness. But there was a definite shift away from the concrete economic phenomena and policies to which these concepts have application, like unemployment, contracts, taxation, and so on. This is not to say that abstract political philosophy can't inform work in political economy, only that extra effort is needed to make it do so.

We would venture that the fragmentation of political economy may not have happened for good intellectual reasons. There are two things we can say about (academic) working conditions in the golden age that do not apply to the 20th century and beyond. The first is quite obvious; the stock of relevant academic knowledge was smaller during the times of Smith, Marx, and Mill. To put it crudely, they didn't have to read as much stuff and know as many different mathematical and statistical techniques to gain competency in their fields. This is not to say they were lazy or didn't consume much material—John Stuart Mill had an incredibly rich life strictly in terms of the material he absorbed, so much so that he missed out on a proper childhood. But it's fair to say that the fragmentation of academic disciplines is partly a consequence of making an academic career more manageable, in terms of how much expertise one is supposed to possess in order to be in a position to write anything on top of it.

A second factor, though related, is less obvious. Academic employment since the late 20th century isn't what it once was. Broadly speaking, academics are expected to demonstrate expertise in the discipline they've chosen to locate themselves. We don't think we'll offend any of our peers if we point out that the easiest way to become an expert in one's field is to pick a very small field. So this is what people do, in order to achieve job security and gain professional esteem. There are other factors, too—small fields lend themselves to nicely sized intellectual communities, and there are only so many people that can fit into a conference. One reason we're writing this textbook is because we both worked in Australia, where at least some academics gain a high level of job security early on and where a smaller professional community somewhat pushes back against specialization. We can afford to get into political economy, but not everyone pursuing an academic career has this luxury.

The good news is that political economy is showing signs of a comeback. Engaging with the ideas of those thinkers in new ways led several thinkers in the mid-20th century to develop a basis for a revived political economy at the beginning of the new century. We will discuss several of these thinkers and their ideas in greater detail in later chapters.

One was John Rawls (1921–2002), the most influential political philosopher in the 20th century, at least in the Anglophone world. Like Smith, Mill, and Marx, he was concerned with how a society could be arranged so as to benefit everyone without leaving anyone behind. Although highly abstract in the manner of 20th-century philosophers generally, the basic idea he developed was to think of society as a "cooperative venture for mutual advantage" that could only expect the allegiance of its citizens if it reliably makes them better off while respecting their basic freedom to live according to their values. As Rawls put it, justice is a matter of hitting on *fair* terms of social cooperation. His ideas, though laid out and defended with practically no reference to real examples from economic life, provide a useful and enduring framework for thinking about economic questions and their relations to social and political life.

Another influential and important thinker during this period was Friedrich Hayek (1899–1992). An Austrian, Hayek was fortunate to take a position at the London School of Economics before the Nazi annexation of his homeland. There, Hayek engaged in a long-running and important debate with the greatest economist of the era, John Maynard Keynes (1883–1946). This debate centered on one of the most important questions of macroeconomics, the business cycle. Specifically, it was concerned with what caused the Great Depression and what the government should do to prevent and end depressions in the future. Keynes argued that depressions are ultimately caused by a lack of consumer spending. Sellers cannot find buyers for their goods and are forced to lower their prices or take losses. To do this, sellers must cut the wages of their workers, who are society's consumers. This creates a vicious cycle, making it even more difficult to get the economy going again. Keynes's solution is that governments could use their spending and borrowing powers to ensure that general gluts don't occur. If an economic downturn does occur, the government can "prime the pump" economically by literally giving money to people to increase spending.

Hayek believed that Keynes's diagnosis was mistaken. Instead, he argued that economic downturns resulted from too many investments in unproductive resources at one time. Sometimes this can be the result of a mania among investors or as a result of mistaken government policy. For instance, Hayek would have argued that the problem in the 2008 financial crisis in the United Sates was that too many investors put too much money in unproductive assets (in this case, subprime housing), encouraged by low interest rates and a lack of oversight. Crucially, Hayek's solution to these problems was not to have the government spend more. Doing so, he argued, would only make the problem worse. In his most popular (and provocative) work, *The Road to Serfdom* (1944), Hayek warned that continued government intervention in the economy and the implementation of economic planning would present a serious danger to democratic government.

We should note that neither Rawls nor Hayek was a political economist in the guise of Smith or Mill. Rawls was a philosopher whose theory of justice is explicitly about the distribution of goods associated with social cooperation. He merely *assumed* that the economy has a productive output whose distribution matters morally. Hayek, on the other hand, was an economist who shied away from moralized thinking. He even claimed that the concept of social justice was a "mirage" and that people when speaking of it didn't really know what they were talking about. Although this element of Hayek's thinking can be taken too far, it shouldn't lead us to discount the value of his thought as a whole.[4] In any case, political economy is often about finding the truth in what seem like opposing points of view.

With the collapse of the Soviet Union in the 1990s, the debate about whether or not we should have democratic and market-based societies effectively ceased as a practical matter. Capitalism proved better than communism in virtually every way. Capitalist-leaning societies are happier, richer, healthier, freer, and better protectors of human rights than any communist or state socialist society. Although this is no reason to become complacent, it is nevertheless true. The debate between communism and capitalism that occupied the second half of the 20th century, however, obscured some of the core questions of political economy. Instead of comparing capitalism and socialism, now the focus is and should be on the shape of our capitalist society. Economists and philosophers are concerned again with questions about why some societies are richer and freer than others and what role institutions and culture play in that process. Concerns about human rights, for instance, are importantly connected to questions about economic development.

Going forward, thinking about the ethics of capitalism will involve thinking about how our democratic capitalist societies can become more

[4] A charitable reconstruction of Hayek's take on justice and why he might have held it is offered by Joseph Heath in his discussion of a just wage (see further reading section in chapter 6). John Tomasi (2012) offers an alternative take on this point in his *Free Market Fairness*.

wealthy, healthy, happy, and free. These are the core questions that we will tackle in the rest of this book.

## 3. The Idea of Economic Justice

In large part, talking about economic justice is like talking about any other kind of justice. When philosophers argue about justice, often under the guise of "social" or "distributive" justice, they are concerned to develop theories about what justice *requires*. This involves developing a view about such things as what it means to respect freedom, to treat people fairly, as equals, and so on. When we think about economic justice, we're trying to develop views about the same sorts of things. But we're trying to do this in ways that have more immediate application to the actual economy. This means that abstract theories of fairness, freedom, and so on might not get us as far as we want to go. We want theories that tell us what fairness in (say) labor markets looks like, given the way these markets work and could be made to work. Similarly, what makes for a just distribution of taxes is going to depend on what taxes are being designed to do and what is feasible with respect to different implementations. It's no good trying to argue that an enormously high tax is just if we take no account of the ease with which people might avoid paying it by changing their economic behavior.

The concept of economic justice is different from various broader concepts of justice. A broad concept of justice is something like "fair terms of cooperation" or a "fair distribution of society's benefits and burdens." These are all quite abstract claims. They may well be plausible, but they're what philosophers call *idealized*. More or less, they aim to say something about what an ideally just society would like, in the event that it would ever exist. And they do not engage much with the realities of the status quo. Rawls is a perfect example of a philosopher whose work was very much in ideal theory. Theories of economic justice might take some inspiration from ideal theories of this sort, but they aim to say something about how the economy, as it currently is, could be made more just. In this sense, theories of economic justice are to some extent *nonideal*.

There's a great deal of philosophical work lately on how to understand this distinction between ideal and nonideal theory. Rather than endorse any elaborate theory of exactly what makes for nonideal theorizing about justice, we'll just give you an example or two of how actual work on economic justice reveals its tendency not to idealize the economy. Chiefly, this is done by noting how economic systems are a certain way, but used to be a different way, and could yet undergo further changes.

One economic practice whose value changes dramatically over time is that of inherited wealth. Prior to the golden age, feudal European societies had laws that required large family estates to pass down the family line without being broken up. This meant that estates couldn't be sold off or divided among different heirs. This practice was known as "entail." It endured for some years in countries like England, even after feudalism began to give way to a more market-oriented society. You may have some familiarity with it if you've read the novels of Jane Austen. Laws of entail often included a requirement of primogeniture, which meant that the lion's share of the inheritance went to the eldest son. This explains why Austen's Bennett sisters had poor prospects, despite being from a wealthy family. It also explains why Mr. Darcy had so much wealth, in spite of apparently not doing a single day's work in his whole life. Austen's work is often read as a comment on the injustice of entail, or at least primogeniture. Adam Smith had much the same view, but he wanted to suggest that entails had gradually become unjust over time.

> When great landed estates were a sort of principalities, entails might not be unreasonable. Like what are called the fundamental laws of some monarchies, they might frequently hinder the security of thousands from being endangered by the caprice or extravagance of one man. But in the present state of Europe, when small as well as great estates derive their security from the laws of their country, nothing can be more completely absurd. (WN III.2.6)

Nobody, including Smith, has been able to work out the whole story as to how some societies came to transition from fragmented tribal systems to larger and more cohesive ones. But a balance of power between a monarch and the nobility might have been an important early enabler of this kind of transition. It was, at least, better than a situation in which the king or tribal leader held absolute power. The presence of entails prior to the 18th century helped ensure that the wealth of aristocratic families didn't fragment as the family tree expanded, which would have broken up their ability to raise armies and present credible opposition to the monarch. But, as Smith notes, times change, and economic and political imperatives change. By Smith's day, Britain had become a "constitutional monarchy," meaning that political authority had largely shifted from the crown to parliament. Aristocracy was becoming increasingly redundant as a valuable branch of real political power, thus undercutting the justification for the large inherited fortunes that maintained it.

Smith argued that the fragmentation of aristocratic wealth, much of which was in land ownership, would spread property around so that working people could become more prosperous. It doesn't *follow* from this, however, that inheritance should simply be gotten rid of altogether. Indeed, the question of how to think about inherited wealth remains one of the enduring questions about how to make capitalism a just economic system. And it provides a good example of a how a question about whether some aspect of the economy is just or unjust can depend on what sort of functional role it plays at the time in question. Something like Smith's method might be applied in the 21st century where tax justice is concerned. Since Smith's time, the income tax has become increasingly entrenched in most developed jurisdictions. We've become so used to paying tax on our incomes that we don't even ask whether it might be odd that *work* is taxed more than, for example, inheritance. While it may not yet be feasible to do without an income tax altogether, it is striking the question of the ethics of taxing income from work, rather than other types of things or activities, barely even comes up.

Inherited wealth is not the only practice that might be assessed differently under different economic conditions. Another good example is the welfare state, which seeks to help people find more productive jobs, typically by providing conditional cash grants to unemployed job seekers. Proponents of the welfare state implicitly assume that it would be a good thing to keep as many people working as possible. If society has reached a stage where less production is necessary, or can be handed over to machines, we may need to take a different attitude about human labor and its (un)employment. Why make cash grants conditional on the recipients finding paid work if there is no work to be done? We come back to this question in chapter 7. Why not let them just keep the money and let the machines do more work instead? We take this question up more fully in chapter 10. The general point we're making right now is that, when doing political economy, we want to keep in mind one of Smith's remarks: "Laws frequently continue in force long after the circumstances which first gave occasion to them, and which could alone render them reasonable, are no more" (WN III.2.4). This claim is still true today, though it probably applies to a different set of laws from those to which Smith wanted to apply it in his day.

There is nothing wrong with philosophizing about concepts such as fairness, freedom, and inequality in abstraction from the changing nature of the economy. But you'll get to different conclusions if you think about these concepts in ways sensitive, to some degree, to prevailing economic conditions. This is what political economy tries to do.

## Conclusions

*This chapter has provided a sense of how political economy, imbued with its preoccupation with moral questions of economic justice, emerged. The prominence of political economy decreases with the increased specialization of academic expertise in the 20th century, but paying attention to this helps distinguish questions of economic justice from more abstract questions of social or distributive justice. The good news is that political economy is making a comeback, and we will be introducing you to many contemporary arguments produced in the last decade or two by currently active authors. But the history of political economy remains influential, and the writers of the golden age will also travel with us in the chapters to come.*

## Study Questions

- The fragmentation of academia has led to the acceptance of economics as a *scientific* discipline, distinct from philosophy or law as more "interpretative" disciplines less concerned with predicting what will happen and more concerned with what *ought* to happen. How intuitive do you find this distinction? What do you make of the fact that, during the golden age of political economy, authors frequently sought to do both at the same time?
- We've suggested that, following Smith's discussion of inherited wealth, we should see the principles of economic justice as subject to change, according to changes in the nature of the economy. Do you find this attractive? Or do you think that principles of justice should be in some sense timeless?

- We've offered the example of the income tax as an element of economic policy that is treated as if it *must* exist, without much reflection, when there might be a case for regarding it as outdated. Can you think of another example of a policy or practice that we just accept, without much reflection?

## Further Reading

*Original "Golden Age" Political Economy Readings*

You may want to engage with the "golden age" thinkers directly and, fortunately, there are now many excellent and cheap editions of their works available.

- *Adam Smith*

The Liberty Fund produces the most commonly used scholarly editions of the collected work of Adam Smith (a version of the Glasgow edition). They have affordable and durable copies of *An Inquiry into the Nature and Causes of the Wealth of Nations* (in two volumes) as well as the standard version of *The Theory of Moral Sentiments*, which are available either individually or as part of the collected works. There are a number of other mass market and scholarly editions available as well. Of note is the edition of *The Theory of Moral Sentiments* edited by Ryan Hanley with an introduction by Amartya Sen published by Penguin. The notes in this edition go far beyond the Glasgow edition, and the commentary by Hanley is valuable. The Cambridge Texts in the History of Philosophy edition edited by Knud Haakonssen will also be of interest to those who want to seriously engage with the text.

- *David Ricardo*

As with Smith, Liberty Fund publishes the collected works of David Ricardo, all of which are also available online in searchable form at the Online Library of Liberty (oll.libertyfund.org).

- *Thomas Malthus*

Both the first and the considerably expanded sixth edition of *An Essay on the Principle of Population* are available online for free at the Online Library of Liberty.

- *John Stuart Mill*

There is no shortage of mass market and scholarly editions of the major works of John Stuart Mill, but Liberty Fund also has the collected work of John Stuart Mill available for free online and the Online Library of Liberty as well as several excellent paperback editions of his major works, including *Principles of Political Economy*.

*Readings on the "Golden Age" by Contemporary Authors*

*The Worldly Philosophers: The Lives, Times and Ideas of the Great Economic Thinkers* by Robert Heilbroner (7th edition, Simon and Schuster, 1999)

Provides an overview of the contributions of the chief figures from the golden age of political economy, such as Smith, Ricardo, Marx, and Mill. Goes beyond the golden age to discuss some more recent figures, such as Veblen and Keynes. Each figure gets his own chapter, and a certain amount of time is spent on autobiographical details. The presentation of the ideas of each thinker is, however, outstanding. (Heilbroner's book went through seven editions, the same number as Mill's *Principles of Political Economy*.)

*A Little History of Economics* by Niall Kishtainy (Yale University Press, 2017)

A very readable survey of the evolution, by stages, of economic thought going back to ancient times and right up to the present day. Although little is said about the gradual shift away from political economy as economics emerged as a narrower discipline, the book is great if you want a snapshot of any period of thought before, during, or after the golden age.

*The Growth of Economic Thought* by Henry Spiegel (3rd edition, Duke University Press, 1988)

This (lengthy!) book gives a detailed, though accessible account of the history of economic thought from the Ancient Greeks to roughly present day. More in depth and less polemical than Heilbroner, this is an excellent work to dive into once you are ready to get into the details of the history of political economy and economic thought. Something to try if you're still hungry after getting through Heilbroner and Kishtainy.

*A History of Economic Thought: The LSE Lectures* by Lionel Robbins (Princeton University Press, 2000)

Lionel Robbins was one of the great economists in the mid-20th century. In this series of lectures, he gives his opinionated and insightful thoughts on the history of economic thought form a point of view that takes the philosophy of economics and political economy seriously.

*The History of Economic Thought: A Reader* by Steven Medema and Warren Samuels (Routledge, 2003).

An excellent collection of primary texts of economic thought from Aristotle to the 20th century. A good companion to the first half of this book and good to have on hand when reading Robbins's LSE Lectures.

# 3

# Getting Out of Feudalism—and Staying Out!

*In this chapter, we'll expand on the concept of feudalism as an economic system. We'll focus on what its central injustices are and how early work on the moral foundations of capitalism sought to emphasize the role of markets in rescuing people from feudal servitude. We'll then look at some important contemporary concerns about the resurgence of some elements of feudal economic order and the sorts of economic injustices to which they give rise.*

## 1. Feudalism and Capitalism

According to the philosopher Elizabeth Anderson, "the ideal of a free market society used to be a cause of the left."[1] That's a striking claim, but it's a plausible one. Nowadays we tend to think of capitalism as a right-wing alternative to the left-wing idea of socialism. One reason that markets and capitalism first gained support on "the left" was that their original proponents had little familiarity with state socialism, which wasn't tried until the 20th century. But in the old days, capitalism was an alternative to something else—feudalism.

There is a debate about where capitalism was "invented" and which society gets to take credit for having been the first to get it started. But we're not going to get into that. For one thing, the question of capitalism's geographic origins isn't essential to understanding how capitalism might be best defended. Furthermore, it is not obvious whether any society has managed to become "purely" capitalist in any case. Various countries have had a go at organizing themselves along approximately capitalist lines, but in different ways, and

[1] See the opening chapter of her (2017) book *Private Government*, in this chapter's further reading section.

*The Ethics of Capitalism*. Daniel Halliday and John Thrasher, Oxford University Press (2020).

DOI: 10.1093/oso/9780190096205.001.0001

with mixed success. And some (like Ancient Rome and Renaissance Venice) went forward and then backward. What we'll do, instead, is give a few historical examples that are most illustrative of how feudalism amounted to an egregiously unjust economic system and how the rise of markets, and associated economic freedoms, made for a dramatic improvement.

But first, some digressive points about terminology. Terms like "left" and "right" are misleading because they encourage binary thinking about what is really (at least) a two-dimensional space of alternatives—remember the triangle from chapter 1. The taxonomy of socialists or communists on the left and supporters of markets on the right is a holdover from the Cold War. A look further back in history quickly shows the inadequacy of this taxonomy.

Nazi Germany, considered the ultimate right-wing society, was hardly an exemplar of market freedoms. Indeed, "Nazi" is an abbreviation of the German for "National Socialist German Workers Party," and the Nazis pursued a policy of economic nationalism that is closer to an industrial version of mercantilism than capitalism. Scholars debate how much the Nazis were ever actually "socialist," but the point to note is that Nazi rule was characterized by a command economy that shared much in common with Stalin's economic system. Similar points apply to other fascist societies in Europe in the early part of the 20th century and in South Africa up until the end of apartheid in 1994.

It's notable that one of the most celebrated political opponents of apartheid, Nelson Mandela, argued that resisting apartheid was quite compatible with supporting a capitalist, market society.[2] The fact that Mandela was branded a communist was partly the work of the apartheid government's propaganda—designed to curry favor with Western governments during the Cold War—and in part Mandela's willingness to ally himself with communists as part of the anti-apartheid struggle. Mandela's own theoretical views combined sympathy for some socialist policies along with recognition that market exchange could promote an equality of status that nonwhites were denied under apartheid.

[2] This claim appears in Mandela's (1956) essay "Freedom in Our Lifetime" and reappears at various points in his (2013) autobiography, *Long Walk to Freedom*. We'd like to emphasize that Mandela gained influence by using reasoned argument rather than mere rhetoric, in ways that recognized the difficulty of theoretical questions about economic justice. His methods suggest that successful political activism can benefit from intellectual rigor.

One reason fascists are anti-capitalist is that properly competitive markets don't distinguish between ethnic or national groups, nor religious affiliation. They don't privilege, for instance, German companies or workers over Jewish companies or workers. Competition is blind to the things that fascists care so much about. There is no market value in "blood and soil." One of the reasons the Jews have been traditionally attacked by nationalists of all stripes is that they are supposedly "cosmopolitan" or "globalists." Admittedly, real-world markets very often depend on or reinforce local social norms. One thing we need to remember is that the norms were already there. We'll come back to this point at various stages in the book.

Originally, "left" and "right" referred to what side of the postrevolutionary French assembly supporters of the revolution and the monarchy were seated. Thus, it came to be that the left is associated with egalitarianism and the right with conserving hierarchy and privilege. It is in this sense that the early defenders of capitalism were on the "left": they wanted to undermine the hierarchical institutions of the monarchical, feudal regimes of their day. But these historical points should remind you that any use of the terms "left" and "right" is likely to oversimplify things. We prefer not to use these terms at all, and they won't appear again in this book as labels for positions about political economy or economic justice. You might yourself try dropping the terms "left" and "right" and see whether you find it easier to articulate your ideas about economic justice.

So what exactly is feudalism? We gave a preliminary answer when we introduced the triangle in chapter 1. A more precise definition says that feudalism obtains when an economy significantly approximates the following conditions:

1. Ownership of physical property (housing, land, and industry) is concentrated into a very small number of private hands.
2. There is a strong overlap between private wealth and political power, with nonwealthy people deprived of political influence.
3. Status divisions have a dynastic aspect: those who are born outside of the elite have little opportunity to join it, and elites enjoy a protected position. One's life prospects are very much dependent one's "breeding."
4. Feudal elites show a tendency to compete for each other's wealth and power, and to maintain their status against any uprising from the lower classes, using violent means.

5. Those who do not own substantial capital find themselves subject to limited freedom of movement, thereby inhibiting their labor market participation.

Although they are probably related to each other, each of these conditions has its own importance when it comes to explaining both the stability and injustice of feudal economic order.

The first condition reflects the way in which the wealth of feudal societies was held by a tiny elite fraction of the population. In the European feudalism that preceded the Industrial Revolution, virtually all land was divided between the monarchy, the aristocracy, and the church. There was no public property in the modern sense and no significant private property dispersed around the wider population. The vast majority of people were peasants, living on land owned by the local nobility. Peasants generally had no means of securing food besides what they could grow on the land, but they were forced to give up much of whatever they could produce thanks to rent and taxes for the local landowner.

Not only did the economic elite own the land on which the bulk of the population lived and worked, but they could basically treat their peasants in any way they liked (conditions 2 and 5). The common people had no "rights" in the modern sense against their lords. Rulers were meant to be restrained by religious and ethical virtues, but these were always imperfectly expressed. The virtues of the church were in any case questionable: peasants were not able or allowed to read the holy books and were expected to conform to the dictates and norms of the church lest they be damned eternally to hell. The commoners of feudal societies were basically viewed as something akin to natural resources: it was prudent for the lords to manage their resources well, but they owed nothing to them and their welfare was unimportant from the point of view of politics. And people, as resources, were quite expendable: feudal landlords generally didn't need to worry too much if a number of their peasants died due to a food shortage, disease, or in a war. If it suited them, the lords might even seek to bring this about quite deliberately.

Condition 3 is also important. One might imagine a sort of "high mobility feudalism," in which elites often fell on hard times and peasants were able to work their way up somehow. Nowadays, mobility often happens when people acquire skills and put them to work, but the rigidity of feudal hierarchies endured partly because people were denied an education. Most peasants were wholly illiterate and had no means of changing this. Further, most jobs outside of agriculture were skilled, artisanal jobs that took a long time to learn properly. These industries were also typically controlled by guilds that protected the occupations of those with the skill by limiting access. In spite of all this, people sometimes did invent new technologies that could have enabled increased prosperity. In such cases, a common response was for the monarch to refuse a patent, meaning that the innovation couldn't go into production.

What of condition 4, about violence? When Adam Smith was a young adult, Scotland effectively went to war with England when an elite family tried to settle an old score. The background to this was complex, having to do with the gradual merger of England and Scotland as nations. But even without the details, it reveals the violent tendencies of feudal order.

In 1745, Charles Stuart, aka "Bonnie Prince Charlie," grandson of the deposed James II (House of Stuart), attempted to regain the throne from the incumbent George II (House of Hanover). The Stuarts had been living in exile since James lost the throne back in 1688. Because the House of Stuart had its roots in Scotland, Charles was able to command the loyalty of the Scottish clan chiefs, who had managed to remain largely independent of the British government in London. (Smith, by the way, was a "lowland" Scot from near Edinburgh, with no clan affiliation.) The clan chiefs were feudal landlords who could conscript their clansmen. To cut a long story short, Charles and the clans had a go at invading England, and nearly pulled it off. But in the end, they failed. The uprising ended with the infamous battle of Culloden in 1746, the last fought on British soil. British government forces massacred the clansmen before embarking on what would now be described as a program of ethnic cleansing in highland Scotland. This culminated in the "clearances," where large numbers of highland Scots were shipped off to North America and Australasia. At Culloden there still stands a memorial to "the gallant highlanders who fought for Scotland and Prince Charlie." Whether the highlanders genuinely fought for the good of *Scotland* is hardly obvious. For the record, Charles managed to escape back to Europe after Culloden—disappointed, but unharmed—such is the way with feudal privilege.

Smith mentions the events of 1745 in his *Lectures on Jurisprudence* (1763). Smith believed that capitalist societies would become less warlike as they destroyed feudal privilege. But the Stuart uprising convinced him that incipient commercial societies might also be vulnerable to hostile feudalist takeovers. The year 1745 was no red herring. Feudal rulers in preindustrial Europe were constantly going to war with each other, typically in ways that granted any spoils to the economic elite while forcing the regular population to be most exposed to the risks. For Smith, the advantage of commerce was that it enabled other ways for wealth to be *created*, rather than merely fought over. Created wealth undermines old elites by disrupting their networks of power and allegiance.

Smith catalogues the various failings of feudalism in Book III of *The Wealth of Nations*. While Smith notes that feudal power means oppression of the great majority of the population, he is keen to emphasize the gross *inefficiency* of feudal economies. This has much to do with the way in which concentrations of wealth corrupt incentives. Because the feudal nobility possessed such large estates, they had little need to ensure that the land was used to its fullest potential. There would always be enough to feed the aristocracy and their families, who wouldn't be much concerned if a few peasants starved. Smith complains about the large "forests" in England in which there were no trees. This sounds odd, but "forest" has a more archaic meaning of "hunting ground." Instead of being used to grow food, land was set aside for the nobility to entertain themselves chasing animals around. Hardly a productive arrangement.

Smith urged that things would only improve when peasants owned the land on which they work, or could at least gain a greater entitlement to the food they grew on it. That would incentivize them to grow more food. More food would not just mean more people fed, but also people freed up to produce other things, such as in industry and manufacturing. Smith extended his case for market society by drawing on the moral psychology that he outlines in his earlier book, *Theory of Moral Sentiments* (1759). Whereas feudal economies are run on coercion, "commercial society" facilitates reciprocal exchange between free individuals, in ways that improve human character. Smith believed that in this lay the route to greater law and order, and peaceful conditions. But such forms of progress will only happen, Smith points out, when something is done to prevent the economic elite from having a stranglehold on productive assets like land.

## 2. Great Escapes: Australian Convicts, American Radicals, and Other Heroes

There is something to be said for looking at countries that, though they may have violent and unjust histories, never really had feudalism. A great example is Australia. We should note that the history of Australia is subject to its own injustices, particularly the genocidal treatment of its indigenous peoples by settler-colonialists, something which still haunts Australia today. But Australia nevertheless had the advantage, not shared by its "mother country" Britain, of being free from a feudal stranglehold on its economy. In its early colonial years, Australia grew fast. By the late 19th century it had one of the highest standards of living, in material terms, of any country in the world.

How did Australia develop so well and so quickly? Convicts were sent to Australia from Britain throughout the 19th century, based on a plan of putting them to work developing Australian industry and agriculture. The plan turned out to require modification: Australia's colonial government found it difficult to simply coerce the convicts into working hard. Australia only really started to develop when convicts were given economic freedoms. They were allowed to be paid and, eventually, to own land and capital.

Many of them prospered, as represented by Abel Magwitch in Charles Dickens's *Great Expectations* (1861), who returned to England much wealthier than when he left. The lot of convicts improved so much that the home country objected—these rogues were supposed to be criminals, not prosperous pioneers! Transport to Australia eventually became viewed as a soft punishment and was discontinued. By this time, Australia had established itself well enough to attract voluntary migrants, and it continues to do so (for example, the authors of this book).[3]

The history of other parts of the world also shows how economic freedom works better than coercion when it comes to increasing the wealth of nations. Another former British colony, the United States, declared independence the same year as Smith's *Wealth of Nations* was published (1776). Two of its main founders, Jefferson and Madison, were great devotees of political economy. The United States quickly went about developing its lands for small, private holdings and, except in the Southern slave states, avoided the large land holdings of the feudal Europe. In those times inherited wealth was even said to be "un-American."[4] Such reforms, along with an addiction to trade, created the dispersed capital (both human and material) conducive to America's rapid economic development.

[3] If you want to know more about the Australian story, we recommend John Hirst's (2014) book, particularly the second and third chapters.

[4] For a discussion of attitudes to inheritance during the American founding, see Beckert (2008). The quote is from p. 183.

These cases remind us that the moral evaluation of a capitalist system (or something approaching it) shouldn't rely on simply pointing out what is so terrible about communism. We should also evaluate today's so-called capitalist societies according to how well they have escaped or avoided the older feudalist systems.

## 3. Signs of a Revival of Feudalism?

Cast in its medieval image, we tend to think of feudalism as dead and gone. But the shadow of feudalism lingers, and it may be starting to darken once again. It might be argued that some European nations never wholly dragged themselves away from feudalism, even the ones that had revolutions, like France, and beheaded their monarchs and nobility. But it may also be said that elements of feudalism are appearing in countries that weren't straightforwardly feudal the first time around, including Australia and the United States.

What's the substance behind this worry? Really, there are two alleged symptoms of a feudalist comeback currently attracting the attention of economists and philosophers. One of these has to do with recent trends regarding increasing material inequality. This concern is especially acute with respect to rising house prices, stagnant wages, and the tendency of income via inheritance to be a greater predictor of someone's prospects than the income they can get from employment. A second concern is that bigger companies are becoming more the norm, creating an imbalance between workers and the owners of capital. Contemporary workplaces are, according to this worry, returning to conditions of employer coercion and domination, thereby resembling the control of labor in a feudal economic order.[5]

Another worry concerns the growing restriction of freedom of movement. Peasants living under European feudalism were often simply prohibited from moving from one estate to another. Modern market economies do not generally impose restrictions on movement of their own citizens. But migration across national borders is another matter. Australia is a leader in this regard: at the time of writing, the government is currently detaining large

[5] We don't make any claim about how far these concerns accurately reflect reality, there is considerable dispute on that point. Regardless, in a democratic society widespread concerns deserve serious attention.

numbers of migrants in terrible conditions on various islands in the seas north of Australia. Though one hardly needs a theory of economic justice to explain what's objectionable about this, it does resemble the highly coercive practices of feudal times. The United States may also be moving in the same direction.

We're about to discuss the first of these three trends in some detail (we'll come back to migration in chapter 8, when we talk about global trade). But we'd like to remind you, first, of the subtle relationship between different economic systems that we pointed out in chapter 1. Remember that ideas like capitalism, feudalism, and socialism represent extreme points in a fairly continuous logical space. Any particular changes in any particular society over time probably represent gradual shifts within this space, as the status quo moves toward one extreme and away from others.

On this note, we should be clear that some elements of preindustrial feudalism thankfully do seem dead and buried so far as the developed world is concerned. The church (and religious institutions more generally) is no longer involved in much economic oppression, nor does it have powers of prosecution and incarceration. Though there are still some theocracies in various parts of the world, nobody gets burned at the stake these days in Europe. Indeed, the current leaders of the major "Western" branches of the Christian church, the Pope and the Archbishop of Canterbury, frequently speak out against economic injustice, often with more substance than politicians.

Also extinct appears to be military conscription, as virtually all of the current capitalist, democratic societies in the world rely on volunteer forces, with some notable exceptions. Although it is possible that compulsory military service could be reinstituted in the event of a major war, even draftees are paid something and are expected to fight for the nation as a whole, rather than particular elites. Scholars have noted a substantial decline in organized violence that coincides with the rise of markets and democracy. Sometimes called the "democratic peace" or the "capitalist peace" or even the "liberal peace" hypothesis, something about the general social systems of capitalist society make war less likely. This is true despite the bloody wars of the 20th century. Steven Pinker in his *The Better Angels of Our Nature* (2011) chronicles this decline in violence. This accords well with Adam Smith's hypothesis that trade and reciprocal relations will humanize people by creating greater opportunities and advantages for sympathy between persons.

Given these facts, nobody would suggest that the economies of current *developed* societies are returning to anything near as bad as the feudalism of medieval Europe. But, keeping the triangle in mind, there is always the possibility of moving in the *direction* of feudalism.

## 4. Inherited Wealth and the Return of the "Rentier"

The old feudal inheritances were substantially reduced by various shocks in the early 20th century: world wars destroyed swathes of private capital, at least in Europe, and governments nationalized a good deal of the industrial capital while implementing increasingly progressive taxation. The decades after the world wars exhibited relatively low levels of economic inequality. People had incentives to work hard in relatively specialized forms of employment, which increased the level of education. Wages rose steadily so that people could "catch up" with those who still benefitted from inheritance and land ownership. The decades after World War II were highly productive ones in countries whose citizens possessed economic freedoms.

Since the 1970s, however, these countries have seen wages stagnate and economic inequality grow. According to the French economist Thomas Piketty (2014), recent trends signal deeper forces lurking within in any market economy. Piketty's line (roughly) is that an economy will tend toward inequality and stagnation unless it is prevented from doing so either by significant government regulation or by more external "shocks," like wars. Because the early and mid-20th century contained some unusually dramatic shocks, which were followed by certain sorts of economic governance, Piketty believes these periods are anomalous decades in the longer run of economic history.

Here is a relatively technical—but helpful—way of describing the sort of conditions that Piketty thinks we're sinking into. Basically, there are two sources of income in an economy. These are labor and capital. Both of these generate "returns" to the people who own them. Returns to labor are salaries or wages. Returns to capital vary, depending on the capital in question (by "capital," here we just mean any tradeable asset that is not labor). Intellectual property might generate royalties, land or buildings will generate rent, shares in a big company will pay regular dividends, and so on. Large holdings of capital will generate incomes that become big enough for owners to live comfortably, without having to save much of their annual return and with no need for wages. These owners of capital become a class of "rentiers," doing little apart from collecting wealth from the wage earners who pay them to rent use of their assets. Under these conditions, wealth is not produced, but *extracted*: the rise of inequality occurs when a small elite suck wealth from the wider population, whereas inequality reduces only when things are arranged so that people can gain a reward for being productive.

There seems to be something to this story, despite recent serious concerns about Piketty's project.[6] The basic worry is easy: if you don't own capital, then you're in trouble. In "developed" nations, people born after 1990, which probably includes most readers of this book, are finding it much harder than members of the preceding generation in getting onto the property ladder. There is considerable anxiety about house prices in major cities outpacing wages. For many people, it may be impossible to buy a home without inheriting money from parents or grandparents. In the words of the British sociologist Danny Dorling, "a whole generation is now growing up with a financial interest in their parents' early death, so that they can inherit a deposit for a mortgage."[7] Of course, not everyone has parents wealthy enough, or generous enough, or ready to die soon enough, for this interest to be satisfied. So unless these young people can squeeze into one of the remaining professions that promise high salaries, they can look forward to a life of renting a home, with all of its hazards, no matter how hard they work. And to whom do the mass of workers pay their rent? To the wealthy or lucky who were able to buy up all the housing, of course—Piketty's extractive rentiers.

If Piketty is right, then capitalism as we defined it in chapter 1 may not be self-sustaining: if we want private property to stay dispersed and for people to enjoy the opportunities associated with competition, then regulations will be needed to stop the drift back toward this sort of quasi-feudal "patrimonial capitalism." Drawing this conclusion *doesn't* show that capitalism is bad, only that it needs to make sure that a large group of people have the opportunity to engage in production and ownership. As we have said, not everyone agrees with the finer points of Piketty's position. But there is an important lesson to be taken from his work: though feudalism is clearly the less just system compared to capitalism, it may yet be the more *stable*. After all, the feudal economies of Europe lasted for over a thousand years and capitalist societies have only recently emerged.

[6] See, for example, the work of economists Richard Sutch (2017).
[7] Quoted from (Halliday 2018, 14); see also Hood and Joyce (Belfield et al. 2017).

## 5. Big Business and Labor Market Domination

Never mind those who don't have to go out and find work. What about those who do? Adam Smith thought that labor markets, in which people actually sign contracts in return for paid work, would be markedly superior to feudalism's method of employment in which landowners coerced peasants and slaves. Smith foresaw "a nation of shopkeepers," in which most workers were self-employed, or worked for small firms, and everyone got on nicely.

Though most workers now have it a lot better than slaves, the story isn't all roses. Despite her appreciation of the egalitarian benefits of capitalism in general, Elizabeth Anderson (2017, 6) writes that "the industrial revolution was a cataclysmic event for egalitarians." This is because the nature of economic production, at least initially, lent itself to large rather than small firms. Once the Industrial Revolution cranked into gear, it became clear that a nation of shopkeepers wasn't the only possibility. In the 19th century, countries became nations of mills, mines, and factories that employed thousands, rather than tens, of workers. These were large operations in which masses of people were employed and controlled by bosses. In the 20th century, many developed countries lost their factories, mills, and mines. They now have employers like big-box retail stores, call centers, and accountancy firms. But one trend has remained: the companies in question tend to be large, with dominant market shares and very large numbers of employees. There are still some small employers and freelancing individuals, but they account for a minority of the workforce (about 10% of the American workforce are self-employed and another 20% work for them).

Why did the rise of large companies take place? One key fact is that some forms of physical capital simply cannot be worked by small groups of people. Think about an ocean liner, an airport, or a theme park. These just don't exist on a small scale, because of the more or less indivisible nature of the necessary capital involved. This might explain the existence of big businesses in some industries, but it doesn't explain the general trend toward bigness in other industries with more divisible capital, like retail. To understand why there are large firms, we need to understand why there are firms or hierarchically structured businesses at all.

Imagine that every part of a Toyota Camry was produced by a different person or group who each individually contracted with the Toyota company to supply them with parts. Then Toyota contracts with a series of people and suppliers for them to assemble this one car and then sells the car to a dealer.

Each contract for parts or labor would be a one-time contract and would specify exactly what was required from the supplier or the laborer. Each supplier or laborer could be guaranteed to get their market rate and would not have to be managed by the Toyota company beyond the current project (meaning Toyota wouldn't have so many employees). This is a radical version of what Smith might have had in mind when he thought about a "nation of shopkeepers." Why don't all the different parts of the divided labor work separately, on their own terms, and contract directly with each other to produce the final product?

Ronald Coase (1910–2013) won a Nobel Prize in Economics for answering this question. The short version of his answer is that firms exist because production is more efficient when it is organized hierarchically. He argued, in his paper "The Nature of the Firm" (1937), that the fundamental question for any firm is whether to "make" or "buy" goods and services. That is, to do something within the firm or to outsource. Doing things within a firm can be more efficient than outsourcing for a variety of reasons that came to be called "transaction costs." Following Coase, Oliver Williamson (1932–)—who also won a Nobel Prize!—argued that the explicit, detailed contracts that are necessary when a firm decides to buy rather than make are extremely costly in terms of time, adjudication costs, and knowledge (Williamson 1983, 1985). When laborers are hired into a firm as employees, rather than treated as independent contractors, their contracts can be open-ended and less specific, giving more discretion to managerial supervision. Oliver Hart (1948–), yet another Nobel Prize winner, has shown that these open-ended contracts have substantial economic benefits in certain circumstances (Hart and Moore 1988, 1990).

While these open-ended or "indeterminate" employment contracts might be economically efficient, they create the need for a hierarchical structure in the firm. Workers need to be told what to do by managers, precisely because the contract doesn't settle everything. Once a firm's structure is in place, it is relatively easy for a firm to become larger, taking advantage of economies of scale and thereby selling its product at a lower price.

Despite the economic benefits, Anderson argues that this type of hierarchy amounts to an authoritarian structure within the firm. Anderson believes that many current employers in the private sector, at least in the United States, are morally equivalent to "dictatorships." She defends this claim by arguing that employers increasingly spy on their employees, both at the workplace and during their officially "private" time, subject employees to burdensome and even cruel working conditions, and suppress means through which employees might seek to exercise any countervailing power, so as to hold their employers accountable. This was never explicitly endorsed by Coase or the other economists who developed the theory of the firm. Nevertheless, once open-ended contracts exist, it is easy for the bossing around to get a bit out of hand.

Anderson backs her claims with a number of examples. We'll repeat a couple here. If you work for the big US retailer Walmart (more on Walmart later), then your boss may change your shift schedule at a moment's notice, irrespective of what difficulties this places on you. If you work for Amazon, in one of their massive warehouses, then you may have to struggle under temperatures of over 100 degrees Fahrenheit and face "demerit points" when you get hospitalized from heat exhaustion.

While Anderson focuses on the injustice of how employees are treated in firms, F. A. Hayek worried about the long-term effects of hierarchical employment, too. In *The Constitution of Liberty* (1960a), he argues that free, democratic, and capitalist societies depend on a sense of independence and fundamental equality, something that is undermined by the servility encouraged in many hierarchical firms. How, Hayek asks, can we expect our citizens to expect and demand freedom in their social and political lives when they spend most of their waking life being surveilled, commanded, and organized by their employers?

Working conditions were, in some ways, better in the small firms that Smith envisaged than in the Amazon warehouse. Those who were in charge worked alongside the mere wage laborers. This probably triggered a degree of empathy. Bosses were at least aware of what they were putting their workers through. A factory of ten workers is small enough to fit into the same pub at the end of the working day. Overall, small workplaces tend to be friendlier, less authoritarian places. In very large companies, bosses either don't know what their workers are going through or don't care. After all, they don't have to look them in the face each day or work in the same overheated room.

Some of you may have watched the popular TV show *Undercover Boss*. Routinely, this show involves some senior executive taking time out from the board room and mucking in with the real workers, usually becoming shocked at the conditions they supposedly haven't seen before. The episodes always end with the boss revealing their true identity to the workers. In the manner of some sort of savior, the boss promises to fix the things that were making the workers' lives so hard. It's unclear exactly what to make of the program, which is designed to be good television. But it's clear that the idea of an "undercover" boss is, just by itself, evidence of where labor markets have got to: the show makes little sense until firms get large enough for the board room to be very distant from the shop floor.

We want to stress that the injustice of labor market relationships is not simply the matter of how much pay the workers take home. The problem that most concerns Anderson is the ability of large employers to unjustly coerce and dominate their staff through the control that they can now exercise over their lives.[8] Of course, this is made easier by low wages, which make it harder for employees to change jobs, since they cannot accumulate enough savings to survive periods of unemployment. They also cannot afford legal fees in the event of mounting a challenge against their employer, even if the law would ultimately be on their side. Nor is being dominated by one's boss entirely about the *type* of work one has to do. For sure, many people have lousy jobs. Some jobs might still be horrible even if the pay is good and you get treated really nicely by your employer. The possibility of work that's awful to perform regardless of the pay and conditions raises an important question that we'll get back to in chapter 5 when we finally get around to talking about Karl Marx and the idea of alienated labor. But the point here isn't so much about lousy work as about lousy bosses and/or lousy employment contracts. The problem is with the quality of labor market *relationships*, which, according to Anderson, are profoundly anti-egalitarian in virtue of unjust hierarchies of status.

Not everyone entirely agrees with Anderson's assessment of economic justice in labor markets. Economies of scale are, of course, not all bad. Like we've said, they enable more things to be produced at a cheaper cost. They might also suppress *some* economic injustices that might occur easily in small firms. The economist Tyler Cowen notes (among other criticisms of Anderson) that if a small operation, like a corner store, refuses to employ homosexual workers, then it is unlikely to reduce business. But if a large company, like McDonalds, is found to be engaging in such practices, then their public image will be hurt simply because word will get around and

[8] Terms like "coerce" and "dominate" have gained technical and different meanings in contemporary philosophy. We're suppressing this difference here. An influential discussion is Philip Pettit's (1999) book, particularly its opening four chapters. See also Robert Taylor's (2013, 2017) work on domination and freedom in commercial societies.

McDonalds relies on being able to attract a customer base large enough to include a variety of sexual orientations.[9]

The disagreement between Cowen and Anderson may lie in how much the remedies for labor market injustice require legislation and how much we can get by on social backlash. In 2016, a British receptionist was sent home from work by Price Waterhouse Coopers—a large accountancy firm. She was actually *employed* by a firm called Portico, to whom PWC outsourced its supply of receptionists. Portico's employee dress code required female receptionists to wear heels between two and four inches long, despite being on their feet throughout a nine-hour shift. The employee went into work wearing flat shoes, which is why she was told to go home and not expect any pay.

In this case, the receptionist was brave enough to mount a protest by starting an online petition to parliament. This got attention on social media, which went viral, as various other women chimed in with similar stories about employer-imposed "guidelines." For instance, some women had been explicitly told by their employers to wear sexually revealing clothes. Much of the public ire was expressed in terms of the oppressive nature of gender norms. That's fair enough. The additional point here, though, is that an economic injustice occurred because an employer was able to *enforce* gender norms because of the power held over an employee. That's an additional injustice, and one that occurs not simply because of prevailing gender norms, but because of the way the labor market has become structured and the way open-ended employment contracts work.

Eventually, the British government responded to the backlash by formally reviewing Portico's practices, concluding that labor market laws had been violated. It is worth considering whether this would have happened had things been different—had the receptionist been less willing to speak up, less able to lose a day's pay, or if social media hadn't been invented. The case reminds us that even when laws exist for the sake of protecting individuals from labor market domination, much else has to happen for these laws to provide the protection intended. It may be that injustice gets addressed most readily when legislation and social movements are able to complement each other.

Of course, not everyone in the labor market has it so bad, and there may be more opportunities emerging to ditch the big employer. There are,

[9] Cowen's comments are included in Anderson's (2017) book, along with comments from other critics and Anderson's replies. Tyler Cowen's *Big Business* (2019) expands on this theme.

increasingly, opportunities for freelance and independent work, especially for skilled and educated workers. This work may or may not pay better than the corporate alternatives, but many like it better because it offers an escape from the hierarchical structure of many firms—as the saying goes, you get to be your own boss. It is worth noting, though, that not everyone likes "being their own" boss. Many people get considerable value out of working with other people and forming workplace relationships. As with many of the other topics we discuss, there is not one way that will appeal to everyone.

One ray of hope is that as the knowledge economy expands and transaction costs decline, we should expect to see more and more of these opportunities. In the "knowledge economy," the means of production—capital—is principally a laptop, wifi, and creativity. This capital does not require a hierarchical firm to make it productive. New technologies are also opening up opportunities in this direction. Companies like Uber and AirBnB have developed digital platforms that make exchanges much easier than they historically have been. Technologies like Blockchain open up the possibility of contracting with very low cost of enforcement.

In the jargon of economics, what's going on here is a reduction in "transaction costs." Finding buyers and sellers and effectively matching them was historically too difficult without the resources of a firm. Once the respective apps were invented, however, there was an easy way to find the service and to pay for it while being tracked and vetted by the app. This provided assurance that everyone would get the service and the payment that they needed to bring their apartment or car into the market.[10] These new technologies might also improve working conditions for many employees, though digital platforms are often accused of depressing wages and treating workers as freelancers merely to avoid demands of employment law (like sick pay). The way these companies operate may lead to substantial social changes. Some of these changes may be unwelcome to some segment of the population. This is an important fact about capitalism in general, its dynamism. Capitalism promotes innovation and change and for those who benefit from the status quo, this change can be uncomfortable and unwelcome. The economist Joseph Schumpeter (1883–1950) described the disruptive change of capitalism as "creative destruction."[11] Capitalism is not sentimental about the past.

[10] For an in-depth analysis of the "sharing economy" and its relation to transaction costs, see Michael Munger (2018).

[11] See Joseph Schumpeter (1994).

Digital platforms are not the only example of technology that has changed labor markets. The development of computers has made it much easier for many people to work from home. Employers are often willing to grant this privilege, as it means they might need less office space in the inner city. Our older colleagues in higher education sometimes lament certain aspects of the job that have disappeared. But the fact remains that we were able to write this book from all sorts of locations, often when we were in different countries from each other, thanks simply to computers, the internet, and the file-sharing service Dropbox. This allowed us to live better lives while meeting our obligations to our employers. More working from home also has wider social benefits, as fewer commutes eases congestion on roads and public transport, and perhaps eases competition for housing close to where employers are located.

The rise of large companies generates worries independent of the increasingly hierarchical character of labor markets and adds another strand to the hypothesis of a feudal comeback. One of these concerns is that big businesses suck wealth out of the geographical regions in which they operate. Walmart, the biggest retail operation in the United States, often sets up in relatively small towns and cities. Before Walmart showed up, a town's local businesses used to reinject their profits into the local economy. Walmart doesn't do this. Instead, its revenues get sent off to other parts of the country by way of shareholder dividends and executive pay.[12]

Overall, there's considerable force behind the worry that labor markets are beginning to mimic the feudal era according to the degree of control that employers now exercise over employees' lives. There is much scope for disagreement about how bad things are getting and what sort of reforms might be most effective. But the status quo is certainly not what Adam Smith envisaged when he thought of labor markets as a route to emancipation for normal working people.

## Conclusions

> *This chapter has shown that at least some contemporary candidates for economic injustice, such as dynastic inequality of wealth and domination in labor markets, may be diagnosed as shifts toward feudalism rather than aspects of "extreme capitalism." Though many societies*

[12] For some discussion of this aspect of Walmart, see George Packer's (2014) discussion of economic decline in the United States.

*managed to escape from the dreadful feudalism of the medieval era, such societies may have to work hard to keep themselves from being sucked back in—feudalism may, after all, be the more stable system. At the root of this is a distinction between economic orders that promote the production of new wealth and orders in which an elite are able to merely extract wealth from others and keep it. Recognition of this danger helps motivate the case for grappling with the sort of challenges discussed later in this book.*

## Study Questions

- According to Adam Smith, the problem with large-scale inherited wealth was that it made society less competitive and kept productive assets away from persons who might make best use of them. How well does this complaint apply to inherited wealth in today's world? In today's much more productive world, is there anything unjust about inherited wealth?
- What do you think of Anderson's concept of "private government"? Does the idea that bosses have a strong tendency to dominate employees represent your own experience (if any) of participating in the labor market? Does self-employment seem more attractive to you than working for an employer? If so, why?
- Is it important that people generally have the ability to own their own home? Is there anything unjust about some people having to pay rent their entire lives, to property owners who might not need to work for a living, being able to live off this rental income instead?
- To what extent should employers be able to influence how their staff dress when in the workplace? What's the moral difference between requiring that employees wear gender-neutral uniforms, and requiring that female staff wear skirts and makeup while male staff wear neckties and shave their facial hair?

## Further Reading

*Private Government* by Elizabeth Anderson (Princeton University Press, 2017)

This book contains an excellent discussion of the unjust conditions of feudalism in England. It also chronicles the rise of philosophical opposition to feudalism and its role in the erosion of English feudal order. It then moves on to a discussion of contemporary labor markets, where Anderson sees a return to conditions in which employers have unjust abilities to dominate employees.

*Note*: This book was based on Anderson's 2015 Tanner Lectures at Princeton University. These can still be downloaded from the Tanner Foundation website:
http://tannerlectures.utah.edu/lecture-library.php

*Why Nations Fail* by Daron Acemoglu and James Robinson (Random House, 2013)

Drawing heavily on economic history, this book links the rise of prosperity to the growth of what its authors call "inclusive" economic institutions that displaced the "extractive" institutions of the feudal era. It also explains why feudalism may be the more stable economic condition, accounting for why initial shifts toward inclusivity, such as Rome and Venice, were beaten back. It also offers reasons why a fuller shift toward markets occurred in England when conditions were put in place for the Industrial Revolution, partly due to the rise of intellectual property rules enabling the patenting of new inventions, displacing the feudal order's opposition to capitalist disruption.

*Capital in the Twenty-First Century* by Thomas Piketty (Harvard University Press, 2013)

Based on a massive trove of economic data spreading across several countries and centuries, this book's central claim is that economic conditions in the 21st century will resemble the 18th and 19th centuries more than they resemble the 20th. This means high inequality and low social mobility, with those reliant on wages and salaries unable to catch up with the minority who receive a large inheritance. It's a long book and its main claims are controversial, but it is written to an impressive level of detail. You can get a good idea of Piketty's main point just by reading the first chapter, as the rest of the book concentrates mainly on showing how the data support its claims.

# 4
# Market Order and Market Failure

*In this chapter, we'll present and discuss the most influential argument in favor of a capitalist economy characterized by widespread economic freedom as opposed to central government planning. This is the argument from price signaling, which draws on the idea of markets as spontaneous orders that work best when left alone. We'll then look at some counterarguments that emphasize the limits of price signaling and other alleged cases of "market failure."*

## 1. Spontaneous Orders and Why They Matter

Common "arguments" in favor of capitalism include the claim that governments are incompetent, that all the smart people work in the private sector, free trade is good, taxation is theft, state spending means hardworking folks subsidizing handouts to the lazy, and so on. You probably hear such talk quite often. It tends not to be put together as proper reasoning, but rather as mere rhetoric. Some of this rhetoric can be built into intellectually respectable arguments, and we will look at some of the more worthy cases in later chapters. But these don't end up amounting to any general argument for or against capitalism, as opposed to more specific or internal aspects of it. We're still early in the book, so for now we want to stay with the big picture and consider what the best *general* argument might be.

The most impressive and influential case for capitalism develops the idea that a market is a *spontaneous order*. This takes some explaining, but it is central to the defense of a capitalist system. Speaking very abstractly, a spontaneous order is any sort of activity involving multiple individuals, which exhibits a definite structure, but which has not been designed or controlled by any overarching power. Or, in the words of Adam Ferguson (1767, 205), a friend of Adam Smith, spontaneous orders are "the products of human action but not human design."

*The Ethics of Capitalism.* Daniel Halliday and John Thrasher, Oxford University Press (2020).

DOI: 10.1093/oso/9780190096205.001.0001

You already know of many spontaneous orders: natural languages, like English, Chinese, and Hebrew, are very straightforward examples. Languages count as *orders* because they are rule governed. As anyone learning a second language soon finds out, the number of rules is often bewildering, and the logic of these rules may seem obscure. But the rules *work*.

Languages count as *spontaneous* because they emerged without any help from government or any other agency who consciously planned or improved them. Their rules are the product of gradual evolution. This *does* mean that they typically emerged relatively slowly.[1] Indeed, the term "spontaneous" is a little misleading. Its point is to refer to orders that are unplanned and change in ways that are hard to control and predict. Such orders are not "spontaneous" to the extent that they come into existence suddenly and for no apparent reason, like so-called spontaneous combustion. Natural languages got here before organized government showed up, but they continue to evolve today. This happens as certain expressions, like slang, become more widely used and others become obsolete—nobody (well, almost nobody) in England says things like "Look here" or "Oh, I say" nowadays, but they were once common. Similarly, new expressions are being introduced into English all the time, like the verbs "to google" or "to uber."

Governments do sometimes *try* to exercise control over natural languages, and the effects are instructive. France has tasked its Académie Française with inventing new French words to replace "Anglicisms" contaminating French conversation. The job of the bureaucrats in the Académie (known as "the immortals") is to mint alternatives for invasive expressions, such as "hashtag" ("mot-dièse"), "spamming" ("arrosage"), and "hacker" ("fouineur"). Readers old enough to remember the 20th century might like to know that the Francophone "baladeur" was assigned to replace the Anglophone "Walkman." (For younger readers, the "Walkman" was Sony's brand name for their portable cassette player, back when phones couldn't store or stream music—and weren't even portable!)

The case of the Académie illustrates an important point, which is that attempts to bring a spontaneous order under control are usually futile. Admittedly, the French government is merely "encouraging" its people

[1] For a fascinating account of how all Indo-European languages emerged from one proto-Indo European language spoken in the Eurasian steppes around 4,500 years ago, see David Anthony's *The Horse, the Wheel, and Language: How Bronze-Age Riders from the Eurasian Steppes Shaped the Modern World* (2007).

to eschew English words. Nobody is going to be hit with a fine, or prison, for saying "email" instead of "courriel"—though parts of French-speaking Canada have laws about what language can and can't be used in certain institutional settings, like schools. People do not choose words because they have any sort of freestanding preference. The force of *precedent* is what really does the work, as with many other norms and conventions. Once a word is established, it is hard for it to become displaced.

Languages evolved to solve a certain set of problems. Broadly speaking, human beings need to find ways to communicate and cooperate. Had we failed to do this, then our genetic ancestors probably wouldn't have reached the hunter-gatherer stage of civilization. Languages developed because of *what worked* when it came to having the sort of communicative signals that could facilitate effective cooperation. This does *not* mean that what evolved was perfect—more on this in a moment. Many words started off as arbitrary noises that got established through precedent. But some terms evolved precisely as a way of communicating something significant about the thing to which they referred. For instance, Australia's Western Brown Snake has an Aboriginal name of "gwardar." This means "go the long way around." If you ever encounter a Western Brown Snake, please remember what the Aborigines call it. All in all, there is a sense in which language takes care of itself.

The lesson here is that if something's not broken, we shouldn't rush to fix it. Spontaneous orders are usually complex orders. Complexity is, by definition, hard to get on top of. When one is dealing with a complex system, it is extremely difficult or even impossible to know how individual elements relate to the overall order. By trying to "fix" or change a spontaneous order, one risks doing more harm than good or even destroying the order altogether.[2] This will usually be on balance a bad thing, even if some minority might benefit in the process. Small changes, like swapping Anglophonic vocabulary for synonymous Francophone terms, will hardly bring the whole house down. But if you somehow designed a language from scratch, you'd struggle to make it nearly as effective as the natural languages already in use.

Another lesson is that not all spontaneous orders are equally good, even when they have evolved to do the same job. Interestingly some languages

[2] This is a result of their complexity, which means that the parts of the system relate to one another in hard-to-predict ways. See Scott Page (2011) for a general account of complexity and Steven Durlauf (2012) for an account of how complexity is important for public policy. For a philosophically rich discussion, see Jennan Ismael (2016).

appear to be better than others with respect to equipping their users with the ability to perform certain tasks. Asian languages are easier to learn than European languages when it comes to number words. European languages have an extra set of terms for the "teen" words, which don't obey the nomenclature used for larger numbers in the twenties, thirties, etc. English, for example, would be simpler if "thirteen" were something like "tenty-three." This extra terminological hurdle means that mathematics develops more slowly in people for whom English is the native tongue. A second problem is that European languages tend to use longer words for numbers, which apparently makes strings of numbers hard to remember.[3] This didn't matter for a long time, as early humans probably didn't need to do very much mental arithmetic. But it makes a big difference in today's world, where mathematical skill impacts substantially one's ability to compete in the labor market.

Evolution allows very complex and sophisticated sets of rules to develop, yet it has something of a randomizing effect as well. Different effects of evolution are seen in different places, even when environmental differences are minor. In Papua New Guinea, much society remains tribal and the population is composed largely of groups that do not engage in cooperation with each other. There are said to be around 800 languages in this part of the world, many of which are mutually incomprehensible. Because of this, large-scale cooperation, such as that needed to build elaborate institutions and infrastructure, is difficult to achieve in Papua New Guinea.[4] This randomizing aspect also explains why evolution often has results that are less than fully optimal, or become suboptimal when conditions change quickly. Biological evolution is not a fast process for complex organisms like humans (though some cultural evolution, like fashion, can advance very quickly). Consequently, institutional, physiological, and even behavioral change typically lags environmental change.

Let us now draw these observations together. Here are some important features of natural languages, which can be traced to the fact that they are spontaneous orders:

1. They got here on their own, developing earlier than (and as a precondition of) government agency.

[3] These cases are discussed by mathematician and cognitive scientist Stanislas Dehaene (2011).
[4] For some discussion of this case, see the remarks in Francis Fukuyama's (2011, xii–xiii) book.

2. An attempt at control or design from outside would be very difficult, perhaps ineffective, probably expensive, and might easily do more harm than good.
3. There are advantages to having a single spontaneous order encompass a large group of people, rather than having a fragmentation of orders covering isolated small groups of people.
4. They have typically evolved in response to local conditions, and they may not be an optimal reaction to those conditions or quick to adjust when these conditions change.

The properties on this list are *also true of markets*. The case for capitalism draws heavily on the *extent* to which this sort of argument can be sustained, particularly with respect to the first three conditions. The first two points feature in the main positive argument for capitalist society and against planned societies such as communism and socialism. The third point (which we come back to in chapter 8) features in arguments for increased global trade and against measures that encourage the global fragmentation of markets, like protectionist import tariffs. The fourth point leads to some qualifications in light of "market failures" and is the more problematic for any unqualified defense of capitalism based on spontaneous order.

Here it is easy to get ahead of ourselves. Let us pause to make an important qualification about the hazards of trying to make arguments out of analogies. We have chosen the analogy between markets and languages because of its high *illustrative* value. It allows us to make various descriptive points about humans' ability to evolve systems of cooperation to solve problems. Languages and markets can embody this sort of system. But it is very important to appreciate that the illustrative value of analogies is nothing more than just that. Further argument is required to show that markets *actually are* spontaneous to the degree that languages are. In general, relying *solely* on argument by analogy makes for quite a limited way of doing philosophy. A better approach is to use analogies to set up a position one might seek to defend, so that it can be readily understood by one's audience. One can then go in search of a more theoretical argument whose persuasiveness does not rely on the analogy, thereby accounting for why the analogy can be made in the first place.

This can be done for the language/market analogy, and we're about to show how, by telling you about an influential theoretical argument wholly independent of the analogy itself. But we want you to know that its degree of success has been disputed. Natural languages are something of an outlier, in terms of the very high degree of spontaneity that they exhibit. Markets are different, though how much different is precisely what philosophers and economists disagree on. Certainly, markets do not get going, or become successful, nearly as easily as languages do. Good evidence for this is that really successful, extended markets have arrived much more recently than languages, *after* the evolution of various supporting conventions and institutions (more on this later).

## 2. Prices and Information

One of Adam Smith's chief insights in *The Wealth of Nations* was that political economy should focus on the average individual rather than on the sovereign or upper classes. This shift in focus was not only moral and political in the way we've already mentioned but also epistemological—it was about the nature of knowledge and information, particularly regarding its dispersal within a population.

Smith saw that positive social effects can arise spontaneously from individuals pursuing their own economic interest, even if they did not intend and were not motivated to achieve those results. Near the beginning of *The Wealth of Nations*, Smith observes:

> It is not from the benevolence of the butcher, the brewer, or the baker, that we expect our dinner, but from their regard to their own interest. We address ourselves, not to their humanity but to their self-love, and never talk to them of our necessities but of their advantages. (WN I.2.12)

Read by itself, this quote can give the impression that Smith saw people as greedy or selfish. Attention to his wider body of work suggests otherwise.[5] Remember that Smith wrote largely to critique feudalism: his point about the butcher and baker is that if we want their meat and bread, then we ought to pay them for it—they're not anyone's slaves. Today, this sounds like a trivial claim (which may be why people think Smith must have been saying something more radical). But in Smith's day, the idea that we could get on better

[5] See, for example, Samuel Fleischacker (2004, 90–94). For more discussion of the "people are selfish" interpretation, see Montes (2016).

by making offers rather than threats was still somewhat new. The key feature of markets is that even though they rely on "self-love," they deliver mutual benefit. We can think of markets, then, as mechanisms for converting self-interest into mutual gain and doing so without requiring any explicit altruism from the people involved. How is this transformation possible?

Markets reward people only for generating something that someone else wants. But if people have market freedom, then they can act accordingly. Smith created an enduring metaphor to explain this idea—the invisible hand:

> Every individual . . . neither intends to promote the public interest, nor knows how much he is promoting it . . . he intends only his own security; and by directing that industry in such a manner as its produce may be of the greatest value, he intends only his own gain, and he is in this, as in many other cases, led by an invisible hand to promote an end which was no part of his intention. (WN IV.2.9)

Metaphors can be difficult to deal with—after all, they are never strictly "true" (there is not really any sort of hand, visible or otherwise, promoting any sort of ends). One way forward is to follow Geoffrey Brennan and Jonathan Anomaly (2014), who think of Smith's invisible hand as a type of spontaneous order having generally positive results. *Spontaneous order*, then, is not a moral concept, but a way of referring to ordered systems that lack a designer or planner. The *invisible hand* is a more specific, evaluative idea about the kinds of spontaneous market orders that can bring about prosperity and, on Smith's view, a more just, equal, and generally beneficial society.

When markets aren't generally beneficial or have serious side-effects, we might say that instead of an invisible hand, we have an "invisible fist." The point is that the spontaneous order of market forces will arise wherever possible, but the results of those spontaneous orders will not always be generally beneficial. Invisible hand processes are those spontaneous orders that arise and benefit everyone. As with markets, they will often require institutional preconditions to function beneficially and continue to do so. Much of what we are concerned with in this book are those very conditions.

In any case, Smith made it clear that he did not see the pursuit of self-interest as *always* leading to mutual benefit. Indeed, his *The Theory of Moral Sentiments* criticizes those who adopted this view. One of Smith's targets was Bernard Mandeville, whose poem *The Fable of the Bees* (1714) scandalously asserted that private vice might be public benefit in the sense that selfishness and greed really do create and sustain beneficial economic conditions. What Smith really believed was that we need properly functioning institutions to *harness* the pursuit of self-interest so that market exchanges can work in mutually beneficial ways. Indeed, the entire work can be read as an analysis of the institutions that work to direct the spontaneous order of the market into invisible hands that benefit everyone. Properly understood, this is to concede that markets are not, after all, quite like languages. The challenge is to achieve this harnessing while remaining appropriately deferential to the fact that we cannot take full control.

It took nearly two centuries before the "invisible hand" was explained in terms of prices and information. Friedrich Hayek gave logical precision to Smith's metaphor in his article "The Use of Knowledge in Society" (1945). For restating and deepening Smith's insight, Hayek was awarded the Nobel Prize in Economics in 1974. Hayek's work does much to make clear the extent to which market order is spontaneous and helps identify what degree of deference is appropriate when it comes to regulation.

Hayek's insight was to see prices as conveying information about quality, scarcity, and urgency. The information conveyed in prices alerts customers and suppliers to the current state of the market and directs them accordingly. Importantly, this information can't be gathered together by anyone looking to control things. It is only available in a dispersed form to the "man on the spot." While each person individually knows rather little about what things are needed and how they get produced, what's known collectively amounts to an enormous amount of knowledge. Although such knowledge remains spread around, enough of it can be passed from person to person, in small pieces, for problems of production and distribution to be resolved.

If there is an insect infestation in Colombia that ruins the coffee harvest, creating a shortage in the worldwide supply of coffee, consumers do not need to be told to consume less coffee. Why? The price, by going up when there is a shortage, tells coffee drinkers to either pay more or consume something else. This price also signals to other coffee farmers that now is a good time to increase production. Doing so will eventually reduce the price overall as the supply increases. Customers and sellers do not need to know anything about the status of Colombian harvests to know that they should decrease their consumption or increase their production; they only need to look at the prices. The "spontaneity" of the market order lies in the fact that the price of coffee works by itself, so to speak. Nobody trying to dictate the price is going to do so with enough knowledge to set the signal in the right place.

It is sometimes said that "knowledge is power." Hayek showed that a strong reading of this claim—that knowledge and power always go together—is profoundly false. While knowledge often confers power, the reverse is not true. Centralizing power over an economy, or any other large-scale cooperative system, does nothing to centralize knowledge of how that system *works* or could be made to *work better*. Knowledge remains dispersed, being passed around in small quantities by people's ability to signal to each other, through prices. In a working economy, nobody knows everything but everybody knows something. And things work best when it's kept that way.

## 3. Can Markets Fail?

Traditionally, the label "market failure" refers to cases where a market is "inefficient." This is a pretty broad usage. There is considerable obscurity and controversy as to what standards should be used to identify when markets have failed or succeeded. Economists since the 20th century have tended to measure a market's success in terms of preference satisfaction: markets work well when they provide alternatives that people generally want and have failed when there exists some (otherwise feasible) alternative preferred by most people and yet not brought about by market activity. Economists often refer to preference satisfaction as "welfare" or "wellbeing." It is, however, unclear as to whether this is the whole of what we should care about when evaluating the results of markets.

One problem is that this technical definition of welfare excludes many things that we might think are important. Market failures, in standard welfare economics, occur when there is some feature of a market that results in an "inefficient" or "suboptimal" outcome. This is a "failure" because markets are considered to "succeed" if and only if they generate an efficient or optimal social outcome. This is a pretty high standard that has a lot of questionable assumptions built into it, but it is nevertheless worth exploring.

When economists talk about "efficiency" or "optimality," they mean something very specific. "Efficiency" in the most general sense means that waste is minimized. An efficient engine is one that produces the least amount of additional heat and friction beyond what is needed. The particular understanding of efficiency used in political philosophy and economics means that some state of affairs (e.g., possible policy outcome, trade, or political regime) is efficient insofar as it is not possible for any reallocation of goods, rights, or whatever to make anyone better off by their own lights without making someone else worse off. This is called "Pareto efficiency" after the Italian economist Vilfredo Pareto (1848–1923). Some state of affairs is Pareto superior to another when moving to it would make no one worse off while making at least one person better off. A Pareto optimal state of affairs exists when it is not possible to make any more Pareto superior or dominant moves, though it is possible for multiple different Pareto optimal scenarios to happen simultaneously.

It is helpful to understand this idea in the single individual case, before looking at two individuals. Imagine that one person, Jack, has a certain amount of money that he wants to spend on dinner. He wants dumplings, but he wants some combination of steamed and fried dumplings. If we imagine that Jack has $20 to spend and that steamed dumplings cost $1, while fried dumplings cost $2, we can represent all the possible feasible combinations of dumplings that Jack can buy in Table 4.1.

In this example, since we can assume that it is impossible to buy half dumplings, this table shows all the possible allocations of steamed and fried dumplings that Jack can buy with his $20. Since we have stipulated that Jack wants to spend all of his $20 on dumplings, each of these allocations is *efficient* in the Pareto sense because there is no wasted money. An allocation of 8 steamed and 5 fried dumplings would be inefficient, however, because $2 would be left in his pocket, without buying any dumplings.

| Steamed | Fried |
|---|---|
| 20 | 0 |
| 18 | 1 |
| 16 | 2 |
| 14 | 3 |
| 12 | 4 |
| 10 | 5 |
| 8 | 6 |
| 6 | 7 |
| 4 | 8 |
| 2 | 9 |
| 0 | 10 |

**Table 4.1** Feasible Dumpling Combinations

The key point to note is that every single allocation pair listed here is identical from the point of view of efficiency. There is no difference, in terms of Pareto efficiency, between getting all steamed or all fried dumplings. We can assume, then, that Jack is *indifferent* between each efficient allocation. We can represent this continuously as what is called an *indifference curve.* Indifference curves for a particular good show what trade-offs between two or more goods an individual is indifferent between.

Consider the representation that follows. We can assume that Jack is equally happy (or indifferent) between any of the allocations on the curve (economists call it a curve, but in this case the line is straight). Indifference curves are typically concave or inward curved because of the "diminishing marginal utility" of most goods. This means that, for most goods, the more I have of it, I won't tend to benefit as much by getting another unit of it as I would by getting a unit of another good. In our case, the more steamed dumplings Jack has, the more likely he is to want to substitute an additional steamed dumpling for a fried dumpling. But, in this case, we have stipulated that there is constant marginal substitution rate between the two kinds of dumplings.

We can also assume that Jack prefers any allocation on the curve to any allocation below the curve. Any allocation above the curve is not feasible since it requires that Jack spend more money than he has available. In this case (but not in all cases) the indifference curve also represents Jack's budget line (see Figure 4.1).

This example illustrates how Pareto efficiency works and how it is related to indifference curves. We have, though, made some simplifying assumptions. As it happens, most indifference curves for normal goods are not straight like

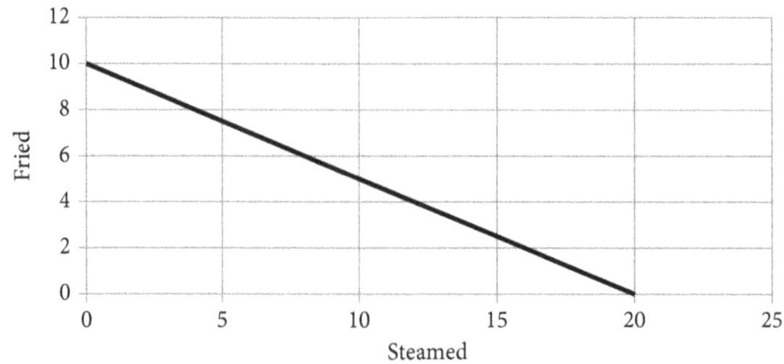


**Figure 4.1** Dumpling Indifference Curve

the one here, but bend inward. That is, they are *concave*. The curves bend inward because with normal goods, we assume there is marginal diminishing utility in the consumption of goods. That is, we assume one gets more utility from the first several units of the good than they get from the later units. Imagine you are walking around in the hot sun, thirsty. The first drink of water will give you a lot of satisfaction, but over time your satisfaction will decrease to the extent that you won't want water anymore.

In Figure 4.2, drinks of water are represented on the *x* axis, while utility is represented on the *y* axis. The dotted curve shows the total utility one gets from drinking water, while the solid graph shows the *marginal utility* of each additional drink of water, that is, how much more utility one gets from having an additional drink. Total utility goes up rapidly at first, but levels off once the drinker gets satiated.

Once marginal utility goes down sufficiently, people will substitute consumption of other goods which have higher marginal utility. This is what is going on with the concave indifference curves. The bending inward represents the marginal rate of substitution for a particular good.

Marginal utility is a crucially important concept in modern economics, and it goes a long way to explain why certain goods are more valuable than others and why scarce goods tend to be more valuable than abundant goods. The prices of goods are determined by the marginal buyer in the market, that is, by the last person that can be induced to buy a good at a profitable rate. (See chapter 6 on how this undermines the labor theory of value.) Cheaper buyers drive down the price of goods so long as there are possible substitutes.

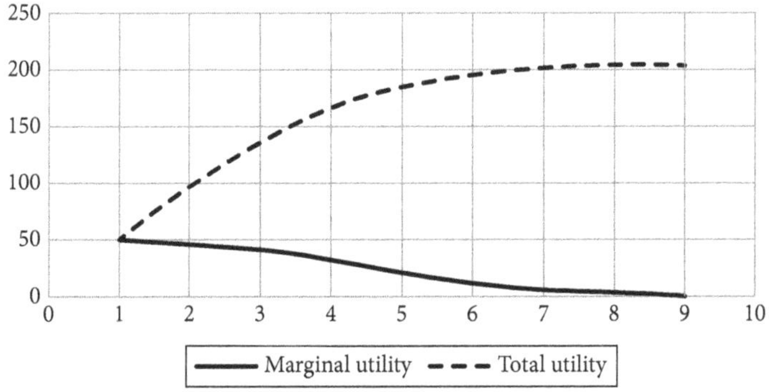


**Figure 4.2** Marginal and Total Utility

Let's return to Pareto optimality or the efficiency of a market as a whole. In a case with more than one person, the set of Pareto optimal possibilities (where there are no more opportunities for efficiency gains) is called the Pareto frontier. The Pareto frontier represents the set of Pareto *optimal* states of affairs, since it is impossible to move from the Pareto frontier elsewhere without making someone else worse off.

Markets succeed when they operate at the Pareto frontier. The standards by which market "success" and "failure" are judged are not neutral, however, and we should not accept them blindly. They make assumptions about the possibility and existence of optimal markets that are both overly restrictive and highly idealized. Instead, we can think of market "failure" more generally as a market that is not an invisible hand, that is, that does not produce what we might generally recognize as beneficial. Of course, there is disagreement about whether a given market is beneficial (as we will see), but in cases where the market creates results that many object to, we can think of a category of "badly behaved markets" that is more general than the traditional category of market failures.

With that caveat, we'll now look at some examples of what some economists and philosophers regard as "market failures" and some cases where markets seem to work less well than they should. While these are sometimes presented as important criticisms of capitalism in a more general sense, the cases we'll discuss in this section are specifically about apparent failures of the spontaneous order of price systems. It is important to note that the solution to market "failure" is typically not to try to substitute command systems (usually government action) instead of markets. Often the solution is to look at the institutional structure of the market and attempt to change those institutions so that the market can function better, with the "failure" removed.

## 4. Markets Behaving Badly

### A. Price Gouging

Let's begin with what an intuitive candidate for a market behaving badly, which is not strictly speaking a case of market failure. Under some conditions, prices suddenly get very high, very quickly. Think again about the coffee case. To be frank, coffee is not really a big deal. We can do without it easily enough.

But what about, say, refrigeration? Suppose a hurricane knocks out the power supply for several days in a large area. People can get by for a while without refrigerated food. But some people, such as diabetics, have a more constant and urgent need to keep medication cool. This explains why, after Hurricane Fran caused extensive damage to North Carolina in 1996, entrepreneurs were able to sell bags of ice for around ten times the normal retail price.[6] The entrepreneurs hired refrigerated trucks and drove the ice in from locations where Fran hadn't knocked out the power.

Some people considered this immoral market behavior. The entrepreneurs were engaged in what is called "price gouging"—charging vulnerable consumers an unjustly high price just because they could get away with it. It is notable that many jurisdictions actually place legal limits on prices, including North Carolina at the time. This reflects the widely held intuition that prices can become *unjustly high*, at least for goods and services whose supply is sometimes a matter of life and death. If this intuition is right, then the refrigeration case appears to be one where markets create injustice. The market did its thing—prices went up in accordance with demand and signaled to producers that there was money to be made by driving bags long distances, which they then did, and satisfied the demand of desperate diabetics. But the result was something going wrong—people being overcharged, exploited, or ripped off. Are people's intuitions, and parallel anti-gouging legislation, correct?

It's important to be clear on what kind of case this is. It's not just any old example of something costing more than we think it should. Sometimes, prices are high because government creates an artificial monopoly by restricting the legal right to trade, as when taxi rides are expensive because drivers must pay off high license fees whose price has been set by policymakers. Hayek would say that the injustice in *these* cases is that prices aren't being allowed to work properly as a signal, because the government has set up barriers to entry that inflate the price beyond the level that would be set under proper competition. But the refrigeration case is different. It occurred because of a genuine lack of supply that nobody engineered. Indeed, the price of ice got so high precisely *because* it was left alone.

Remember the definition of market failure from the last section. Is there any inefficiency here? Diabetics need something to keep their insulin cold and entrepreneurs arrive with ice from other areas to satisfy that need. Given

[6] Thrasher first encountered this example in a talk by Mike Munger.

the shortage of ice, the marginal value of the ice is very high, which is reflected in its price. If the sellers were to charge less, people would consume more than they need and some people would be unable to get the ice that they need. It seems like the market is working as it should in this case.

These facts lead some philosophers, such as Matthew Zwolinski (2008), to reject the intuition that there's anything unjust about the price in these types of cases. Zwolinski makes explicit use of Hayek's reasoning: if ice had stayed cheap, then the beer drinkers, being no doubt more numerous than diabetics, would have consumed the ice first. In fact, things probably wouldn't even have got that far: the entrepreneurs would have no incentive to rent trucks and drive ice so far, so they wouldn't have taken the trouble. The diabetics would have been the biggest losers, and there would have been no winners. The price spike did not create the exploitation of the diabetics. Instead, it came to the rescue.

Critics of Zwolinski have offered various replies. One is that price signals may not be as crucial as they were in enabling information to move around. After all, it's not as if we find out about hurricanes only when people are suddenly paying over the odds for ice. We have weather forecasting and news reporting, both of which are more effective than they were in Hayek's time, let alone Smith's. So we don't need a price signal to know that *some* people are in dire need of alternative refrigeration. If we spent money on rescue services, we could get ice (or some other alternative) to the diabetics without them being "gouged."

Hayekians might counter that the state would still have to work out *which* people need the ice, which might be difficult. The entrepreneurs simply set up shop and let the diabetics come to them, which worked easily and efficiently. Another counterargument points out that not everyone has equality of purchasing power. Some beer drinkers may be wealthy and willing to pay extra to chill their beer. Diabetics may simply be too poor to compete, even though, on any plausible measure, they need the ice more than anyone needs a cold beer. Here the Hayekian response would emphasize that capping prices still wouldn't ensure the ice got to the diabetics. Plausibly, then, the problem is a deeper one about background inequality or poverty, not the prices as such.

The refrigeration case puts pressure on the idea of a *fair price*. Hayek would say that a *correct* price is whatever sends the right signals to consumers and suppliers. This may conflict with certain intuitions we have. But Hayek's view supplies a serious explanation for why we ought to revise these intuitions. If you think that the refrigeration case involves an unjustly high price, then you might be able to work with some of the considerations about alternatives to prices where the flow of important information is concerned. But those considerations may be peculiar to the refrigeration case and may not arise with respect to other intuitive cases of "price gouging." If you want to respond in ways that equip you with a means to process other cases, then you need to offer an alternative theory of a fair price. That's not easy, though we will examine some ways of approaching this challenge when we talk about exploitation in Chapter 6.

## B. Positional Goods

Higher prices make it apparent that some good or service is needed, thereby inducing an increase in supply. But what about goods whose supply cannot be increased, simply as a matter of logic? Goods like this include what we call *positional goods*. How strong were your high school grades? Well, that depends partly on what grades other students got. The value of your grades was all about the *position* they gave you in the ranking of grades held by all students in your peer group. Educational grades are a classic positional good. Markets in positional goods are often badly behaved without being traditional market failures. Like the price-gouging case, markets with positional goods seem to work as they should but, in the process, create negative effects for a lot of people.

In the market for education, consumers often find themselves in relations of mutual conflict. Education is now one of the fastest growing costs associated with raising a child in developed countries. In some places this has led to an "arms race," in which children are being worked harder and harder so that they don't fall behind other children. And parents are spending more and more money to pay for this. This goes against what the optimists of the golden age had hoped for. Adam Smith was aware that status mattered to those who were comfortable enough not to worry about a roof over their head or food in their belly. Indeed, he criticized the wealthy for what he saw as the childish ways in which they competed for status. But he didn't appreciate that, as total wealth increased and more people were lifted out of poverty, demand for positional goods might grow. It's no accident that the more serious consumer arms races occur in countries with large middle classes, like the United States and South Korea.

Positional competition is a problem because a rising price can't induce greater supply. Educational grades aren't like bags of ice: if you give out more of what people want (top grades), you just devalue them and then nobody will be satisfied; they will just compete harder for other means of distinguishing themselves. This is what it means to say that logic itself limits the supply of a positional good. We'll come back to them in Chapter 9.

## C. Public Goods

What about goods that can't be given a price in the first place? These are public goods, which represent perhaps the most studied kind of market failure. Classically defined, a public good is "nonrivalrous" and "nonexcludable." Put simply, a good is nonrivalrous when its consumption by one party doesn't reduce the quantity or quality left for others. A good is nonexcludable when it is difficult or impossible to stop people from consuming it once it is produced. The "textbook" cases of public goods include law and order, coastal flood barriers, free-to-air broadcasting, and national defense. Markets, according to the "textbook" theory, cannot supply goods of this type at efficient levels.

The problem with nonrivalrous goods is that it is difficult to capture the cost of production: extra consumers do not require extra "units" of the good, and so there isn't really a per-unit cost that can be passed on to each consumer. If a good is nonexcludable, there will be little incentive to produce it since it will be impossible to recoup the full production costs. If I build a coastal flood barrier, then I can't "switch it off" for anyone who refuses to pay. This is an especially difficult problem if the good requires collective action to produce. Individuals will have an incentive to sit back and let others bear the cost of producing the good since, once it is produced, everyone can benefit whether one helped to produce it or not. In this way, nonexcludable goods enable "free-riding." Some nonrivalrous goods can be made excludable, for example, when walls are built around a baseball game so that spectators need to pay to come inside. We call these "club goods."

In accordance with the classic definition, we can distinguish these different categories of goods in Table 4.2.

One classic argument against markets was that it is impossible to supply public goods through the market alone. Free-riding (in the case of common pool resources) and underproduction (in the case of pure public goods) would make the production of essential public goods economically

| | Non-Rivalrous | Rivalrous |
|---|---|---|
| **Non-Excludable** | Pure Public Good (Broadcast Radio) | Common Pool Resource (Public Restroom) |
| **Excludable** | Club Good (Baseball Game) | Private Good (Laptop) |

**Table 4.2** Types of Goods

impossible. This "public goods argument" has often been viewed as *the* justification for state authority.[7]

While there is certainly a role for the state to produce certain pure public goods, it is important to remember that many things meeting the classic definition are now being produced without coercive taxation. The internet and other technologies have allowed the provision of what would have been previously thought to be impossible. One of the most widely used websites is the online encyclopedia Wikipedia, which hasn't even tried to make a profit. Wikipedia has been a great success in displacing traditional encyclopedias that were published in excludable form (as books or on cd-rom) and sold for a price. Elinor Ostrom won the Nobel Prize in 2009 for showing that many common pool resource problems can be solved voluntarily.

We should be wary of concluding that, when something is a public good, it follows that the government should just ensure its supply at any cost. Governments are often prone to their own public good–type problems, sometimes called "government failures." Some coastal flood barriers are better than others. Sure, it may be that everyone wants some kind of barrier. But do they want a bargain one or a top-of-the-range one? Ultimately, the decision here will be about how much tax to levy on people to fund the barrier's construction. Here there are no easy answers. And that's before we talk about public goods that some people want but others do not. A massive fireworks display may be both nonexcludable and nonrival. But does that mean that (all) taxpayers should be made to pay for it?[8]

[7] See, for instance, David Schmidtz's *The Limits of Government* (1991).
[8] If you want to know more about such difficulties, read Anomaly (2015).

## 5. Market Failure or Government Failure?

Well-behaved markets make all parties to an exchange better off. The reason is simple. People who are free to say "no" in a market will not agree to an exchange unless they think they will be made better off by it. This is not true, however, if coercion is used to force (or block) an exchange. When a robber demands "your wallet or your life," a kind of exchange is being proposed. The difference between this case and the market case is that only the robber is a net beneficiary of the exchange. In markets, both parties should see net benefits over the status quo; under coercion or threat of coercion, one party intentionally makes or threatens to make the other party worse off in order to force a transaction.

We can think of markets doing their job when they ensure and facilitate *mutually* beneficial exchange. When all the mutually beneficial exchanges that can freely be made have been made, economists call the market efficient. If we think efficiency is an important feature of market success, then making sure exchanges are made freely and without coercion is an important part for the institutional background that contributes to market success.

Market exchanges often have by-products that affects some third party. Economists call these "externalities." Pollution is a good example: we are happy to pay an energy company to burn coal to produce energy that we want, but many others have to deal with the pollution that the coal plant produces. Currently one of the worst places for air pollution is South Korea. According to some results, around 20,000 people may suffer premature deaths from air pollution every year there. While much of the air pollution comes from Korean production, a large amount, perhaps as much as one-third of the air pollution that affects urban areas like Seoul, comes from Northern China and is blown across the Yellow Sea (the name doesn't come from the pollution, but from the older effect of the Gobi Desert sand on the sea's color). The Chinese are not intentionally polluting Korea, but the Koreans are suffering nonetheless.

When dealing with these kinds of problems, the most desirable solution is to "internalize" the externality. For instance, if polluters have to pay for the full cost of their pollution, we might still get some pollution, but energy producers would have to calculate carefully how much pollution is needed to produce the energy that we all want. Which is to say that they will be forced to be more efficient. The trouble is that in many cases, we just don't know how to internalize the externalities.

At the same time, we must stress that not all externalities are bad. Some "positive externalities" are the result of what economists call "network effects." Think of the benefit of having a Facebook account. The authors are old enough to remember when Facebook was only available to certain university students and even when it wasn't available at all and people had to make do with now defunct websites like Friends Reunited and Orkut. If you're not from India or Brazil, then you probably haven't heard of Orkut. But you can find out about it for free on Wikipedia (another positive externality). Back then, it was somewhat interesting to have a Facebook account, but it only became really useful later when Facebook became open to everyone. More people on the social network makes the social network more valuable to each user.

When we see something that looks like a market behaving badly, sometimes the right response is to think of ways to improve the market. The alternative—government action—must rely on coercion or the threat of coercion. In some cases, this makes sense. In the American South until the 1960s, state "Jim Crow" laws prevented a variety of exchanges between whites and blacks. Black southerners were prevented from buying the same train and bus tickets as whites and were not allowed to stay in the same hotels and eat in the same restaurants. After the Civil Rights Act of 1964, the federal government used its coercive power to prevent the southern states from continuing these "Jim Crow" measures. The result was a clear decrease in the net level of coercion and an elimination of coercive blocks on exchanges (of all types) between whites and blacks. But really this was about *reducing* the degree of coercive planning in the market order. Jim Crow laws were not a market failure, but a government failure.

A generalized concern about "government failure" has been developed by the branch of scholarship known as public choice theory. One of the key ideas in this theory, developed in large part by James Buchanan (1919–2013), who won a Nobel Prize in Economics in 1986, is that whatever motives, good and bad, and whatever cognitive limitations we ascribe to ordinary people in the marketplace, we should also be aware that those same limitations and motives apply to people in government, including voters, politicians, and government officials or bureaucrats.

One important idea from public choice theory is the concept of "rent seeking." Broadly speaking, rents refer to incomes that are parasitic or extractive, or which don't reward genuine productivity. More technically, a "rent" to an economist is just a return that is higher than the "opportunity cost" of the good or service in question. Opportunity cost is the value of the next best use that one could put a good or service to—what you have to give up for something. So if you are deciding whether to spend an hour studying or watching TV, the opportunity cost of studying is what you need to give up in order to do it, in this case watch TV. Let's say you would rather watch TV than study, but if someone game you $20 to study, you would much rather study than watch TV, but if they offered $19, you wouldn't. We can now put a (rough) price on the value you get out of watching TV over studying; you like watching TV (all things equal) $20 more than studying. We can say the opportunity cost of studying is equal to $20. Now, if I offer you $30 to study rather than watch TV, I am offering a return $10 higher than the opportunity cost and that $10 is technically a "rent."

Markets are good at eliminating rents through competition and innovation, but governments are experts at creating rents in the form of monopoly privileges that protect certain parties from competition. One of the most vocal opponents to ride-sharing apps like Uber and Lyft are taxi companies One reason they are upset is something we mentioned earlier. In most cities, taxis are required to buy licenses to legally operate. Now, thanks to Uber and Lyft, individuals and companies that paid for these licenses find that they are worth far less, perhaps nothing at all. The point of these licenses was to increase barriers to entry into the taxi market, giving a rent to those who bought entry. Other government licensing schemes have similar effects. The moral of the story so far is that we shouldn't think that government intervention is always or even likely a solution to problems that we see in the market. Government action risks enriching those who speak the loudest and contribute the most to the campaign coffers of political parties. People are people and the problems we see in the market are often likely to be replicated or exacerbated when those same people are given coercive power to make changes.

Once again, though, other government "innovations" that have done much to aid the development of commercial society. There are many examples, such as the provision of bankruptcy protection, guaranteed education, safety nets, and so on.[9] If these actions are about facilitating the quasi-spontaneous order of a market economy, and insofar as they don't create too many privileges or block or force too many exchanges, then there can be a lot to be said for them.

Finally, we should want to be clearer about how we describe government actions when it comes to the economy. The production of cash, bankruptcy

[9] If you want to know more, take a look at Mariana Mazzucato's (2015) book in this chapter's Further Reading section.

protection, and the guarantee of a lender of last resort aren't really ways of *interfering* with an economy. Or at least they need not be. They can be, in some circumstances, more like enabling conditions for markets than interventions. Much rhetorical "defense" of capitalism suggests that *any* government action is an "interference" in a market that would otherwise be more "free" and better flourishing. This is highly inaccurate. The fact remains that trade is often facilitated when certain assurances are backed up by effective institutions and rule of law. Only then will they be prepared to fully trust strangers. Not all of these need to be done by the government, but some surely do.

If we accept that the market will work better given certain background provisions, there's a question about how far this should go. Bankruptcy protection provides businesses with insurance against catastrophe if they fail to be viable in a competitive market. If we provide such protection for businesses, then why not do something similar for individual workers in the event of unemployment or ill health? Hayek himself was willing to acknowledge as much.[10] We'll come back to this important question when we discuss the welfare state in chapter 7.

The bottom line is that, no matter how many concessions we make on grounds that the spontaneous order needs to be helped along, there has to be a sense in which we respect the fact that prices cannot simply be invented by anyone working outside of the effects of the widely dispersed information about supply and demand. Generalizing, we must accept that markets are to some degree a spontaneous order, meaning that we cannot look to government as the source of all economic prosperity. There'll always be a reasonable debate about how far the legacy of Smith and Hayek can go in the name of limiting (while sometimes vindicating) what government does. But it's so far stood the test of time as an account of how to make sure that we all have enough to eat, and then some.

## Conclusions

*This chapter has showcased one very important argument for capitalism, which is that an economy will work best if power is dispersed, so that the exercise of economic freedoms can enable information to move around a community through price signaling. Insofar as this happens when people are left to be free, rather than coerced, markets count as spontaneous orders. They are, however, not fully spontaneous*

[10] See for example his remarks in (Hayek 1960b, chap. 19).

*as governance is needed for various assurances and other enabling conditions. And prices cannot always be relied on to get the job done, as in the cases of alleged market failure that we've discussed. The invisible hand—the tendency of some spontaneous market orders to deliver mutual advantage and greater justice—usually requires certain background conditions. The cases of market failure are evidence for this, and raise questions about how to refine capitalism, but they do not rebut the basic point that price signaling needs to be allowed space to work.*

## Study Questions

- We have suggested that governments do not just "intervene" with markets but that they sometimes support, enable, or expand markets. How easy is it to draw the line between these different types of government action? How important is it to do so when evaluating market society?
- Imagine a society in which everyone (butchers and bakers included) was a moral saint—they worked tirelessly for the sake of others and not at all for personal gain. Do you think such a society would be able to produce everything that it wanted, or more than it could if it relied on prices?
- What are your intuitions about the refrigeration case and "price gouging"? Is it unjust to allow prices to spike in this way? If so, how do you decide what's a fair price? What else might be done besides legally capping prices?
- Can you think of any examples of public goods that it might be questionable to force people to fund through their taxes?
- Can you think of some more examples of both market failures and government failures? Once you've thought of a few, can you gain of sense of which might represent the greater social problem and which might be the harder to solve?

## Further Reading

*The End of Socialism* by James R. Otteson (Cambridge University Press, 2014)

Part one of this book provides a more extensive account of the way in which price signaling solves the problem of getting various goods and services supplied. The author also goes into much detail as to the difficulties of solving these problems through the alternative of centralizing power, as in a socialist economy.

"The Use of Knowledge in Society" by F. A. Hayek, *The American Economic Review* 35 (4): 519–530

Older, shorter, and less well known than his later works like *The Road to Serfdom* (also worth reading), but perhaps Hayek's most concise and readable articulation of the signaling argument laid out in section 2 earlier. This and other essays are also found in the excellent collection, *Individualism and the Economic Order*.

*The Entrepreneurial State: Debunking Public vs Private Sector Myths* by Mariana Mazzucato (2nd edition, Penguin Books, 2018)

Although not seeking to criticize any ideas about the importance of price signaling and spontaneous order, this book is a comprehensive attempt to document various ways in which government innovations have paid dividends, even if much of the praise has gone to entrepreneurs in the private sector whose creative efforts depending on these prior government efforts. Examples include the development of smartphones and solar panels.

*The Logic of Collective Action: Public Goods and the Theory of Groups* by Mancur Olson (Harvard University Press, 1965/1971)

This book was one of the first "killer apps" of public choice theory, applying the ideas to a variety of important topics. One of the important ideas Olson championed was the idea that government failure is so pervasive because of "concentrated benefits and diffuse costs." Those who benefit from government protection have a huge incentive to seek it, while those who will be harmed often do not. We will look at this idea in more detail in later chapters. This book also effectively demolished Marxist-style class analysis for the purposes of respectable social science.

*Free Market Fairness* by John Tomasi (Princeton University Press, 2012)

In this book, Tomasi attempts to combine a Rawlsian emphasis on fairness and equality with Hayekian insights about economics and society. The result is a defense of what Tomasi calls "market democracy." Overall, his work is a sophisticated and important contribution to capitalist theory and liberalism.

# 5

# So Why Not Socialism?

*In this chapter, we'll consider some of the more influential arguments for socialism. These turn out to support different guises of socialism. Two key internal questions for socialists are (1) whether a socialist economy is based on coercion or voluntary cooperation, and (2) whether production should involve markets and competition. Different combinations of answers serve to separate utopian, Marxist, and market socialism from each other (we also comment briefly on anarchism and fascism, which can be seen as retaining elements of socialism). The goal of this chapter is to compare and contrast these different schools of socialist thinking, with a view to seeing how each variety of socialism can be defended.*

## 1. The Century of Socialism

It is no exaggeration to call the 20th century the "century of socialism." On this historical narrative, the 20th century begins with a bang in mid-1914 with the assassination of Archduke Ferdinand by Serbian nationalist Gavrilo Princip. This act set in motion a comedy of errors leading to the globalized slaughter of World War I. By 1917, Germany was struggling to fight on two fronts. In an effort to destabilize the Russian government, they sent an exiled Russian revolutionary back to St. Petersburg—V. I. Lenin. With Lenin's return, the revolutionary Russian Marxist party (Bolsheviks) would topple the provisional Kerensky government that had taken over following the Czar's abdication. This led to the institutionalization of the world's first and most powerful Marxist country, triggering a series of revolutionary movements until the fall of the Soviet Union in early 1990s. Marxist socialism is still with us (in some form) in the People's Republic of China, Cuba, and to some degree in Laos and Vietnam. We suggested in chapter 3 that the Democratic

*The Ethics of Capitalism.* Daniel Halliday and John Thrasher, Oxford University Press (2020).

DOI: 10.1093/oso/9780190096205.001.0001

People's Republic of Korea (North Korea) is more feudal than socialist, with a hereditary monarchy—the Kim dynasty—in charge.

Marxist communism was not the only form of socialism to fire the imaginations of millions in the 20th century. Britain, United States, and most European countries practiced a kind of welfare state capitalism that mixed elements of socialism with capitalism. Latin America and Africa saw periods of socialist governance. The emergence of an independent Jewish state drew on the ideology of "labor Zionism," which (arguably) remained prominent in the early governments of Israel. So socialism has gained fans in many places and continues to appeal to many people worldwide. As of this writing (2019), several presidential candidates in the United States are self-described socialists and many more flirt with socialist policies. Several recent (2019) polls find that around one-third of American millennials identify with socialism in some sense. This raises the important question of what socialism is and whether it is a viable alternative to capitalism.

## 2. What Is Socialism?

How did socialism get popular? The short answer is that socialists are appalled at the myriad injustices of the economic status quo. They are upset by poverty and low wages, whose persistence they see as ever more perversely unjust in an era of high economic production. Socialists are also appalled by the power that private-sector employers have over their workers, wage levels aside.

This answer is incomplete. We say this because it is possible to share much the same indignation about the economic status quo and still defend capitalism. This is possible because the economic status quo is not a perfect instantiation of capitalism. Proponents of socialism very often refer to the status quo as "capitalism," though this can easily be questioned using the reasoning in both chapter 1 on defining capitalism and in chapter 3 on feudalism's comeback. The economic state of things in the real world is some mixture of feudalism, capitalism, and even socialism. The precise composition varies from country to country and from decade to decade. While it might be true that many, or even most, societies are closer to instantiating capitalism than the other two alternative systems, it doesn't *logically follow* that present economic injustices should be blamed on capitalism. It could even be that the status quo would be more just if it were purged of noncapitalist elements.

Socialists will want to say, of course, that moving the status quo toward a position of economic justice instead requires purging any capitalist and feudalist elements currently present in the mixture. But this takes arguments. It is *not* an adequate defense of socialism to just label the status quo as "capitalism," and argue from there, relying on the patent injustice of feudalism to leave socialism as the last alternative standing. What we want, instead, is a positive account of why socialism is the best system around when it comes to realizing justice. We are going to evaluate socialism in this chapter by considering attempts by socialist proponents to do this.

Before we ask what's morally attractive about socialism, we should ask, what is socialism? This question can provoke heated arguments. Just like the question of how to define capitalism, there is no consensus answer. Even so, socialism involves some combination of the following conditions:

1. Explicit planning of the economy; that is, most important decisions about who gets what and who owns what in society are *not* made by consumers in markets.
2. There are limited or no opportunities to own private property, especially private property used for production.
3. Most major and minor industries are owned and run by the state.
4. The types of legal employment contracts are severely limited.
5. International trade is limited in important ways.
6. Social class distinctions (particularly between workers and capitalist owners/employers) do not exist, or they are on a path to being erased.

The attentive reader will notice that the first three features are mirror images of the features we claimed were key elements of capitalism. Socialists believe that some other institutional structure besides the market should decide allocation and distributive questions in society (though some socialists still think markets have a place, as we shall see in the case of John Stuart Mill and his followers). Even socialists who see a role for markets want the market to do something other than merely serve consumer demand. As we emphasize in the next section, there has been considerable dispute among socialists about what these alternative institutions should be, but there is consensus that they should not be markets based on private property. Still, there's a lot more to socialism than the idea that private property and profit are bad, and that the government should nationalize things. In fact, insofar as intellectually serious socialists do believe these claims, they hold them not as first principles but as *conclusions* of arguments beginning with rather more sophisticated first principles.

## 3. Types of Socialism

There are several "flavors" of socialism that have been popular at various times in history. The most influential, both intellectually and politically, has been Marxism. But it was not the *first*. It is important to look at pre-Marxist socialisms both to understand Marxism as a system that grew out of these earlier ideas, and to get a sense of which other forms of socialism might compete with Marxism.

### A. "Utopian" Socialism

During the golden age of political economy, the Industrial Revolution caused both dramatic increases in productivity as well as huge dislocations of populations. Seeking to participate in the new economic opportunities, many people migrated to urban areas. The major European cities at that time lacked the infrastructure to support so many new occupants. Living conditions among the poor were horrendous. Working conditions in the new industries were often very bad, too. Long working days, hazardous workplaces, and little recreation meant a hard life for many. Many novels of the time, notably those by Charles Dickens, make some of these miseries explicit. But even novelists can disagree. In her *North & South* (1855), Elizabeth Gaskell portrays work in the "dark satanic mills" of England as liberating for many of the characters, especially the women in the novel.

The conditions of the workers led many people to conclude that markets were bad news for social justice.[1] These included a factory owner named Robert Owen (1771–1858). He was interested in creating working and living conditions that expunged what he saw as the degrading and damaging aspects of the new market economy. Owen, like many socialists after him, believed the character of individuals to be largely shaped by their living and working environment. The working conditions in the new economy created

[1] You can get more detail on utopian socialism from the further readings in chapter 2, such as the books by Heilbroner and Kishtainy.

the many vices of the working class. Their long hours and repetitive work made them idle unless they were overseen by managers. Without education or the possibility of decent recreation, they were given to drunkenness and vice when not working. Their health became poor and their life expectancy decreased. The urban workers of the Industrial Revolution in England and southern Scotland were typically several inches shorter than rural agricultural workers due to bad air/smog and poorer sanitation.

Owen thought he could remake Britain's workers into a virtuous and happy group if only their working conditions could be reformed. A utilitarian (influenced by the anarchist and presocialist utilitarian thinker William Godwin [1756–1836]), Owen was convinced that the dream of the "greatest good for the greatest number" could only be achieved if cooperation replaced competition. To that end, he set up an experimental community called "New Lanark," to the southeast of Glasgow. In this community, there would be no direct competition, education would be available for all, and young children would not work. Owen also believed, like Ricardo, that labor was the ultimate source of economic value. Because of this, he instituted a system whereby all purchases would be made by trading hours of labor rather than money.

Owen's experiment embodied a countercultural socialist strategy that would bypass state power. His utopian communities were voluntary, not centrally controlled or designed. These communities were copied by other countercultural reformers in the United States and Britain.[2] The term "utopian" socialist was an insult that Marx leveled against all his socialist forbearers, but in the Owenite sense, there label is more accurate than insulting: the Owenites were interested in utopian experimentation as its own distinctive project.

The two-other important "utopians" were St. Simon (1760–1825) and Charles Fourier (1772–1837). St. Simon was a French thinker who wanted to "rationalize" economic life. He argued that markets were unscientific because they left the allocation and distributional questions of society to the seeming anarchy of individual choice. Simon believed that this process should be put under rational, scientific control. Fourier, like Owen, believed

[2] Owenism was quite popular in the United States. Two such communities, Utopia and Modern Times, were founded by American Owenite Anarchist Josiah Warren. In these communities, money was substituted for "labor notes" and goods were traded directly for labor. One such "time store" was opened in downtown Cincinnati, Ohio. On Josiah Warren and American individualist anarchism, see Jennings (2016).

in creating ideal communities of noncompetitive workers who would be organized into "phalanxes" of 400 families. Groups this size, Fourier thought, were big enough to cooperate effectively, but small enough for everyone to form a strong community bond.

Fourier believed that besides competition, the main problem with capitalism lay in the work that the poor must do. They tend to hate their tedious jobs (more on this in chapter 6). To alleviate this, Fourier thought workers should rotate into different jobs every few hours so that they didn't get too bored of any individual task. Sharing Owen's belief in the importance of education, Fourier also predicted a coming 8,000-year-long socialist paradise where the seas would turn to lemonade, temperatures would warm, and each woman would have four husbands. For Fourier, "the life of the Phalanstery is a continual orgy of intense feeling, intellection, & activity, a society of lovers & wild enthusiasts."

Despite his strange views about the future, Fourier was extremely influential. Not only were his phalanxes tried in several parts of the United States and England, but many of his ideas about education, work, and even sex were adapted by later socialists. His ideas were especially influential in the work of the early socialist anarchists.

## B. Anarchism

The utopian socialists didn't advocate much by way of state action. Instead, they focused on practical experiments in living that they hoped would demonstrate the superiority of socialism. In this way, they shared much with the great liberal thinkers of their time. They both believed that reason and demonstration would show that their social ideas were superior.

Another group took the idea of the importance of voluntary association much further. Whereas the utopian socialists merely aimed to bypass the state, this group, the anarchists, believed that organized coercion and violence in the form of the state should play no role in social life whatsoever.

Three anarchists stand out and deserve mention. The first is Pierre-Joseph Proudhon (1809–1865), a Frenchman who is generally believed to have coined the term "anarchism." Proudhon developed a theory of *mutualism* that owes much to the ideas of Ricardo. Like Ricardo, Proudhon believed that only income that derives from labor could be justified, leading him to famously claim that "property is theft." What he meant, though, is that *most* property is theft because it is derived from nonlabor sources. It is possible to have property and engage in trade justly, Proudhon thought, in an economy based solely on labor value and voluntary association.

Other influential anarchists from around this time include Mikhail Bakunin (1814–1876) and Peter Kropotkin (1842–1921). Bakunin is the most colorful personally, and Kropotkin is the most interesting theoretically. Bakunin was jailed in Siberia at one point for his part in various uprisings. He managed to escape to the United States, eventually returning to Europe. He is notable as a fierce critic of Marx, especially his idea of the "dictatorship of the proletariat" (more on this later). His greater fear was that Marxism would eventually vest some small group with absolute power, making them worse than the most authoritarian state:

> They [the Marxists] maintain that only a dictatorship—their dictatorship, of course—can create the will of the people, while our answer to this is: No dictatorship can have any other aim but that of self-perpetuation, and it can beget only slavery in the people tolerating it; freedom can be created only by freedom, that is, by a universal rebellion on the part of the people and free organization of the toiling masses from the bottom up.

In this way, his criticisms of Marx and Marxism accurately predicted the horrors of Marxist states in the 20th century.

In the United States, Owenite socialism, Herbert Spencer's views on evolution, and Proudhonian anarchism combined into what became known as "individualist anarchism." Like Proudhon, these anarchists did not reject capitalism and markets as such, rather they rejected what they saw as the unproductive aspects of the economy.[3] Many of these anarchists like Lysander Spooner and Benjamin Tucker tended to disagree with their European comrades over economics, however. They saw any strongly collectivist form of socialism as comparable to the state in its oppressiveness, and they strongly preferred mutualist markets and voluntary cooperation when possible. Anarchism, though its theoretical defense has evolved in the years

[3] Although not an anarchist, Henry George believed in a freer and fairer world close to one envisaged by socialists. His book, *Progress and Poverty*, was one of the great bestsellers of the of the 19th century. Many contemporary thinkers are either influenced by Goerge (such as so-called left libertarians) or have revived noticeably Georgist ideas in a more sophisticated form (especially Eric Posner and Glen Weyl's [2018] *Radical Markets*).

since, continues to be a serious research program attracting serious theoretical defenders.

## C. Marxism

For many socialists in the 20th century and even today, Marxism *is* socialism. This is because, more than anyone else, Karl Marx (1818–1883) created a socialism embodying a unified economic, political, and philosophical vision. This actually makes it hard to give a concise overview of Marxism. We noted in chapter 1 that, in the academic community, being accused of misinterpreting Marx is tediously common. What we say here is likely to be rejected by some Marxists, both academics and activists. Do keep this in mind. Of course, the best way to decide for yourself what Marx really thought is to go and read his texts, copious as they are.[4]

Following the German philosopher G. W. F. Hegel (1770–1831), Marx believed that history follows certain laws. Hegel believed that world history was the progressive realization of self-consciousness, which would culminate in a state of mutual recognition, justice, and freedom. Marx believed, instead, that history was driven by the development of the organization of economic life. The process of history is the accumulation of "contradictions" at one stage of history that must be resolved by moving to a new stage of history. Marx saw capitalism as the natural successor to feudalism, with communism the natural progression from capitalism.

Marx saw socialism as inevitable because capitalism would lead to the immiseration of the working class. The workers would ultimately revolt, installing socialism. Marx labeled his version of socialism "scientific" in contrast to the "utopian" socialism of those who came before him. The difference, he argued, was that he gave an economically sound argument for why socialism is necessary and why it will be salutary when it comes. The utopians didn't do this. Even though they did try to put their ideas into practice, usually on a local level, they lacked particularly sophisticated accounts of the mechanism of production and distribution to guide them. Marx, on the other hand, thought he did.

[4] We'd recommend beginning with *The Communist Manifesto* (1848) or perhaps the *Economic and Philosophical Manuscripts* (1844), rather than the much longer *Capital* (1867), even though we quote from it in this chapter. An easy way in to Marx's writings is Jonathan Wolff's (2003) excellent short book, in this chapter's Further Reading.

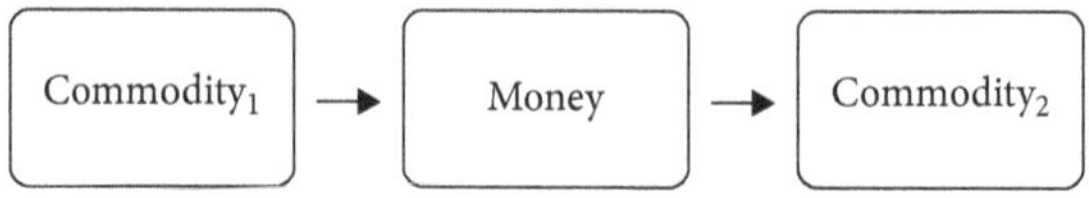


**Figure 5.1** C-M-C Circuit

Marx adopted the labor theory of value. He writes, "as values, all commodities are only definite masses of congealed labor-time."[5] But economic value is not a unitary concept, according to Marx. Marx followed Smith in identifying a difference between "value in use" (e.g., the value I get out of using a hammer) and "value in exchange" (e.g., how much money I can get in trade for that hammer). Marx went beyond Smith in suggesting that capitalist economies cause value in exchange to get divorced from value in use, in ways that create problems.

We can see this in what is called the C-M-C circuit and the M-C-M circuit (see Figure 5.1). In the first circuit, we trade one commodity (say corn) for money in order to buy another commodity (say wood). This can make sense, because even though the two commodities may have the same value in exchange (they cost the same), they can have different value in use. I might need more wood than corn, for instance. Simple economies, according to Marx, have this form.

Capitalist economies, however, are different. Capitalists raise money in order to buy commodities in order to make more money. This inverts the original formula. Suppose the capitalist buys corn on the market when it's cheap and sells it later when it's scarce. According to Marx, the capitalist has merely increased the value in exchange without increasing the value in use. But how is this possible? Marx argues that $M_2 = M_1 + \Delta M$, which means that the second and greater value in exchange must equal the original value plus some incremental increase. Where does this increase come from?

Marx believed the answer was labor *power* (e.g., the power to work eight hours) is what is sold on the labor market, not labor itself. Labor power has value in exchange, but not value in use. Marx argued that the full labor power of the worker was being used by capitalists, but only some fraction of that was going back to the worker as wages.

The missing value in the M-C-M circuit (see Figure 5.2) is the *surplus* value that capitalists are effectively stealing from the workers when they

[5] See the opening chapter of his magnum opus, *Capital*.

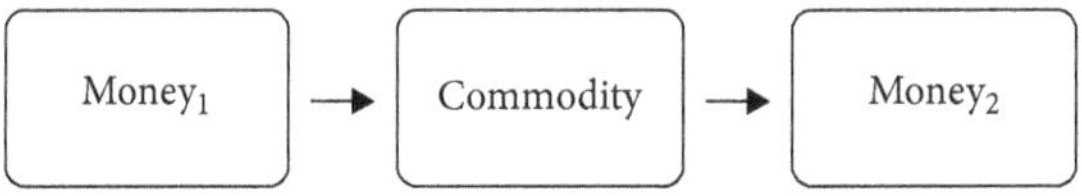


**Figure 5.2** M-C-M Circuit

trade with them (hence, the exploitation lies in the worker getting back less than their labor power has allowed them to put in). Capitalists can do this because of the bargaining power they have over the workers: the capitalists own the means of production, but the workers do not.

More on the moral significance of Marxist exploitation in the next chapter. For now, remember we're emphasizing Marx's theory of history—the mechanisms through which capitalism emerges (according to Marx) before being displaced by socialism. Marx argued that, over time, capitalists would reinvest more and more of their profits into machinery that would help to automate more and more work. Consequently, the number of jobless workers would continue to grow, creating a "reserve army" of the unemployed—so-called because they can be relied upon by capitalists to replace any workers who strike or walk away. As such, a constant degree of unemployment would maintain the bargaining position of the capitalist over the worker, allowing the capitalist to pay even less for labor power. Over time, the working class is driven to complete misery:

> It follows therefore that in proportion as capital accumulates, the lot of the laborer, be his payment high or low, must grow worse. The law, finally, that always equilibrates the relative surplus-population, or industrial reserve army, to the extent and energy of accumulation, this law rivets the laborer to capital more firmly than the wedges of Vulcan did Prometheus to the rock. It establishes an accumulation of misery, corresponding with accumulation of capital. Accumulation of wealth at one pole is, therefore, at the same time accumulation of misery, agony of toil slavery, ignorance, brutality, mental degradation, at the opposite pole, i.e., on the side of the class that produces its own product in the form of capital.[6]

This "antagonistic character of capitalist accumulation" eventually leads to revolution and the replacement of capitalism with socialism. Interestingly,

[6] These remarks come from later in *Capital*, chap. 25.

though, Marx says very little about how socialism will actually work. In the real world, states that have ostensibly identified as Marxist have been heavily committed to centralized economic control through coercion. These ended in disaster (see later). Thoroughgoing Marxists may blame this on the Russian and Chinese revolutions coming too soon: both countries switched to communism without first "graduating" from feudalism to capitalism, and then waiting, contrary to Marx's theory of history.

In addition to the possibility of a premature revolution, it is not obvious that Marx was wedded to the idea of permanent central coercive economic planning. Indeed, one of the most intriguing Marxist predictions was of the eventual "withering away of the state," as people learned to be productive without government, and true *communism*, as opposed to socialism, could finally be achieved.[7]

## 4. Market Socialism

Marx was suspicious of labor markets largely because of class conflict. But could a system in which people sold labor for wages exist without the division between workers and capitalists? John Stuart Mill thought such a system was possible and used this idea to develop a different kind of socialism.

One of the most philosophically interesting chapters in Mill's *Principles of Political Economy* is the seventh chapter of book four, titled "On the Probable Futurity of the Labouring Classes." Mill was disdainful of people whose ownership of capital granted them idleness while workers suffered. Evidence for this can be found scattered around *Principles*, but the following remark is representative:

> I do not recognize as either just or salutary, a state of society in which there is any "class" which is not labouring; any human beings, exempt from bearing their share of the necessary labours of human life, except those unable to labour, or who have fairly earned rest by previous toil. (IV.vii.2)

[7] The phrase was not actually used by Marx but by his associate, Friedrich Engels, in a book called *Anti-Duhring* (1878), which discussed some contemporary criticism of Marx. For a full discussion of the ways that socialists interpreted the coming socialist utopia, see Yuri Slezkine's (2017) *The House of Government* on the Russia Revolution and Leszek Kolakowski's (2008) *The Main Currents of Marxism*.

This sounds like the stuff that might be used to argue for a welfare state, or massive redistribution of wealth. Mill believed in some redistributive policies, such as inheritance taxes. But the main agenda of the chapter on the workers' "probable futurity" is about workers gradually taking over the system of production.

Mill's is an early version of what's now known as *market socialism.* There will be no owners of capital besides workers (or perhaps retired workers) who work on that capital. This goes all the way to the top where firm hierarchy is concerned: managers are to be elected not by a board or external shareholders, but by the workers themselves. What we have is still a market society, but one in which production is enabled by worker cooperatives, rather than standard hierarchical firms with internal hierarchies, against a background of class distinctions.

Mill found market socialism attractive because of his optimism about the human condition and the tendency of human relationships to work better when based on reciprocal exchange rather than hierarchical pressures. In this way, he was applying the defense of market society that runs through Adam Smith. Indeed, Mill claims in the preface to his *Principles* that his book is really an attempt to update Smith's ideas in light of evidence made available by the Industrial Revolution. Mill's case for market socialism is clearly egalitarian. Other remarks in the "futurity" chapter make this explicit:

> The form of association, however, which if mankind continue to improve, must be expected in the end to predominate, is not that which can exist between a capitalist as chief, and work-people without a voice in the management, but the association of the labourers themselves on terms of equality, collectively owning the capital with which they carry on their operations, and working under managers elected and removable by themselves. (IV. vii.21)

Mill favored allowing people greater freedom to participate in positions long reserved for the economic elite. Indeed, this chapter also sees Mill defend the right of women to enter male-dominated professions—a radical view at the time. But widening participation leaves things open as to whether workers should all draw the same salary. Some modern market socialists believe that, in a proper worker cooperative, all workers should be paid the same. Another view is that those elected to managerial positions, with greater responsibility and (perhaps) burdens, may be entitled to larger salaries, as might those performing especially unpleasant tasks.

As the earlier quotation reveals, Mill also thought that market socialism was *feasible*. He believed that, as education improved, more power and trust would be given to workers. Ultimately, "the relation of masters and work-people will be gradually superseded by partnership."[8] The fact that Mill saw this outcome as very *likely* perhaps explains why his moral defense of market socialism does not go as far as it might.

Is market socialism really socialism, or just a modified sort of capitalism? On the one hand, Mill was adamant that competition was a good thing and that worker ownership retained it.[9] And Mill distanced himself quite explicitly from other types of socialism. On the other hand, Mill did actually describe himself as a socialist—something that came out in his posthumously published (and unfinished) *Chapters on Socialism*.

We have included reference to the ending of class distinctions among our central tenets of socialism earlier. Whether endorsing this condition without the others meant Mill was right to self-identify as a socialist, and whether he did so when he wrote *Principles*, continues to be the subject of disagreement among contemporary scholars. What's most important is that market socialism remains a contender in contemporary thinking about how to address economic injustice and that Mill's work is an important landmark in making it a contender. If socialism is about removing hierarchical class conflict, then yes, market socialism really is a form of socialism—just keep in mind that it rejects most else of what's in Marxist socialism.

Whether market socialism is feasible depends on how easily an economy can move beyond the current state of having companies reliant on wage labor instead of worker ownership. More on this later. It's also unclear whether we could transition to market socialism without a good deal of state coercion and whether maintaining it might, after all, require more of the same. Proponents of market socialism often suggest that even a costly transition of this sort is better than the Marxist alternative of a revolution, which after all will probably get many people killed. They have a point.

[8] PPE IV.vii.14).

[9] See the closing remarks of the chapter: "Instead of looking upon competition as the baneful and anti-social principle which it is held to be by the generality of Socialists, I conceive that, even in the present state of society and industry, every restriction of it is an evil, and every extension of it, even if for the time injuriously affecting some class of labourers, is always an ultimate good" (IV.vii.65).

## 5. Problems with Socialism

According to some sources, the death toll attributable directly to socialism in the 20th century is around 125 million people.[10] Why has socialism has been so spectacularly unsuccessful and brutal everywhere it has been tried? Several different reasons stand out.

The first is that socialists were empirically wrong about capitalism. The average wage and income of workers has risen substantially since the 19th century in all countries that have allowed economic freedoms (and hence markets) to operate, even if (and maybe because) they have substantially regulated their economies.

In terms of life prospects, there is no comparison between, for instance, the United States of the 1850s and the United States in the 21st century. All Americans, even the poorest, are many magnitudes richer than at any time in the past. This is true elsewhere (recall the list from chapter 1). The only places where this is not true (parts of Africa, Asia, and South America) is where noncapitalist approaches (primarily some form of socialism) were extensively tried.

Marx and other socialists were just wrong that moving toward capitalism would impoverish workers permanently (that is, until a revolution). In fact, the exact opposite has happened everywhere capitalism has been tried. The rise of markets has universally (though not uniformly) enriched workers, while socialism has impoverished them.

This fact is compatible with the view that economic justice requires some state ownership of industries like healthcare and that markets work best given some important elements of state support, not least because a system that delivers benefits on average in the long run will usually create losers, too. Indeed, as we are emphasizing throughout this book, most successful societies are not purely run on markets and competition. Where we find success, however, we—without exception—find markets not centralized planning. Indeed, an explanation for why Marxists were empirically wrong is largely provided by the argument about spontaneous order and price signaling given in chapter 4.

The second is that the core of Marxist socialist theory, the labor theory of value, is false (recall chapter 2). Indeed, virtually all the core *economic* ideas of socialism are false. The reason for this is simple, but nevertheless

[10] On this point, see *The Black Book of Communism* (Panné et al. 1999).

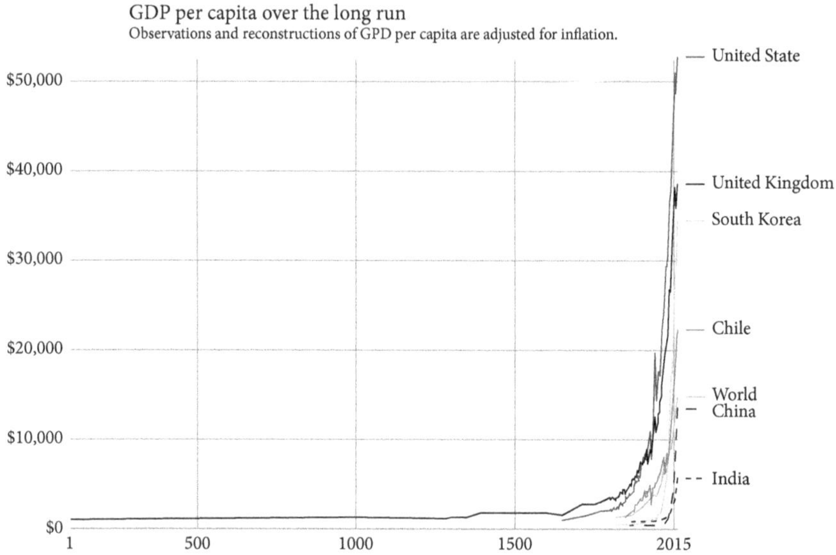


**Figure 5.3** Long Run per-capita GDP
Chart from Max Roser (2020).

important. Socialist economics, especially in its Marxist form, became tied to political movements and to institutionalized communist ideology. This made free thought and innovative socialist economic thought very difficult during most of the 20th century. Any deviation from the Marxist party line was seen as an attack on socialism and was therefore discouraged. This is a problem because virtually the year that Marx's master work *Das Kapital* was published, a revolution occurred in economic thought that would sweep away the labor theory of value—the entire engine of Marx's theory of exploitation and history.

These ideas, developed independently by three different thinkers (Jevons, Menger, and Walras),[11] showed that economic value is best understood as subjective and that prices are related to the "marginal" value of a good, not its total value (see Figure 5.3). Effectively, all economic value is exchange value. This may sound abstract—a simple way of putting it is to note that the price of just about anything will drop when it has been produced in very large quantities, or if demand drops for some reason, such as a change in

[11] You can find larger discussions of these figures and their influence in the Kishtainy and Heilbroner books from the Further Reading section in chapter 2.

fashion, or a new alternative product is brought to market. The price of analog cameras dropped dramatically with the introduction of superior digital cameras, and analog photography, once huge, is now a tiny niche market. (If you were born in the 21st century, you may not have heard of Kodak, but it was a more valuable company than Coca-Cola until shortly before you were born.) But this has got nothing to do with the labor that goes into producing analog cameras or any other product that enables them to be used. This has important consequences for what Marx wanted to say about the role played by capitalists in exploiting workers, but we'll come back to this in chapter 6.

The third is what we can call the "incentive problem." As we have seen, socialists going right back to Robert Owen believed that individuals are strongly shaped by their work environment. Marx believed this as well. Capitalism, according to the socialist, perverts our motivation and desires so that we are only interested in working on the basis of monetary incentives rather than for the common good or for the community. This will change, they believed, once communism is established.

This socialist acceptance of central planning is an extreme example of the belief of what Adam Smith called the "man of system":

> The man of system . . . is apt to be very wise in his own conceit; and is often so enamoured with the supposed beauty of his own ideal plan of government, that he cannot suffer the smallest deviation from any part of it. He goes on to establish it completely and in all its parts, without any regard either to the great interests, or to the strong prejudices which may oppose it. He seems to imagine that he can arrange the different members of a great society with as much ease as the hand arranges the different pieces upon a chess-board. He does not consider that the pieces upon the chess-board have no other principle of motion besides that which the hand impresses upon them; but that, in the great chess-board of human society, every single piece has a principle of motion of its own, altogether different from that which the legislature might chuse to impress upon it.[12]

The socialist planner, like the man of system, is enamored with the beauty of their ideal form of society and attempts to realize that social order without considering whether the members of society are also interested this goal.

[12] These lines come (perhaps surprisingly) not from Smith's *Wealth of Nations* but from his *Theory of Moral Sentiments*, which was written earlier (1759): VI.ii.42.

This is not to deny that a work environment can be a horrible place (Smith claimed as much, even though he wrote before the Industrial Revolution filled England with "dark satanic mills"). Human beings, as Smith argues, have their own interests and desires, which may or may not accord with the plan of the socialist. By trying to force individuals into socialism, we can expect resistance and disorder.

Indeed, this is what we did see in actual 20th-century societies that identified as socialist. Millions died in the 1932–1933 terror-famine in Ukraine (the Holodomor) after the forced collectivities of farmers mandated by the Soviet State.[13] The so-called Great Leap Forward in 1958–1962 Maoist China resulted in an estimated 55 million deaths due to famine and state-sponsored violence.

Perhaps the most extreme example of the imposition of a socialist plan on an unwilling population was in Cambodia. In 1975, the communist Khmer Rouge came to power and declared "year zero." The city-dwelling population was driven into the jungle to live and work as teams of farmers and laborers. Educated people such as doctors, teachers, and lawyers were targeted as class enemies and killed, as were ethnic minorities. Estimates put the death toll at around one-third of the entire Cambodian population within just a few years, before the Khmer Rouge was toppled by a Vietnamese invasion in 1979.

More prosaically, incentives in socialist societies are often skewed away from what people want and toward, instead, what the plan or planner wants. There are stories from the Soviet Union that when the incentives were based on quantity quotas, for instance, the number of screws produced in one week, workers would make a huge number of tiny or easy-to-manufacture screws. When the planners wised up and changed the quota to the overall weight of the screws, the workers would make a small number of very large and heavy screws.

Underlings in a planned order are generally under pressure to tell their superiors what they expect or want to hear, rather than what is actually true. It is said that when Mao Zedong toured China by train during the Great Leap Forward, each local authority moved bushels of wheat from miles around into the fields by the railway line. Local officials behaved in this way to ensure that Mao did not learn the truth about the famine, as this would certainly lead to their being punished.

[13] See Robert Conquest's (1987) *Harvest of Sorrow* and Anne Applebaum's (2017) *Red-Famine*.

It is notable that these problems are by no means confined to economic production but extend—in very parallel fashion—into other contexts in which centralized power tries to control things. In the early 1980s, Soviet spies were told to gather evidence "confirming" belligerent intentions in Western governments. Rather than risk dismissal for being "unproductive," spies in NATO countries sent concocted or exaggerated reports back to Moscow, which merely reinforced the paranoia that had convinced politburo members that Western hostility is precisely what spies *would* discover. Paranoia became so heightened that the Soviets temporarily misinterpreted a NATO military exercise as the real thing and almost started a nuclear war.[14]

Last, but not least, there is the "knowledge problem." This relates directly to the incentive problem and Smith's criticism of the man of system. The problem is that in the market, individual consumption decisions work to determine the price of goods (consumer sovereignty). The problem, as F. A. Hayek (1940, 1945) argued, is that in the socialist economy, there are no prices to send the signals about what needs to be produced (we covered the details of this argument in chapter 4). Planners in the socialist economy must try to simulate prices, but they will never have all the information that they need. Chaos and shortages are inevitable.

This creates a dilemma for socialism. Either simulate the market in order to have as close to an efficiently functioning economy as possible or give up on prices entirely. The Soviet economy initially took the second route in its "war communism" phase (1918–1922), but huge shortages and economic chaos led them to introduce the New Economic Policy (1922–1928), which replicated certain aspects of markets. They did this to prevent unrest and revolt. For the rest of the Soviet era, planners set prices and production quotas centrally and attempted to engineer the economy. This was never very successful, and black markets flourished.

A similar problem has haunted all other attempts at establishing socialist economies. These considerations count against the "diehard" Marxist claim that the likes of China and the USSR would have fared better if they had put up with a century or so of capitalism prior to having their revolution. While a period of capitalism may have meant some valuable capital left over from

[14] For the full (and rather terrifying) story, read Downing (2018). To be fair, the US military, perhaps the most elaborate planned order in the capitalist world, also works in ways that reportedly increase the possibility of unintended nuclear war. See especially Daniel Ellsberg's (2017) *The Doomsday Machine*.

the revolution, this would not have been enough to forestall the incentive problem or the knowledge problem.

But what about market socialism, of the sort favored by John Stuart Mill? The only difference is that the workers own the capital on which they work. Why should this stop them from responding to price signals? The short answer is that it doesn't. Indeed, market socialism may well be immune to the knowledge problem and the incentive problem. And this explains why some worker cooperatives exist and why a number of them can compete with conventional firms.

But market socialism has other problems. One is that the worker cooperative may not be very scalable. Workers squabble a lot when given power. Shareholders are a more passive type of owner. A company whose owners stay quiet while a small group of executive directors make all the decisions may simply stand a better chance of getting things done than a company that tries to devolve all of its ownership rights to a large body of workers, all of whom must simultaneously be kept happy by the managers. These considerations approximate the theory of the firm (recall chapter 3), which Mill did not anticipate. This is not to say that Mill's vision is completely unfeasible—some industries seem to allow worker cooperatives to flourish. And it might be a good thing if more cooperatives could find ways to be competitive. But it remains difficult to figure out what, if anything, would help them become the norm.

What we can say, however, is that while it might not be easy to abolish the conflict between owners and workers, it might often be possible to do something to increase workplace democracy in ways that reduce the antagonism of class conflict without removing it entirely. Market socialism, or at least something closer to it than the status quo, would almost certainly advance justice in labor markets. Workers might not be given ownership, but they can certainly be given more rights, particularly with regard to countervailing powers with which they might hold their managers to greater account. Much is up for debate about what possibilities exist when it comes to increased worker ownership or control of firms, and how desirable they might be.[15] But more experimentation in firm organization might create competitive pressures that could at least make worker control more widespread.

[15] See, for example, the survey article by Frega, Herzog, and Neuhauser (2019).

## 6. Ideals and Reality

Confronted with these problems and with the abject failure of all attempts at socialism, committed socialists might be tempted to argue that none of the actual versions of socialism so far attempted were *real* socialism. Instead, they were all impure corruptions of what remains an attractive ideal.

This response raises an interesting question about how to evaluate economic and political systems more generally. As we noted at the beginning of this book, and again at the start of this chapter, it is common to attribute many problems in our society to problems with *capitalism*. There are, as we have shown in the last several chapters, many problems that arise in capitalist economies, but usually the solution—insofar as there is one—is not to get rid of capitalism.

Still, if we can evaluate socialism at least partly on the basis of its historical success, that is, if we consider the reality of socialism as a historical phenomenon and institutional practice, surely, we must do the same for capitalism. Here we follow John Stuart Mill:

> If, therefore, the choice were to be made between Communism with all its chances, and the present state of society with all its sufferings and injustices . . . to make the comparison applicable, we must compare Communism at its best, with the régime of individual property, not as it is, but as it might be made. The principle of private property has never yet had a fair trial in any country; and less so, perhaps, in this country [Britain] than in some others. (PPE II.i.16)

This remains a sound methodological point; the status quo should not be compared to an idealized version of socialism. Capitalism has its warts, but all existing functioning societies do. Mill is right that there is no benefit to comparing mundane reality to idealized utopias.

Comparing actual socialism to actual capitalism gives us no reason to prefer socialism. It is still possible, though, that ideal socialism might still be better than ideal capitalism. If so, the problem with all the historical examples of socialism is that they perverted the socialist ideal in some important way. Even if this is right, we might think that there must be something so difficult about socialism that every attempt to institute it has failed to live up to the ideal.

A final move might be to reject economic arguments for socialism altogether and argue for socialism on purely ethical grounds. This is what some late 20th-century defenders of socialism did, most notably the philosopher G. A. Cohen (1941–2009), who is the subject of the next section. It is worth noting, before we turn to his arguments, that this is an important change to how socialism was defended throughout most of the 20th century. During that time, the key claim in favor of socialism was that it would outcompete capitalism. That by replacing the "anarchy of the market" with rational planning, waste would be reduced and efficiency would increase. Seeing that socialism produced exactly the opposite results, supporters (apart from those who were simply led by the evidence to change their beliefs) moved to ethical arguments.

## 7. Ethical Socialism

Cohen concedes that capitalism may work better for us now, but he claims this only shows that *we* are defective, not socialism. If we were better people, he argues, socialism would be possible.

In his (2009) book *Why Not Socialism*? Cohen asks us to consider a group of people who have decided to go camping together. Wouldn't it be better, he asks, if the camping trip were run along socialist rather than capitalist lines? Wouldn't it be better if all the campers shared their food and if they go out fishing, they share their catch with everyone, as people do on camping trips? Surely, Cohen argues, the egalitarian, socialist camping trip would be preferable to the alternative. Imagine instead that the camping trip is run along capitalist lines. According to Cohen, this would be a disaster. The best anglers would refuse to fish unless they are paid by the other campers. Some of the campers who brought more food or drink wouldn't share it with others unless they are compensated. Overall it doesn't sound like much fun. Generalizing, Cohen concludes that the difference here is about *community*. Socialism preserves community, whereas capitalism kills it.

One criticism to raise about Cohen's camping trip example is that he's overlooked Mill's advice about comparing systems like for like. In the socialist camping trip, everyone behaves well and the socialist community works out perfectly, but on the capitalist camping trip, people are greedy and mean spirited. Jason Brennan (2014) in a reply to Cohen titled *Why Not Capitalism*? turns this story on its head. He argues, using a similar example, that a society of well-behaved capitalists interacting on free, voluntary terms would be even better than the community described on the camping trip.

Brennan thinks that justice involves free and equal people pursuing their own values through voluntary cooperation—capitalism is more in line with these values. Cohen would counter that effective incentives don't make for a valuable community. Markets, as Smith pointed out, do *induce* individuals to serve one another. But even though individuals are helping one another under capitalism, they are doing so because they are seeking their own gain, not because they see each other being directly worthy of aid. By "community," Cohen means "the anti-market principle according to which I serve you not because of what I can get out of doing so but because you need my service" (G. A. Cohen 1989, 217). Socialism, according to Cohen, is better than capitalism because it is presupposed on just this sort of community.

One view is that community is not as valuable as Cohen thinks it is. According to James Otteson, a philosopher much influenced by Smith and Hayek, "socialist-inclined policy conceives of people's group membership or class identity as more important than their individuality" (2014, 131).[16] Otteson regards this as "socialism's greatest mistake." There remain serious questions about the importance of group identity in society, and how much a theory of justice needs to attend to it. An intuitive suggestion is that most of us care to some degree about being able to identify as a member of some group, while also caring about being allowed to be an individual. But we won't settle such questions here.

Another view is that Cohen's position fails on its own terms. Camping trips are not the only sort of small group in which goods and tasks need to be distributed. One other such group is the family. As philosopher Miriam Ronzoni (2012) has pointed out, reflection on the family may be a more informative test of the desirability of socialism than reflection on camping trips. In a family, goods are distributed according to norms of community (in Cohen's sense) rather than the market. Children, by and large, get to eat for free, while parents go out and work so that this can be possible. And that's the way it should be.

But families are not like camping trips. For one thing, not *everything* is shared. Siblings do not have a right to just wear each other's clothes. And privacy needs to be respected—family members should not just barge into each other's bedrooms. Most important might be the facts that, while the camping

[16] Otteson's arguments against this position are laid out in the chapter that follows it.

trip only lasts a few days, families last *much* longer, and that some of their members (at least the children) have not joined voluntarily. It's also hard to withdraw from a family, whereas if you don't like a camping trip you can just "go home," but typically back to a family. Ronzoni suggests that Cohen is able to motivate socialist sentiment with the camping trip case *only because* he has picked an example of a social setting that is short-lived and voluntary. Would you want to go on a camping trip that lasted decades, and do so with persons who weren't already your friends, but might have little in common with you? Probably not. That might tell us something.

## Conclusions

*This chapter has shown that socialism comes in many varieties, not just the familiar Marxist sort. In practice, socialism has not done as well as capitalism in terms of welfare or justice. But the argument does not and should not end there. Moral defense of socialism remains possible, but it is important to be clear about what the challenges are. A defense of Marxist socialism will continue to run up against the problem motivating the Smith/Hayek defense of capitalism that we saw in chapter 4, namely, the fact that information and incentives don't get distributed effectively in a centrally planned socialist system. There remains a case for market socialism, but this is likely to be implemented only in degrees, with its own problems. Philosophical debate continues about whether socialism captures something desirable about community that market norms abandon.*

## Study Questions

- Do you agree with Mill that there's something less than ideal about any society in which workers do not share ownership of the firm in which they work? Even if you disagree, do you think that workplace democracy must remain greatly limited without market socialism?
- Is utopian socialism useful when it comes to working out how to pursue economic justice, or does its name suggest that it's just wishful thinking?

- If you were a really talented individual, how would you feel if society forced you to use your talents for the greater good without any extra reward? Would it make any difference if this were how all talented people were treated? How would you feel if you were an untalented person?
- What do you think of Mill's methodological point about comparing capitalism and socialism in ways that avoid idealizing either one any more than the other? Is this possible?
- Do you enjoy going on camping trips, or engaging in similar practices in which production and distribution are based on friendly sharing rather than any market-like principles? What does your answer show (if anything) about the comparison between capitalism and socialism?

## Further Reading

*The Philosophy and Economics of Market Socialism* by Scott Arnold (Oxford University Press, 1994)

A very thorough discussion of both the feasibility and (moral) desirability of market socialism, building on the ideas originally developed by Mill, and asking further questions. Of particular interest are the chapters on whether market socialism could really remove all of the symptoms of status quo labor market injustice, such as the threat of unemployment and low wages.

*The End of Socialism* by James Otteson (Cambridge University Press, 2014)

Develops a case against socialism inspired largely by the Smith/Hayek outlook developed in chapter 4 of this book. Engages usefully with G. A. Cohen's work from the point of view of the positive moral case for capitalism.

*Why Not Socialism?* by G. A. Cohen (Princeton University Press, 2009) and *Why Not Capitalism?* by Jason Brennan (Routledge, 2014)

These books, complement one another dialectically a Marxist might say.

*Why Read Marx Today?* by Jonathan Wolff (Oxford University Press, 2002)

A very concise summary of Marx's writings and their enduring relevance, written by a first-rate political philosopher. Perfect if you've no prior experience with Marx, but still very good if you've read many of Marx's writings already.

# 6

# Low Wages and Lousy Jobs

*In this chapter, we address some principal questions about labor market justice. Some of these are old concerns about the persistence of poverty due to the forces that keep wages low among unskilled workers. This leads to worries about exploitation. We'll also introduce the concern, most often associated with Marx, that much paid work is of a character that is detrimental to human flourishing. We'll then move on to more recent trends, such as the rise in executive pay and other aspects of "labor market polarization." This will help us grapple with whether it's unjust for a few people to earn so much more than everyone else.*

## 1. The Old Stories: Malthus, Mill, and Competition among the Unskilled

Poverty is the oldest problem of political economy. The thinkers of the golden age were among the first to propose solutions.[1] The rise of markets since the 18th century rescued *many* people from poverty, but poverty remains stubborn. It's natural to wonder why we don't or can't help the others left behind. This remains a key question of political economy today.

The golden age generated different explanations of poverty's stubbornness. The pessimists argued that we'd be stuck with poverty in the long run, whereas the optimists suggested that poverty would continue to decrease, perhaps indefinitely. This chapter is really about the pessimists' arguments.

[1] Before the golden age, many who were privileged enough to write about anything displayed a striking indifference to poverty. It was even said by some that poverty reflected a divine plan. This was what John Stuart Mill had in mind in his *Principles of Political Economy* when speaking of "the base doctrine, that God has decreed that there will always be poor" (II.xiii.5). For more on intellectual attitudes to poverty before the golden age, see Fleischacker (2004).

*The Ethics of Capitalism.* Daniel Halliday and John Thrasher, Oxford University Press (2020).

DOI: 10.1093/oso/9780190096205.001.0001

We'll start with Thomas Malthus, whose ideas on poverty were laid out in his *Essay on the Principle of Population*, published in 1798 (after Smith but before Ricardo and Mill). The "essay" was long (300 pages), but its central point was simple: Malthus believed that population growth would outpace growth in the production of food (see Figure 6.1). As he put it, population increases "geometrically" while food production can only increase "linearly." This idea represents the first real mathematical model in economics (don't worry, it's also one of the easiest). The point here is that population growth surpasses growth in food production—past the dashed line. This will leave the poor without enough to eat.

The basis of Malthus's pessimism was that the prospects for keeping birth rates under control were poor. Contraception was illegal in England at the time, and methods were primitive (there are records of early condoms made from lambskin). According to Malthus, if the poor became better fed due to an increase in wages, they would just beget more children, or else waste the money on vice. Malthus was skeptical of the prospects for people to moderate their reproductive behavior so that food production could keep up with population. In short, either there would not be enough food, or an increase in food would mean an increase in mouths, and soon enough there would again not be enough food.

Malthus's arguments went further. He claimed that donating money to charity was not a genuinely benevolent thing to do, since "poverty and misery have always increased in proportion to the quantity of indiscriminate charity." Here is a longer passage that gives a sense of his outlook:

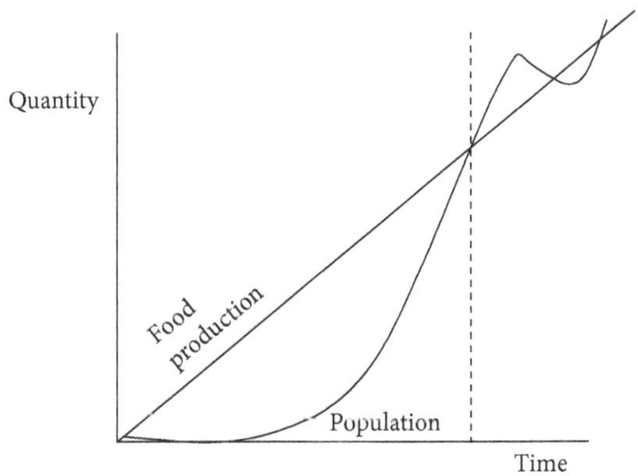


**Figure 6.1** Malthus's Model of Population

> It is a general complaint among master manufacturers, that high wages ruin all their workmen; but it is difficult to conceive that these men would not save a part of their high wages for the future support of their families, instead of spending it in drunkenness and dissipation, if they did not rely on parish assistance for support in case of accidents. And that the poor employed in manufactures consider this assistance as a reason why they may spend all the wages they earn, and enjoy themselves while they can, appears to be evident from the number of families that, upon the failure of any great manufactory, immediately fall upon the parish. (1992, 101–102)

This sounds harsh, though Malthus was genuinely concerned about the welfare of the poor. A devout Christian and Anglican priest, he organized family planning information for workers, and many of his followers became birth control activists. But these efforts were compatible with his belief that, unless and until the poor controlled their number voluntarily, famine and disease would take care of the job.

An effective rejoinder to Malthus came, later, from John Stuart Mill. In the 18th century, a large factor behind high birth rates was *women* lacking freedom. Mill argued that reproductive freedom overlaps with market freedom: if women could go out and get jobs, then less pressure would be put on them to get pregnant instead. Mill also suggested that women were perfectly deserving of being paid the same as men, and he claimed that this failed to happen either because of "prejudice" or because women saw little point in seeking better paid work when their father or husband was able to take the money off them.[2] This argument continues to have application today, though Mill perhaps failed to anticipate that women's entry into paid work has not been accompanied by an appropriate change in social norms on which women are expected to do the bulk of unpaid domestic labor.[3]

Clearly, the force of gender inequality is better at explaining high reproductive rates in a population than the cruder Malthusian idea that poor people "lack restraint." But Malthus was at least right about the ratio of maximum population growth to maximum food growth. In the 21st century, the global population is becoming more urbanized and reliant on food grown

[2] See the remarks in *Principles* at II.xiv.25. Mill's more complete views on the injustice of gender inequality are laid out more fully in his shorter book *On The Subjection of Women* (1869).

[3] Something similar has played out with the use of microcredit—loans to women in the developing world, where social norms don't lend themselves to women having economic freedoms. For discussion, see Serene Khader's (2014) article.

by someone else. There are serious questions about how to ensure we all get fed in an increasingly crowded world. There is also something to Malthus's claim that charity can do more harm than good, though it is hard to make generalizations about this.[4]

David Ricardo was the next of the golden age pessimists. Where Malthus's views were specified at the micro level (the behavior of individual people or families), Ricardo focused on the macro. He believed that poverty would endure because of the stranglehold that landowners held on the production of food. As population expanded, the owners of agriculture would extract ever-higher rents for use of their land. Ricardo's was an early attempt to explain the persistence of poverty and inequality by appealing to distinctions between *classes* of people whose interests do not align. It's about social structure rather than individual psychology, more like Marx than Malthus.

For a time, Ricardo's pessimism was thought to be defeated by industrialization, as people could make money from the new industrial capital, with land no longer the only source of wealth. But Ricardo's outlook is making a comeback of sorts. Thomas Piketty (recall chapter 3) has suggested that what Ricardo predicted for agricultural land in the 19th century is beginning to play out for real estate in the 21st century—Piketty even calls this "the Ricardian apocalypse." Ricardo's view is complex, and its macro focus takes attention away from the dynamics of labor markets as an explanation for poverty and other injustices. We mention his views here mainly to avoid a gap in the narrative.

After the Industrial Revolution, poverty became increasingly blamed on the power that the property-owning class held over the working class. This had more to do with who controlled *distribution* than the landed aristocracy's ancient stranglehold on production. Important here was the way in which industry changed the nature of work itself.

As we indicated in the last chapter (recall the discussion of utopian socialism), worker migration and the growth of cities is typical of any country's transition from an agrarian to industrial economy—the recent history of China and India confirms this. Since agricultural life is hard, poverty decreases during this period in absolute terms, but it becomes more concentrated and has different effects.

The Industrial Revolution brought with it *divided labor.* When describing the rural worker, Adam Smith noted how the character of farm work varied

[4] For a skeptical view, see Angus Deaton's (2013) book *The Great Escape*, especially chap. 7.

with the seasons. Thus, "the ploughman, the harrower, the sower of the seed, and the reaper of the corn, are often the same" (WN I.i.4). This isn't to say that agrarian workers had it really good. They were often peasants who labored in "servile dependence" for their masters (recall chapter 3). The point is that rural labor was less *specialized.* In this way, it contrasts sharply with industrial labor.

The best way to get at this difference is to look at Smith's own description of industrial work. This begins with one of Smith's best-known examples.

> To take an example, therefore, from a very trifling manufacture; but one in which the division of labour has been very often taken notice of, the trade of the pin-maker; a workman not educated to this business . . . could scarce, perhaps, with his utmost industry, make one pin in a day, and certainly could not make twenty. But in the way in which this business is now carried on, not only the whole work is a peculiar trade, but it is divided into a number of branches . . . One man draws out the wire, another straights it, a third cuts it, a fourth points it, a fifth grinds it at the top for receiving the head . . . and the important business of making a pin is, in this manner, divided into about eighteen distinct operations. . . . I have seen a small manufactory of this kind where ten men only were employed . . . But though they were very poor, and therefore but indifferently accommodated with the necessary machinery, they could, when they exerted themselves, make among them about twelve pounds of pins in a day . . . Those ten persons, therefore, could make among them upwards of forty-eight thousand pins in a day . . . But if they had all wrought separately and independently, and without any of them having been educated to this peculiar business, they certainly could not each of them have made twenty, perhaps not one pin in a day. (WN I.i.3)

In other words, deskilling is an important enabler of teamwork so as to enable production well beyond that of a bunch of skilled individuals working independently. It's intuitively quite obvious that teams can often do what individuals can't achieve separately, though the degree of difference (forty-eight thousand versus twenty pins!) may surprise us.

The deskilling process usually means a general worsening of the work itself. This important point needs to be weighed against the value of increased productivity. It is probably more *interesting* to make a pin from scratch than to spend one's entire day on a single subsidiary task such as "drawing out the wire." At any rate, the deskilling of work involves turning it into a form such that anyone can do it. If I'm to make a pin from scratch, then I'll probably get better (and quicker) at it over time. This gives my employer a reason to try and hang on to me, rather than replace me with someone who has to learn the set of skills from scratch. But once a factory has been arranged so that workers each perform more simple tasks, this problem disappears. So the process by which labor becomes divided has two *very important* consequences. First, the work becomes more specialized and monotonous. Second, the worker becomes easier to replace.

Deskilling makes work easier *only* in the sense that it does not demand skills that are hard or slow to learn. It does *not* mean that the work is "easy" in the sense that it is *pleasant* or *safe*. Many factories are noisy, hazardous places. Living in an industrial city often means exposure to pollution and other health hazards when one is not at work. In addition, the monotonous tasks associated with divided labor often lead to physiological problems, like repetitive strain injuries. If you work on a factory production line, pulling a lever so that (say) a screw gets drilled into the side of a fridge, then most people could do your job, irrespective of how burdensome it is. To obtain and retain such unskilled work, you face stiff competition. Your employer could very easily replace you if you walked away. For this reason alone, unskilled work is poorly paid.

This goes some way to explaining how poverty endures even after production has gone up enough for everyone to eat. The problem is that the productive process does not pay everyone enough to ensure that the output gets *distributed* in ways that actually relieve poverty, because the very increase in production has been largely enabled by making it easier and cheaper to put people to work.

These two concerns about the consequences of divided labor—degradation of the work being performed and the downward pressure exerted on wages—can be developed in different ways. We'll examine them in turn.

## 2. What Makes a Lousy Job Lousy?

For Smith, the problem with deskilled work was that it basically fries your brain:

> The man whose whole life is spent in performing a few simple operations, of which the effects are perhaps always the same . . . has no occasion to exert

> his understanding or to exercise his invention . . . He naturally loses, therefore, the habit of such exertion, and generally becomes as stupid and ignorant as it is possible for a human creature to become. The torpor of his mind renders him not only incapable of relishing or bearing a part in any rational conversation, but of conceiving any generous, noble, or tender sentiment, and consequently of forming any just judgment concerning many even of the ordinary duties of private life . . . But in every improved and civilized society this is the state into which the labouring poor, that is, the great body of the people, must necessarily fall, unless government takes some pains to prevent it. (WN V.i.178)

This passage is less famous than the one about the pin factory. This may be because it occurs much later in Smith's massive book. While the earlier passage can give the impression that Smith welcomed divided labor for its dramatic impact on productivity, these later remarks show his awareness of its downside for those who had to perform it.

Smith advocated creating more educational opportunities for workers to partially alleviate some of these problems. He argued that education for the poor should be funded at public expense, though he didn't believe the state should run or fund the schools directly as it tends to do now (WN V.1.182). There are many who still believe that greater education is among the best solutions to poverty. This makes some sense—when deskilling occurs, we can fight fire with fire by giving workers fresh skills that they can use to gain better wages in other sectors of industry. But it may yet prove an exercise in fighting a losing battle.

The golden age's greatest critic of divided labor was Karl Marx, who spoke of "alienated" or "estranged" labor. This concept is in many ways an extension of Smith's outlook. Indeed, Marx's thinking about alienation is one of the most difficult of his views to interpret, though not because it lacks power, and its plausibility does not depend on Marx's theory of history, whose problems we discussed in the last chapter. Marx himself developed different refinements of what alienated labor might actually amount to. But broadly speaking, it involves some sort of disconnection between the labor that a person performs and the person himself. Philosopher Jonathan Wolff, a Marx scholar, says that there are at least three senses of alienation that appear in Marx's writings.

First, there is alienation from the *output* of one's labor. One consequence of industrial capitalism is the sheer scale and complexity of the things that are produced. This leads to a situation in which the products of our labor become dominant over the people that have produced them. In the industrial era, many products are hard to understand, as is the full extent of the market in which they are exchanged. We, the coauthors, typed this textbook on computers. We took the power of these machines for granted, just like most people do. But we had little sense of how they worked and how they got produced. In this sense, we were alienated from them.

Is this bad? Were we *dominated* by our computers? Well, we had a very strong dependence on them—we would have struggled, physically, to write this textbook by hand. To be honest, we probably wouldn't have bothered if we had to produce written work this way. Of course, things used to be different—Marx had no computer and wrote copious reams by hand. Were Marx, Smith, and others less dominated by the products of their age? This isn't obvious, as they were still dependent on pencils and such. The more important point about domination is that the market, aside from any specific product bought or sold within it, sets the agenda with regard to how we ought (rationally) to act. In some sense, which may be hard to pin down, the market has decided that we all need computers now, along with a bunch of other things. Maybe that is a form of domination, but it could be liberation. There are millions of people today who are able to use technology to do and make things that would have been impossible otherwise.

The second kind of alienation attaches to the way in which markets have an individualizing effect: by and large, life in a capitalist economy makes us concerned about making enough money. Though we may still have families, we tend to have a preoccupation with going out and getting money to feed them as a central goal in life. This transforms our interactions with other people. In our struggle to earn enough money, we come to see colleagues, strangers, and perhaps even friends as elements of this pursuit, rather than as proper people. Marx might be drawing here on Aristotle, who famously said that "man is a political animal." He wasn't saying that man (or people) enjoy getting involved in politics. Aristotle meant that humans flourish by existing in groups and interacting quite directly with each other. In this sense, we are like other social animals, like lions and seals, which also live in groups, and unlike solitary creatures, like leopards and pandas. But we'll only flourish if our interaction goes in a certain kind of way.

This second type of alienation isn't really connected with divided labor and could, therefore, conceivably arise in an agrarian economy. Really it is about the role of money and credit in shaping our lives and how we *perceive* our labor and each other. Money drives a wedge between ourselves and other people. It deprives us of the opportunity to interact with others for its own sake, as fellow humans. It is interesting to consider how much of a departure this view marks from the earlier optimism of Smith, who saw market interaction as a means through which human relations could be strengthened, due to the virtues of reciprocal exchange between individuals of equal status. Marx is perhaps not denying that view, only adding that the system of money and credit (which was less developed in Smith's time) will muck things up.

Finally, there is perhaps the most philosophically compelling of Marx's ideas about alienated labor. This is about alienation from our work *itself*. Humans seek to be creative, and we all have potential to be creative in our own individual fashion. In his *Economic and Philosophical Manuscripts* (1844), Marx used this idea to distinguish humans from animals. He notes that many animals engage in productive activity with respect to external objects (ants build nests, beavers build dams). But they do so on instinct, without individual direction or variation. Humans, by contrast, differentiate when producing instances of the same type of thing. When comparing humans with animals, Marx notes that "man produces even when he is free from physical need and only truly produces in freedom therefrom." Humans shape their life activity to their will. Our productive activity has to come from within, so to speak, if it's to help us flourish.

All of this is quite intuitive. If you listen to music and get to know different bands, composers, and so on, you can usually tell them apart and even recognize a new song or piece as created by a specific artist. People who engage in pottery, carpentry, and so on tend also to develop certain traits in the output of their work. Birds' nests, on the other hand, hardly look different from each other. There may be minor variations, according to which twigs have been used, but one never looks at a bird's nest and sees in it the individual style of some *particular* bird.

The process of deskilling robs our work of this creative potential, Marx argues. In the first part *Communist Manifesto* (1848), Marx writes that the specialized industrial-age worker "becomes a mere appendage of the machine." He adds that "work . . . has lost all individual character, and, consequently, all charm for the workman." This seems correct: When you work on a production line, your being replaced by another worker will have no impact on the character of what's being assembled. Contrast this with the earlier examples of music and pottery—if I take over from you at the pottery wheel, the output will probably look different. As Wolff notes, having to perform deskilled labor makes us more like animals—like ants building one big ant hill—than humans each doing our own thing.

In his book *Nicomachean Ethics* (circa 330 BCE), Aristotle argued that different creatures can be distinguished according to their different *essential functions*. In order to flourish, a creature must perform the essential function of its species. Thus, a beaver flourishes when it builds dams, because dam building is in the essence of beavers. Essential functions also attach to inanimate objects: the essential function of a knife is to cut. A good knife is one that cuts well.

In effect, Marx's view adapts Aristotle's. For Marx, performing work, in ways that leave "our stamp on the world," is our essential function, or what he called our "species being." Performing industrial labor is incompatible with acting out our essential function. Aristotle's view is a controversial one about wellbeing, and there may be reasons to doubt that humans and other creatures really have a function that *defines* them in relation to other species. But in claiming that human flourishing requires some creative productive activity, Marx need only be making a somewhat moderate version of Aristotle's claim: what matters is that we have certain capacities that we need to exercise in order to live well.

We're going to focus most of our remaining discussion on this third sense of alienation, and on whether it signals a special injustice, or bad consequence, of labor markets since the Industrial Revolution.

## 3. Is Alienated Labor Underrated?

Britain's Royal Navy once ran a recruitment campaign with a catchy slogan. It went: "Who wants to be a cog in a machine? Depends on the machine." You can still watch this advertisement online.[5] Maybe it's not so bad slaving away in a monotonous job if you're doing it for Queen and country, rather than for some big company making its shareholders rich off your alienated back. Generalizing, people often care about being part of something big and important. They might *still* care even if their being replaced by another worker

[5] For example, visit https://www.youtube.com/watch?v=yf3hPzMQfos

would make no difference to the output to which their labor contributes. So even if the *character* of labor is degraded in the manner that Marx describes, might its *output* be a source of job satisfaction and, ultimately, human flourishing?

If we agree with the Royal Navy, then we might disagree with Marx and Aristotle. We might reject the view that the *only* way to flourish is through producing outputs that have our own individual style impressed on them. This might be *sufficient* for a flourishing life, but it is not obviously *necessary*. Maybe the Marx/Aristotle view is just too narrow.

No doubt *some* people become less happy when they have to perform alienated labor. Academics moan about doing administration. They often want to get back to research, so that they can do things that leave their stamp on the world. Many academics (including the authors!) also enjoy teaching and regret the professional pressure that takes them away from it. But here we may be speaking about a biased sample group: people who become academics typically have a prior disposition to avoid alienated labor and seek out careers that allow them to make their stamp on the world, even if they know, deep down, that this stamp will be pretty miniscule. But a lot of other people are relatively happy to perform alienated labor because their priorities are different. Maybe it's OK for people to want different things in life, and adjust their labor market goals accordingly. One of the problems with Marx and Aristotle is that there is a specific sense in which they were not *liberals*—they held a view about human flourishing on which everyone is supposed to flourish in a very similar way.

Another response to Marx is that alienated labor is not *necessarily* burdensome—being a cog in a machine might sometimes be comfortable. Some people like to "switch off" while at work, and not have to think too hard. Others simply aren't very creative and have no particular ambition to be. Liberals about wellbeing can accommodate the idea that there's nothing necessarily wrong with such people. The Marx/Aristotle view, on the other hand, is a philosophically controversial view about wellbeing, known as "perfectionism." Broadly speaking, perfectionists believe that the good life is a matter of achieving certain specified goals associated with "perfecting" our human nature. This approach has its philosophical competitors. Hedonists, for example, believe that there's nothing to wellbeing besides having the right kind of psychological states, like pleasure. Simply assuming the truth of a controversial view like perfectionism, in order to evaluate the character of much paid work, may be problematic, or at least needs defense.

Alienated labor can also be *compensated.* Plenty of well-paid jobs involve what Marx would see as alienated labor. Corporate lawyers have to work very long hours doing rather monotonous tasks (for example, sifting through reams of documents looking for esoteric information). This is not creative work. It is well paid because it is relatively *skilled*—corporate lawyers need to know a lot of law, and there are relatively few of them as a result. Firms must attract and retain them, and the pay reflects this. Law firms nevertheless practice highly divided labor, as individual lawyers work on relatively specific parts of a project.

Modern corporate lawyers are evidence that deskilling and divided labor are not equivalent, even though they very much coincided in 19th-century manufacturing. On reflection, this should be unsurprising: alienated labor is all about the *character* of the work as something that we perform, whereas deskilling is really about *how many people* can perform that work. It's quite possible that our intuitive aversion to alienated labor is being influenced by a sense that it must be poorly paid. But take any lousy job and imagine it with higher pay. If you no longer have moral discomfort about some people performing that work, then your sense of injustice may not really be tracking alienated labor, but rather poorly paid labor.

So there's room for disagreement about the extent to which alienated labor is bad or unjust in itself. Still, Marx's concept of alienated labor does help explain certain social phenomena, particularly behavior *outside* the workplace. One of Marx's famous lines is that "religion is the opium of the people."[6] His point was that people turn to organized worship for relief from the daily grind. Though religious observation has declined in "Western" market societies, there is still plenty of activity aimed at diverting people from the drudgery of working life. Any examples would be controversial, and we want to avoid making any strong claims about what sort of activities are most conducive to true human flourishing. But if you've spent a working week doing some mind-numbing monotonous task, you often just feel like getting drunk and watching bad television. And one could certainly argue that loyal supporters of soccer teams are engaging in activities a bit like organized religion, especially when the team keeps losing. Again, it's unclear what sort of general conclusion this warrants about capitalism and justice, but it's evidence of how Marxist thought retains relevance even if we're not all working down in the mines or in the factories.

[6] This line appears very early in his *Contribution to the Critique of Hegel's Philosophy of Right* (1843).

We'd like to squeeze in a few more observations about Marx's other thoughts on alienated labor. Recall the second refinement of the idea, the one associated with the corrosive effects of working principally for money. Professional athletes sometimes report losing their love for their sport once it becomes their source of income. Andre Agassi, one of the most successful men's tennis players ever, says in his autobiography that he came to "hate tennis." This may indicate some damaging effect of pushing for "success" in a market economy. Agassi might have been happier, though poorer, in the amateur era prior to the rise of television and the money it injected into many sports. And this may be because he would have played tennis (if he'd played it at all) largely for its own sake. To put yourself in Agassi's position, consider whether you'd welcome the opportunity to pursue one of your hobbies full-time, for a regular salary, perhaps involving a larger time commitment and/or intensive travel schedule. If this would corrupt what's valuable about your hobby, then this shows that Marx was onto something, though precisely what remains up for debate.

A final concern about alienated labor is its tendency to homogenize human beings. Adam Smith said that another thing distinguishing humans from animals is that "the most dissimilar geniuses are of use to one another" (WN I.ii.5). The thought here is that different people have different talents, and we'll have a more interesting society if people can life appropriately differentiated lives. Industrial labor may increase the output of physical goods, but it may decrease the less tangible output associated with diversity among individuals. One who later developed this idea in much more detail was John Stuart Mill. While Mill had little to say that was directly about alienated labor, he believed that leisure time could do much to help humans conduct "experiments in living," something that industrial labor continued to obstruct in Mill's day. More on this in chapter 10. Mill and Smith were both liberals, not perfectionists, and this may have made it easier for them to reach such claims about diversity.

To summarize: The concept of alienated labor is certainly an important one—labor markets are much changed since the Industrial Revolution, though they are hardly free from drudgery. Perhaps alienated labor is an injustice of some sort in its own right. Or perhaps it merely correlates with certain other injustices or helps explain (causally) the existence of other things that might attract our concern. These matters are far from being settled. Philosophers continue to offer new thoughts about what makes a lousy job lousy and what makes a better job better. Many of these thoughts raise questions beyond the Marxist preoccupation with alienated labor specifically.[7]

## 3. Exploitation—Not Getting Out What You Put In

Karl Marx's other big idea about labor market justice was that capitalism exploits workers. Very simply, this occurs because workers don't get paid what they (or rather their work) is really worth. The capitalists, who employ the workers, do no real work themselves. They merely own the means of production and make contracts with workers who have only their labor to sell. Because the capitalists add nothing, they rely on being able to sell the output of the worker's labor (recall our description of this in the last chapter). When they do this, of course, the capitalists keep the bulk of the revenue for themselves. They only give a very small part of it back to most of the workers—perhaps only enough to keep the workers and their families alive. In this way, the capitalists have "extracted" much of the value of the workers' labor. The degree to which they extract such value is equal to the degree to which they *exploit* their workers.

In developing his theory of exploitation, Marx relied on the *labor theory of value*, something we've come across a few times already. The labor theory helps make sense of exploitation in quite a compelling way: the workers in a Ferrari factory cannot afford the cars they produce. But let's assume, for the sake of argument, that a worker's annual salary would be enough to purchase the raw materials for one Ferrari. If the worker could afford the raw materials, but not the car that she assembles from these materials, then there's a sense in which she's been robbed of some value that *she* has added to things that at one point she could afford. The capitalist, who merely owns the Ferrari factory, has been granted the power to extract this value by being able to retain some, perhaps nearly all, of the revenues from the sale of the factory's outputs, that is, the cars. The worker loses out. That's Marxist exploitation.

The problem with Marx's theory of exploitation is that the labor theory of value is false (again, something we've touched on a few times already).[8] Labor

[7] See, for example, the article by Anca Gheaus and Lisa Herzog, and the longer book-length discussion by Andrea Veltman, both in the Further Reading section.

[8] Even those sympathetic to the general Marxist criticism of capitalism like John Roemer (1985) and Jon Elster (1985) admit that without the labor theory of value, little remains of Marx's theory of exploitation.

is no doubt a factor influencing exchange values. But it is manifestly not the only factor. Just to stop you from getting bored of hearing this, we'll give you a new example. Some production creates multiple outputs at once, which have different exchange values: heating crude oil in a fractioning column (those skinny flame-topped structures in oil refineries) creates a range of different oil products. Kerosene, from near the top of the tower, has a much higher exchange value than diesel oil from lower down. But both were produced using precisely the same labor, that is, whatever labor was necessary to fill the column with crude and keep it operating.

Kerosene sells for higher prices because it has certain uses, for which people are willing to pay more (you can't fly a plane on diesel oil). Of course, prices that we actually pay are also affected by various "artificial" factors such as taxation, and some products are taxed at different rates from others. But correcting for such things is not going to restore the labor theory of value. So variations in labor are neither necessary nor sufficient for prices to change. This is a big problem for the labor theory of value. As such, it is a problem for the Marxist's theory of exploitation as well. If exploitation is to be identified in labor markets, we must find some other way to detect it.

## 4. Exploitation—Alternatives to Marx

The moral force of Marxist exploitation lies in some sense of unfair dealing: the worker puts something in to the production process, but doesn't get out a proportionate reward, compared to the reward that accrues to her employer, the capitalist. The labor theory of value is merely *one* way to measure the degree to which unfair dealing is occurred. That is to say, the labor theory provides a *baseline*, representing a "fair" price for labor, against which actual wages can be compared. But philosophers have since provided some alternative baselines.

Broadly speaking, intuitive cases of exploitation, including labor market exploitation, exhibit certain features quite consistently: they involve big disparities in bargaining power, which result in unequal payoffs for those involved; those who are exploited are in an apparently desperate situation, needing to make a bad deal with an employer or suffer grave consequences. None of these considerations, by itself, appears to reveal precisely what is wrong with exploitation, or what distinguishes it from other morally objectionable acts. But they're a start, and they avoid commitment to anything like the labor theory of value.

One philosopher, Alan Wertheimer (1999), asks us to consider a person drowning in a lake. A passerby is in a position to rescue this person by tossing in a life preserver, but offers to do so only on agreement that the rescued individual surrenders half of his annual salary for the rest of his life. Certainly, this is an intuitive case of exploitation, and most of us would think that the rescuer is doing something morally wrong, even though the drowning individual is likely to accept the offer, given his desperate situation.

Wertheimer's observation about this case is that there's a lack of other individuals who can compete with the rescuer's high price. The rescuer has a monopoly on rescuing services, which is why the rescuer can charge so much. Were the lakeshore lined with throngs of people, each possessing a life preserver that they could throw to the drowning individual, then the price would quickly come down. (Yes, the example is a bit weird, but you get the point.) It's hard to say how low the price would drop, but we'd be less likely to think of the case as an extreme instance of exploitation if it were, say, five dollars or the promise of a beer in the lakeside bar.

For Wertheimer, this is precisely how we should measure exploitation. The nonexploitative price for an exchange is the price that would be reached in a properly competitive market. Wertheimer maintains that his view provides an effective alternative to the Marxist theory of exploitation. Nevertheless, Wertheimer is able to accommodate some of the concerns that motivated Marx without buying into the labor theory of value. Marx observed that one effect of divided labor is to increase competition among workers but not among employers, thereby bringing down wages. In effect, Wertheimer is trying to make this observation do the bulk of the work by itself.

One criticism of Wertheimer is that he leaves it unexplained precisely *why* we should think that fairness involves conformity to competitive prices. After all, a competitive price could be anything. The actual large salaries of some athletes and film stars might be competitive, because their talents are so scarce. But it's odd to say some of the world's highest earners would be exploited if they were paid a bit less. There are other cases of exchanges at uncompetitive prices that we do not regard as morally very troubling, much less exploitative. Ruth Sample, another philosopher, offers the case of a wealthy tourist who visits poor countries without researching the state of their markets. Arriving in some far-flung locale, the hungry tourist may pay a whole dollar for a pineapple, even though locals typically exchange pineapples for 10 cents. Has the tourist been wrongfully exploited? Our intuitions say "no." But Wertheimer's theory treats the case pretty much the same as the lake case, allowing perhaps for a lesser degree of departure from the competitive price.

In place of Wertheimer's, Ruth Sample (2003) provides her own theory. It says that exploitation attaches to exchanges where one party "takes advantage of another in a way that fails to respect the inherent value in" them. By seeking to extract a huge chunk of money from a drowning swimmer, one treats the swimmer as a mere means to making money. Generalizing, if employers are able to use workers' vulnerability (in terms of workers' desperation to find enough money to survive) to turn a profit, then they're ultimately being disrespectful. There is something quite compelling about this view: at any rate, there's something intuitively plausible about the idea that people are not instruments, and that vulnerability and desperation make it easier for more fortunate people to treat them as such.

Sample's theory disqualifies the case of the tourist, who is not really vulnerable or desperate, only ignorant. The tourist is being overcharged for a pineapple, but not exploited. Similar things could be said about pay cuts for top-earning athletes. But Sample's position has its own problems. Is it really true that paying someone a low wage is tantamount to treating her as a *thing* rather than a person? After all, when we do interact with things, like machines, we typically don't pay them *anything*. Of course, there may be other ways in which employers frequently *do* express disrespect for their employees. Recall here the sort of labor market domination we discussed in chapter 3. But, as we said at the time, the disrespect here is not inherent in the wages paid. Low wages may reflect the enabling conditions of disrespectful domination (these being principally the worker's vulnerability due to a lack of alternative job options), but not count as *constitutive* of disrespect. The disrespect "kicks in" once employers start bullying workers, demanding sexual favors, spying on them, and so on.

The work of Wertheimer and Sample represents the best contemporary theories of what exploitation is and what makes it unjust. But skeptics about exploitation in labor markets are also quite numerous in political philosophy. The fact remains that many intuitive or alleged cases of labor market exploitation are mutually consensual and mutually advantageous. They simply wouldn't exist otherwise. For this reason, skeptics suggest that hiring the citizens of poor countries at apparently low wages is the lesser evil compared to just simply sitting on the sidelines. Matthew Zwolinski (2008), for example, ventures that firms employing sweatshop workers are hardly doing anything worse than people who don't hire labor in the developing world, which is almost all of us, including those condemning the various multinational firms doing the hiring.

The burden of proof is on those who want to explain the wrongness of exploitation. Philosopher Joseph Heath (2010) claims the idea of a fair price is a central fallacy of what he calls "left-wing" thinking on economic justice. A less skeptical view is that our intuitive sense of exploitation is a proxy for something else. One might think that, generally speaking, we just have a moral duty to help vulnerable people and not seek to gain as much as we would if trading with nonvulnerable people.[9] Exploitation is very much an enduring bone of contention in political philosophy. It may be fair to say that the topic started with Marx, but also that it remains far from finished.

## 5. The New Story: Runaway Incomes at the Top

Poverty continues to persist while some people earn huge amounts. Are today's highest salaries unjustified? Or, to put it another way, are some people paid too much? We'll close the chapter by looking at some interesting cases where this might be so.

In many industries where they now occur, massive salaries are a largely recent development. In the 1950s, there was a breed of British comedian who would tour around the country appearing at what were known as "variety shows" or "music halls." Professionals of this sort would show up in a given town, perform for one night, and then move on to some other town. These comedians would roam around telling the same tried and tested jokes, perhaps for years on end (how's that for alienated labor?). They were able to do this because they almost never faced the same audience twice.

Nowadays, comedians and other paid performers don't have it so easy. Developments in technology, especially communications technology, have caused what's known as *audience concentration*. Historic fragmentation of many separate audiences has been converted into a smaller number of larger audiences. In practice, this means a population who would otherwise have gone to small local theatres spread across a country (or even multiple

[9] One such view about exploitation has been developed by the philosopher Robert Goodin in his (1988) book.

countries) are now all watching the same show on TV. This means that fewer performers are required. It also means that those performers who do make the grade can expect to be paid more than those who worked during years of lower audience concentration. The effect is most dramatic in professional sport. Spectator sport became popular during the Industrial Revolution, when urban populations started to get a bit of leisure time. In the early days, many people attended a local stadium in person, but audience concentration was low. But thanks to the advertising and sponsorship potential enabled by TV, top athletes in sports like soccer and tennis now make hundreds of thousands of dollars *per week*, just because so many people are watching them.

Two important factors emerge here. One of these is what the economist Robert Frank calls "winner takes all markets."[10] The other is known as "labor market polarization": Respectively, these labels refer to the tendency of top earners to be only *marginally* better than those who miss out, and to the fact that there is little middle ground when it comes to the range of salaries available (and often less than there used to be). This isn't just true of professional sports. The Berlin Philharmonic Orchestra will pick some incredibly able individual to be its next violinist. The next best violinist might be *less* skilled, but only to a really tiny degree, noticeable only to experts and music connoisseurs. Most people who actually pay to go and watch the Berlin Philharmonic, or purchase their recordings, really wouldn't notice the difference if the orchestra swapped one of its regular violinists for one of the best ones it rejected. If most people can't tell the difference, then there's a sense in which there's *no* difference in talent between the hired violinist and the runner up—the latter would not reduce the orchestra's ability to sell its product. Are high salaries unjust simply because the runner up is almost as good and yet gets paid much less? That's hard to believe. But we can also use this kind of case to establish a contrast with other some other cases of recently inflated incomes.

One good example here is the rise in so-called executive pay, that is, the salaries awarded to those who occupy the most senior positions in firms. While wages on average have largely stagnated in most "Western" economies over the last few decades, the very top executive salaries have grown well. This can't be explained in the same way as the somewhat parallel growth in the salaries of paid performers like athletes. Executives do not have a newly

[10] See especially Frank and Cook (2010).

concentrated "audience" consuming their services. So we might treat them differently.

One philosopher who has written extensively on executive pay in recent years is Jeffrey Moriarty. Moriarty's (2009) main point is that top executives have fiduciary duties to shareholders. Broadly speaking, a fiduciary duty is a moral or legal requirement to act in the interests of some designated party. Such duties typically emerge out of some sort of special relationship. Social workers, for example, hold fiduciary duties toward clients like vulnerable children, elderly individuals, or recovering drug addicts. Social workers are often paid by the state, but there is nothing unusual about fiduciary duties emerging from a relationship in which the person being protected is also the one who pays the duty holder, as when a lawyer or surgeon is paid by their client.

A core objective of an executive's job is to increase shareholder value. This is quite widely accepted even there is reason to believe that executives must act to satisfy other requirements, including moral ones. Shareholders basically entrust executives to look after their interests concerning their property, relying on executives' superior abilities to do so. In this way, the relationship of a shareholder to an executive resembles the relationship between a patient and a doctor. If I need a hip replacement, I'm not in a position to perform the relevant surgical procedure on myself. So I pay a doctor to do it, relying on this doctor's superior ability. Accordingly, the doctor accrues some fiduciary duties to take care of me properly.

When executives bargain for very high levels of pay, they decrease shareholder value. This is true just because the pay of executives is among the firm's costs, which affect what the firm is worth. Executives ought, morally, to accept what Moriarty calls the "minimum effective compensation" for their work. If executives take more pay, *even if they are offered it voluntarily*, then they are violating their fiduciary duties to shareholders. Although Moriarty doesn't offer any such analogy, one might think that executives who accept more than minimum effective compensation are rather like surgeons who perform hip replacements but, during the operation, cut off part of the hip bone to sell to some laboratory that wants to conduct research on it. While it might be permissible for me to offer parts of my body to such third parties, it is wrong for my doctor to do it for their own personal gain.

For this reason, argues Moriarty, executives are morally distinct from other top earners. Athletes, actors, novelists, and the like do not owe fiduciary duties to those paying them for their labor. Consequently, their acceptance of high pay does not reduce the degree to which they act in accordance with any such duties. So the point is not that executive pay, though very high, is too high per se. Instead, the point (according to Moriarty) is that it's too high *given the sort of work that executives are being paid to perform.*

As with people being paid too little, the question of someone being overpaid requires a baseline against which to assess whether a salary is too high. If Moriarty is right, then it's easier to identify a baseline for executive pay than for the pay of some top performers. What else might bear on the justification of high salaries? One possibility is lack of job security. Although most jobs are not as secure as tenured professors at major universities, most of us can reasonably expect to have our job beyond the next week, month, or quarter. This is not true of many CEOs, athletes, or performers. CEOs can be fired at the whim of the Board of Directors and athletes may get injured with no notice. This can change the structure of the pay that they find attractive. They can price in the risk of losing their earning potential into very large lump-sum payments. Some sports leagues, most notably the National Football League in the United States, have limits on what most players can earn. This reduces very large salaries, but it also makes being a professional football player a riskier enterprise. One either needs to be a top draft pick and get the bonus that comes in that "winner-takes-all market" or survive long enough to go on the free agent market when one's best playing days are largely over. We may tend to think that very high salaries for athletes are obscene, but once we factor in the risk and insecurity, we might moderate our judgment—a bit.

More could be said about other very high salaries. Extremely high incomes can be earned working for leading investment banks, hedge funds, and the like. But what do such industries *produce*, exactly? One of the problems with financial markets is that the products and the mechanisms through which they are sold are themselves very hard to understand—how many people really know what a "credit default swap" is? It is tempting to suggest that a lot of what banks do is more destructive than productive, especially given their apparent role in the Global Financial Crisis, in which large numbers of mortgage holders lost their houses. That being said, the "classic" function of banking, namely creating a medium of contact between borrowers and savers, clearly *is* a valuable service. Some of the more forceful objections to the workings of financial markets draw on concerns that the financial sector has come to enjoy a regulatory environment that is anti-capitalist, in which profits can be kept while losses are absorbed by taxpayer bailouts.[11]

Similar things might be said about the high incomes accruing to owners of intellectual property, such as the patents attaching to pharmaceutical products. Here, again, everything depends on the decisions made by legislators when it comes to the degree of monopoly privilege granted by intellectual property laws. Many patented and copyrighted ideas clearly have some productive output, whether it is relief from painful symptoms in the case of headaches, ease of writing a textbook or assignment in the case of computer programs, or the possibility of growing a crop that's immune to a certain pest, in the case of genetically engineered seeds. But much actual legislation extends intellectual property rights given rather arbitrary and minimal changes to whatever it is the patent or copyright is held in. If a pharmaceutical company is able to preserve the market value of its product only by suppressing the ease with which competitors emerge, then it is clearly working against the wider interests of society. Indeed, lobbying for protection against the import or patenting or competing products is a bit like a bottled water company lobbying against the supply of tap water—an activity that, if successful, may inflate an income greatly, but hardly with justification.[12]

It's fair to say that the moral evaluation of high incomes shouldn't proceed on a case-by-case bases, but should be guided by moral principles that might tell us much about how to distinguish the high incomes of an athlete, CEO, and hedge fund employee. One worry is that winner-takes-all markets are going to become more the norm, as audience concentration increases. The rise of automation may also chip away at middle-income jobs by taking the skill out of them, resulting in more polarization (more on robots in chapter 10). How serious a threat this presents depends, of course, on how the state responds to the fact that labor markets create winners and losers. This will occupy us in the next chapter.

[11] A good short discussion of the (mis)regulation of financial markets is Roberts (2019)—see Admati and Hellwig (2013) for a similar discussion in greater detail. Philosophical discussion of financial markets and justice can be found in the collection edited by Lisa Herzog (2017).

[12] For a sustained discussion of intellectual property, see Robert Reich's (2016) book, especially chaps. 4 and 5.

## Conclusions

*This chapter has shown a variety of problems with labor markets. Among these, it is important to distinguish between concerns about income inequality and/or exploitation, and concerns that are really about the character of certain forms of burdensome work rather than its remuneration. We have also seen that the challenge of vindicating our intuitive moral discomfort about exploitation is perhaps greater than intuition suggests, though we've looked at some interesting attempts to pull it off. Similar points about the nature of work may apply to wages at the "top end" of the income distribution. Rather than just eyeball the large salaries that some people earn, we should ask whether high salaries are compatible with the sort of work that is being performed. Our answers may vary from one case to another.*

## Study Questions

- Is the problem with divided labor that its monotony deadens the mind, as Smith seemed to think, or is it that it deprives workers of an ability to be creative, as Marx emphasizes? Or both? Or something else? What do *your* experiences of lousy jobs suggest?
- What is the point of the concept of alienated labor? Is the mere existence of such labor an injustice in its own right? Or is it more of a useful explanatory concept, for example, for making sense of why people pursue hobbies and "escapism" during their leisure time?
- Can you think of any good reasons why a top athlete should have their pay taxed at a different rate from a CEO who has the same salary? If so, which of these parties should pay the higher rate of tax? What about people who gain a similarly high income by doing something else, such as writing a novel?
- Do you think it is reasonable for members of the public to know how much money you make in a year? If you're uncomfortable about people knowing what you earn, then why shouldn't high earners, like corporate CEOs, make the same point about their financial affairs?
- Is it ever morally wrong to make someone an offer, which merely supplements that person's existing options? If this is wrong, can you

think of the reason why? If not, does it follow that there's no such thing as wrongful exploitation?

- Almost everyone who has accepted a job would have turned it down had some other employer offered superior pay for the same work. Does it follow that almost everyone in the labor market is being exploited due to their limited bargaining power?

## Further Reading

*On the Very Idea of a Just Wage*, special issue of *Erasmus Journal of Philosophy and Economics* 11 (2) (2018), edited by Huub Brouwer and Thomas Mulligan

A great recent collection of articles by leading scholars in political economy, debating various questions to do with labor market fairness and wages. A great place to start getting deeper into some of the questions summarized in this chapter, and to get an impression of where the current debate is up to. The *Erasmus Journal* has the added benefit of being freely available online: https://www.ejpe.org/journal

"The Goods of Work (Other Than Money!) by Anca Gheaus and Lisa Herzog, *Journal of Social Philosophy* 47 (1): 70–89

An excellent article presenting various ideas of why it might be important to have a good job, for reasons other than (though not necessarily contrary to) the Marxist idea that we need to avoid alienated labor. Among the ideas discussed here is that a good job involves access to a community and a source of recognition by others, which (according to the authors) are not substitutable for and cannot be obtained with merely gaining better wages.

*Meaningful Work* by Andrea Veltman (Oxford University Press, 2016)

A longer discussion of what makes some jobs lousy and other jobs part of one's flourishing. Probably the only recent book-length philosophical discussion of this topic, and a good place to start if you want to dig more deeply into this chapter's issues.

# 7

# The Welfare State and Its Rivals

*In this chapter, we'll look at some leading proposals for dealing with the fact that the labor markets confer rewards unequally. Over the years, governments have made various attempts to correct for this by regulating or intervening with the labor market. We'll examine some of these methods in this chapter. In addition, we'll look at some proposals that have not (yet) been widely implemented through labor market legislation, but which have interesting philosophical arguments behind them and which seek to improve on what governments currently do.*

## 1. Labor Markets and the Minimum Wage

Labor markets create winners and losers: some people take home high salaries for fulfilling work while some get neither. This chapter covers the most influential ideas about why this is so and the responses that this has generated.

An intuitive perversity of the labor market is that the worst jobs seem also to have the worst pay. Here's John Stuart Mill on this:

> The more revolting the occupation, the more certain it is to receive the minimum of remuneration, because it devolves on the most helpless and degraded, on those who from squalid poverty, or from want of skill and education, are rejected from all other employments . . . hardships and earnings, instead of being directly proportional, as in any just arrangements of society they would be, are generally in an inverse ratio to one another. (*Principles of Political Economy* II.xiv.8)

Mill's intuition—that wages for unpleasant and/or unskilled work are unjustly low—is a common one. Things are not nearly as bad (in developed countries) as they were in Mill's time; but the disparity still exists. Think

*The Ethics of Capitalism*. Daniel Halliday and John Thrasher, Oxford University Press (2020).

DOI: 10.1093/oso/9780190096205.001.0001

about a job that you'd regard as horrible to perform—chances are the pay is low, too.[1]

From the start, we need to be clear about what *causes* low wages. Recall, from chapter 6, that wages drop *when workers are easy for employers to replace*, either by other workers or by machines. Mill was at pains to establish this in the text surrounding the quoted passage earlier. Fundamentally, wages are low when there are many workers willing to work a given job at a particular wage. In this sense, the price for labor is no different from the price for commodities.

There are interesting exceptions to this rule. Universities in Australia and the United Kingdom use the same salary scale for academic staff in all departments. But it would be *much* easier for the university to replace staff in the philosophy departments than in law or medicine. Most likely, the university does this simply to avoid grumpy and resentful staff. Pay of academics is not completely flattened—promotion, for example, might be slower where staff are easier to retain. But the difference is not as big as it would be if academic salaries were governed by ease of replacement, that is, the demand for labor.

Moral intuitions don't always track the causes of the injustice that triggers them. This doesn't mean those intuitions must be wrong, only that they don't focus our attention on the cause. This impairs our ability to propose plausible solutions. It is sometimes said that low wages are evidence that the workers in question are "undervalued" by society. Low wages may sometimes be bad; but we shouldn't explain this by way of ascribing human-like agency to the economy, as if society is itself an employer making decisions about how much workers ought to be paid. Remember, the main cause of low pay is relative demand for labor. Pay can stay low even when consumers are willing to pay highly for the output of the labor in question. Remember Adam Smith's puzzle about diamonds and water. Diamonds are very expensive, but water is not, despite the fact that we need water to live. The relatively lower price of water does not mean we value it less, though.

Here's one way to tackle the problem of low wages: force employers, by law, to pay higher wages. Many countries practice a version of this strategy. An increased minimum wage is among the more popular proposals in grassroots political campaigns. American readers, for example, will be familiar

[1] It is worth noting that many, though certainly not all, dangerous jobs are highly paid. Reflecting on why this is so for some jobs but not others is instructive.

with slogans like "fight for fifteen" in the United States (advocating for a $15/hour minimum wage).

The standard argument *against* a raised minimum wage begins from a theoretical account of how labor markets work. Absent intervening regulation, workers and employers possess freedom of contract. Workers are free to offer their labor and employers are free to offer wages (and other benefits) in return for it—or not. Consequently, workers and employers can, and will, draw up mutually advantageous, consensual employment contracts. But employers will only offer wages at a level they can afford to pay. If some law says an employer can only hire people by paying them more than is possible, then the consequences are simple: to avoid breaking the law, the employer will simply refrain from hiring as many workers as they would have otherwise. Inability to hire may mean firms cannot grow to meet demand for their product. It may also mean that although someone has an idea to start a firm, they can't afford to do so.

The biggest losers, though, are the workers themselves, for whom the supply of jobs dwindles even further due to the costs of hiring. In this way, minimum wage laws may, in fact, *intensify* competition among those who can only sell their labor at low prices. This may mean that work that would have otherwise been paid somewhat above the minimum wage level now drops closer to that level. Some employers will hire illegally, "under the table." But this is often bad for workers, too. For one thing, they cannot easily report an abusive employer without simultaneously exposing themselves to prosecution.

This standard argument has been around since the golden age, partly because it is so straightforward.[2] If the government passed a law stating the minimum wage must be millions of dollars a year, then most of us would be out of a job. The standard argument is often wheeled out when someone with a platform wants to resist calls for a higher minimum wage. Nevertheless, it has weaknesses: it trades on a highly simplified and idealized portrayal of most labor market exchanges. Chief among these is the assumption that labor is relatively fluid; that workers can easily move between employers as and when superior offers become available. Adam Smith was optimistic about capitalism partly because he made this assumption himself. He thought that as workers moved to towns, the greater choice of jobs available within the same locality would lead employers to compete by raising wages.[3] Smith's

[2] For example, see PPE II.xii.
[3] See the remarks in WN I.x.1.

reasoning makes some sense, but changing jobs typically imposes substantial disruption on a worker's life. These relate to one's pension scheme, health-care plan, place of residence, children's school, and so on. It is also time consuming and costly for employers to find and hire new workers.

These "frictions" in the labor market are so important that there are entire subfields that study them. The cost of changing jobs and of hiring new workers is a special case of "transaction costs" in the labor market. Hiring (and firing) is expensive, so employers would like to have a degree of worker retention. It is also expensive for the worker to have to move between jobs. Because of such costs, labor markets price in many of these factors in hard-to-predict ways. This means that even though the standard argument against the minimum wage is accurate for *some* maximum (i.e., competitive) wage, we can't be precise about what that maximum is in any given industry, time, and place. Much of the debate between those who favor higher minimum wages and those who are opposed concerns where the competitive wage would lie. This is compounded by the fact that it is in the interest of workers and employers to speculate as to where that margin is.

So, while the standard argument is certainly plausible, it only really establishes that the minimum wage ought not to be set above a competitive level. Any minimum wage above the competitive wage will hurt the lowest skilled workers on the margin, but we don't know precisely where that margin is. The minimum wage will also likely help existing and higher productivity workers. Minimum wage laws will often redistribute from lower to higher productivity workers at the same wage since if someone needs to be let go, it will likely be the lower productivity worker. For the same reason, they will also tend to incentivize firms to look for high productivity low cost replacements for workers in the form of automation or the elimination of services.

There are other worries about a minimum wage. Sometimes particular professions carry low wages because of overcrowding by a demographic excluded from entering other professions. Historically, women have been overrepresented in professions like teaching and nursing, which are not especially well paid despite requiring skilled workers. A large part of the explanation is that women have traditionally had fewer skilled labor market options elsewhere. Such trends have sometimes motivated proposals to legislate for higher wages for nurses, teachers, and other so-called pink collar industries. Such proposals don't really address the underlying injustice, however, which is that women's access to other sorts of skilled work has been blocked in the past legally and socially by men. Raising wages within the sectors that *do* admit women may simply encourage more crowding. It would probably be better to locate and fix the cause (i.e., lack of proper freedom of contract), not the symptom (low wages in the limited space where this freedom can be exercised).

Another perverse effect can occur when minimum wage legislation is applied differentially. This happens when the rate of pay is allowed to vary in ways unrelated to the nature of the work itself or the labor demand. Two such variables are the *time* at which the work is being performed and the *age* of the worker. In Europe, North America, and Australasia, there is a long tradition of legislation requiring that workers be paid extra on Sundays and public holidays. Historically, such legislation may have had some moral basis: for years, public transport in major cities was poor or completely absent on Sundays. A higher rate of pay provided some compensation for this. There might also be moral reasons to ensure that the bulk of the working population gets its leisure time at the *same* time, particularly if congregating on days off is an important means for workers to exercise political participation.[4]

But should the minimum wage really be higher on certain days? An increased rate for Sunday work can have some undesirable, perhaps even unjust effects. Some workers get shifts allocated to them by middle managers. This is true of many service providers such as restaurants, hotels, and retailers. In these industries, Sunday work is often coveted precisely for the higher rate of pay it confers. This means that managers have a degree of (arguably) arbitrary power over their workers, as they may withhold Sunday work from staff they dislike or who do not perform certain favors. This sort of thing is hard to police. Thus, Sunday wage law may lead to increased labor market domination by managers, even if favored workers receive higher incomes.

It is also noticeable that shops and businesses that might otherwise be open on Sunday either close early or don't open at all in order to keep the wage bill down. This might seem like a trivial issue, but it can mean that workers will have to find time when they are also working to do their shopping. Allowing more flexible labor contracts for people who might be more willing to work on weekends could solve this problem.

Ultimately, some minimum wage may be morally defensible. But it is unlikely that raising wages to a morally desirable level can rely on legal

[4] This view is defended by philosopher Julie Rose in her book *Free Time* (2016).

stipulation alone. This is just to say, however, that increasing wages should not typically be done *directly* through legal fiat. Opposition to a higher legally mandated minimum wage is really only opposition to using government powers to coerce our way out of a problem by declaring its symptoms illegal. Time to look at some other proposals.

## 2. The Classic Welfare State

At the highest level of abstraction, a welfare state approximates any system of government-managed assistance provided to adults temporarily unable to find paid work. Unfortunately, the welfare state is routinely misrepresented in public debate. Before we can get into the proper merits and shortcomings of a welfare state, we want to set the record straight.

The prevailing popular view of the welfare state is of a system of handouts. One sector of the population works and pays taxes, while another lives off these taxes while doing little or no paid work themselves. Politicians have, unfortunately, sought to make political capital by promulgating this view. In Australia, we hear about "leaners and lifters." In Britain, it's "skivers and strivers." In the United States, "makers and takers." A candidate for president there once suggested (not knowing he was being recorded) that "47% of the people . . . believe that they are victims . . . that the government has a responsibility to take care of them . . . I'll never convince them that they should take personal responsibility and care for their lives." Though the rhetoric differs, the substance of all these claims is the same: they promote the impression of the welfare state as a program of more or less constant *redistribution* from hard-working to idle sectors of the population.

This is not what the modern welfare state actually is, or was ever supposed to be, however. A welfare state in the original, classic sense is not a system of constant redistribution, but rather a system of social *insurance*. These are different things, though they may look similar in the right light.

The classical welfare state was laid out in a report, written for the British government during World War II, chaired by the civil servant William Beveridge. The Beveridge Report took it for granted that most people would experience ebbs and flows in labor markets—periods spent in work and periods spent unemployed looking for a job. The proposed solution was to use income tax revenues to fund payments to workers during periods of unemployment. In this way, the welfare state was meant to be precisely like any other insurance scheme since it *pooled risk*. It secured cooperation between a large group of otherwise disconnected people, so that when some of their number suffered misfortune, they could draw on each other's resources. Indeed, this is exactly what various "friendly societies" and mutual aid organizations in Britain and the United States did before the development of the modern welfare state.[5]

Insurance payouts shouldn't be equated with raw redistributive transfers. We can see this just by reflecting on how insurance works in any other context. If I go out snowboarding and break my leg, my travel insurance company will pay for my rescue and treatment. This will almost always cost more than whatever I might have paid to purchase the insurance. The extra cost is, of course, covered by the payments made by the scheme's other customers. But we do not normally regard the recipients of private insurance payouts as "leeching" off those who bought the same insurance but didn't submit a claim. This is basically because we understand, at some level, that when people group together to pool risk, they're cooperating.

What Beveridge assumed about ebb and flow is more or less right: most people who suffer unemployment at certain times are working, and paying income tax, at other times. Beveridge made conspicuous use of phrases like "interruption of earnings" rather than the more permanent-sounding "unemployment." If unemployment is temporary, then the welfare state ought to end up funded by its own beneficiaries: if you receive assistance while out of work, we can see (in some sense) that you are receiving what you helped pay for while you were in work and will help pay for when back in work.

Insurance schemes need to be designed against abuse. If all snowboarders purchased insurance, then applied for a payout by simply claiming they'd had an accident when they in fact didn't, the scheme would collapse. This is why, if your house burns down, then the home insurance company will usually be interested in confirming that you didn't start the fire on purpose and why there are laws about insurance fraud. Any benefits that the welfare state confers on the unemployed are *conditional* on recipients meeting some other criteria so as to ensure that the system of payments is similarly protected. In some way or another, recipients need to demonstrate that they are unemployed through no fault of their own—that is, that the system really is working as insurance.

[5] See David Beito (2000), *From Mutual Aid to the Welfare State*, for a detailed history of some of these organizations.

We can all accept that insurance is unworkable without protection against abuse. But questions remain about whether such protection can be achieved for a welfare state without some serious moral cost. Philosopher Jonathan Wolff has developed this point in some detail.[6] Generally speaking, states tend to make unemployment assistance conditional upon showing up at some office and convincing some state official that you've been trying (but failing) to find work. Wolff observes that this can be humiliating and shameful. What's more, the very idea of being told one must demonstrate that one is not gaming the system may signal distrust, which may reinforce the stigma of unemployment.

How deep are these concerns? As Wolff explains, we need to figure out which problems are hazards of institutional design that might be overcome and which problems might prove to be unavoidable. Good training can ensure that state officials are sympathetic and polite when assessing welfare recipients rather than aggressive interrogators who compound the harm of unemployment. But there is no getting away from the fact that a welfare state requires scrutinizing the unemployed about their lack of *talent*. Wolff argues that, in any market society, it is unrealistic to think that unemployment will never be a source of shame:

> Think how it must feel—how demeaning it must be—to have to admit to oneself and then convince others that one has not been able to secure a job, despite one's best efforts, at a time when others appear to obtain employment with ease. This removes any last shred of dignity from those already in a very unfortunate position. . . . Thus the unemployed must give a humiliating answer to a question it is humiliating even to consider, in order to qualify for welfare benefit . . . one is required to reveal facts that one finds demeaning or shameful, even humiliating. Surely it is very difficult to retain any sense of oneself as an equal under such circumstances.[7]

Having to persuade the state that one is unable to succeed at getting a job is never going to be like the relatively dignified process of (say) demonstrating that one's house burned down because of faulty electrics.

[6] See Wolff (1998).

[7] Wolff (1998, 114). If you're getting tired of reading, an excellent movie is Ken Loach's *I, Daniel Blake* (2016)—a darkly humorous depiction of how the running costs of a welfare state tend to be absorbed by those it is supposed to serve.

Another set of worries has to do with the sheer fallibility and inefficiency of welfare state programs. Whatever sort of experience it puts people through, the act of scrutiny itself carries substantial running costs. Officials need to be employed, data need to be stored, buildings need to be spread around the country so that the unemployed can access them, and so on. States can try to keep these costs down, but this will often reduce the quality of service as a result. This can make unemployment far more stressful than it might otherwise be. Poor quality of service can even make the welfare state self-defeating by making unemployment a trap.

A challenging concern about welfare states is the possibility of creating long-term dependence on unemployment relief. In 1984, Charles Murray published a controversial study on long-term trends of American welfare policy from 1950 to 1980 called *Losing Ground*.[8] His claim was that American welfare policies had discouraged work and led to intergenerational poverty. Many have disputed his findings, but this study and others like it were influential in the United States—so much so that Bill Clinton promised to "end welfare as we know it" in his 1992 run for president. In 1996, he signed a bipartisan bill that more or less did just that. It required every recipient to begin working after two years of benefits and put restrictive limits on lifetime benefits. The effects of this policy (and welfare in general) are still being debated.[9]

Although we have been mostly discussing the classic idea of the welfare state as unemployment insurance, existing welfare states are somewhat different in their goals. This is especially true in the United Sates, where, since 1996, traditional unemployment insurance welfare payments are an incredibly small part of the overall federal budget. Other transfer programs, mostly old-age pensions and medical care, make up the vast majority of the federal budget. In 2018, for instance, 64% of the budget or $2.33 trillion is spent on Social Security (mostly old-age pensions and disability payments) and healthcare. Whatever we say about these programs, many of the outlays go to elderly citizens who tend to be wealthier overall than the median worker. This raises additional questions about the justice of these transfers that are somewhat different from the questions about unemployment insurance.

[8] See Charles Murray (2015) for an updated edition. Murray (2016) argues, in more recent book, *In Our Hands*, that the welfare state should be replaced by a form of universal basic income.

[9] A good debate on the topic by Robert Goodin and David Schmidtz can be found in *Social Welfare and Individual Responsibility* (1998).

## 3. Subsidized Idleness or Empowerment for the Masses? The Case for Universal Basic Income

A simple way to protect people from unemployment is to break the connection between unemployment and loss of income. The idea of universal basic income (UBI) is that everyone, or at least every adult citizen or permanent resident, be given financial support irrespective of what they do (or don't do) in the labor market. UBI is *universal* in that the support it provides is not dependent on meeting any particular criteria—even the wealthiest members of society receive it. And UBI is *basic* in that it is supposed to provide enough to purchase basic necessities, like food, clothing, and shelter, but perhaps not much else. It is worth emphasizing that UBI is not normally envisaged as providing anyone with more support than unemployed workers receive under a welfare state. Its defense rests on *how* it provides support, not on how *much*.

There are important "internal" questions about the format of a UBI. One question, naturally, is how much counts as "basic." Another question concerns how and when the grant gets paid. Some proponents favor a regular, cash grant akin to a salary.[10] Other proposals involve large "one-off," lump-sum payments, given to people at reaching adulthood, sometimes called stakeholder grants.'[11] A regular cash grant might provide effective security against poverty. A stakeholder grant, on the other hand, might provide potential for embarking on ambitious projects relatively early in life, like an expensive program of higher education, which might increase one's standard of living later on. These internal questions are interesting, but we'll have to pass them by, though you can learn more by consulting the secondary literature. In what follows, we'll mainly discuss UBI on the model of regular payments of a modest cash grant, though most of the discussion could be developed with reference to stakeholder grants, too.

UBI strikes some people as ridiculous. But something of this sort has been dished out for years by the state government of Alaska. Since 1976, the state has paid all residents an annual dividend funded by its mineral revenues. The payment is not exactly "basic"—it is usually under US$2,000 per year. But it may be the closest thing to a UBI anywhere in today's world. At the time of writing, UBI is being taken quite seriously by some governments.

[10] This is the version of UBI defended, over many years, by Philippe van Parijs (1998).

[11] The most influential recent discussion of stakeholder grants is Bruce Ackerman and Anne Alstott's (2000) book, *The Stakeholder Society*.

Switzerland held a referendum in 2016 on adopting a form of UBI (it didn't pass). So UBI is not as "utopian" as it initially might sound.

Although it's getting increased attention, UBI is an old idea. Its defense dates back to the golden age and even predates the Industrial Revolution. Thomas Paine (1737–1809), the American (and French) revolutionary, was its intellectual pioneer.[12] In his pamphlet *Agrarian Justice*, Paine developed Adam Smith's complaint about the concentration of land ownership into a small number of aristocratic hands. Paine thought that every person had an equal right to a share of the world's natural resources and that this right had been grossly violated by the fact that land was owned by so few. He recognized, however, the impracticability of dividing up land so that everyone had some relatively small share. His solution was to leave the land distribution as it was and use taxation: those with substantial land holdings would pay a "ground rent" into a fund to be shared around. Most important, Paine wanted his grant to be paid to every single person, including wealthy landowners, "to prevent invidious distinctions." Paine likely realized that assistance has a stigmatizing effect when it is provided in such a way that marks certain people as needy, or as failures. As a practical political matter, making the payment universal also creates a constituency that is difficult to divide. In the United States, Social Security payments work the same way.

UBI is sometimes viewed as a "leftist" idea, perhaps because of its apparently barefaced redistributive agenda. But the arguments for UBI are not *only* arguments pushing the benefits of redistribution. Setting aside our dislike for the "left/right" dichotomy, it is worth noting that UBI, with its low running costs compared to the welfare state, often appeals to thinkers largely opposed to substantial government efforts to move wealth around. F. A. Hayek, for example, advocated a basic income, albeit in a somewhat fleeting manner and without much elaboration.[13] The economist Milton Friedman (2002) endorsed a "negative income tax," which is functionally very similar to a UBI, and Charles Murray (2016) has advocated a UBI as an alternative to the welfare state. Being skeptical about government economic planning is *not* the same as thinking that poverty is morally unproblematic or that it is just something that we have to accept as a result of a proper labor market

[12] Paine only makes a cameo appearance in this textbook. For some good secondary literature on Paine's proposals in *Agrarian Justice*, see Elizabeth Anderson's (2015) paper.

[13] What he actually said, in his 1960 book *The Constitution of Liberty*, was: "We shall . . . take for granted the availability of a system of public relief which provides a uniform minimum for all instances of proved need, so that no member of the community need be in want of food or shelter" (1960b, 261).

process. The chief question, for Hayek, was "of how and by whom . . . assistance should be provided," not whether it *should*.[14]

So the moral and practical case for UBI is a varied one, with many forceful points of emphasis. But UBI is still morally controversial. We'll now talk you through some of the reasons that lead UBI's opponents to reject it.

First, there is the concern that the introduction of a UBI would induce laziness on an industrial scale. This objection really divides into (at least) three worries about giving people an incentive to stop working. The first is that laziness is just a bad thing, for the person who indulges in it.

The second concern is that, for the sake of UBI's feasibility, we can't *all* be lazy. The standard assumption behind a UBI is that it would be funded largely out of income tax revenues. For most countries, the feasibility of UBI depends on some people deciding to go out and work so that the state can raise the necessary funds. What this means, obviously, is that a UBI will fall flat on its face if everyone, or enough people, simply decide to opt out of the labor market. In the jargon, the worry is that a UBI is *collectively self-defeating*.

Though different, both of these concerns can be addressed by denying that laziness is an automatic consequence of being given money for nothing. Paid labor is not the only sort of productive activity. It may just look that way so long as it's the only sort of productive activity that most people can perform while avoiding poverty. UBI grants freedom for valuable unpaid activities. This includes various sorts of charity and voluntary work, as well as raising children. People who perform this sort of work are not engaging in *paid labor*, but they are, surely, still *working* in ways that have valuable outputs. Indeed, it may be seen as a historical accident, or product of social evolution, that some very important categories of labor are not paid in the first place. Really, mothers probably ought to be paid for their reproductive labor. After all, society needs more human capital and we all benefit from it. UBI partly recognizes this. (In making this reply, it is worth noting its departure from Paine's view of UBI as compensation. UBI is nowadays frequently defended as an enabler of productive activity of the sorts not rewarded by labor markets.)

A third concern about laziness is that it's being subsidized by someone else, namely whoever continues to enable UBI via income tax payments. A general way of expressing this complaint is to say that basic income violates

[14] For more discussion, consult Matthew Zwolinski's (2011, 2015) articles.

*reciprocity.* The idea of reciprocity is, roughly, that people should respond in kind to each other's acts. Society is, after all, a cooperative scheme (planned or unplanned). If some people are working hard to put something in to the big scheme of society, then others should not simply take the benefits but put something back in also. UBI recipients, who use the grant to opt out of the labor market, appear to be doing precisely this—they're *free-riding* on those whose work makes UBI sustainable.

On the worry about collective self-defeat, UBI's fans typically concede the logic of this point, but they deny that such a scenario would ever come to pass. The fact is that many people will *want* to work. Some will be attracted to specific jobs, and others will generally want to take home a bit more income than the UBI allows. So people will still get off their couches and go and find work. The point is that the UBI will allow them greater freedom when doing so. Philippe van Parijs is a Belgian philosopher who has been one of UBI's stalwart proponents over the last few decades. He emphasizes that "it is of the greatest importance that our tax and transfer systems not trap the least skilled . . . in a situation of idleness and dependency."[15] His point is that we need to help the unskilled so that they don't simply compete with each other and stay poor. The welfare state doesn't do this—it pushes people back to the unskilled jobs from which they have been ejected, before turning its attention to the next lot of unemployed workers to be spat out of the system. This is due to its central preoccupation with getting people back into work without really trying to evaluate, much less change, the system itself. Van Parijs calls this "work fetishism." Instead of caring about what sort of work people actually do, inside the labor market or out, the welfare state just tries to keep everyone busy as if employment is an end in itself. Proponents of UBI think they're doing better than this.

There are other arguments for UBI. One is that it may help disrupt gender hierarchy. There's a long (and continuing) history of women getting less out of the labor market than men. There is also a long history of spousal domestic violence, overwhelmingly against women. Now, women often remain in abusive relationships because they lack the financial means to escape.[16] Even in

[15] Van Parijs makes these remarks in an edited collection dedicated to discussions of his defence of UBI—Cohen and Rogers (2001).

[16] Though here we risk oversimplifying. There is, for example, important evidence suggesting that victims of spousal violence in upper-income families incur a certain stigma when disclosing; see Weitzman (2008).

relationships that are not straightforwardly abusive, there may be a problem with unequal bargaining power so long as men enjoy larger earnings. A UBI may correct for these problems somewhat. UBI is also supposed to help exalt the status of unpaid work that has been traditionally performed by women, which of course includes domestic work. It is sometimes said that UBI will make men more willing to stay at home and change nappies (etc.), making it easier for female spouses to go out and do something else.

Plenty of UBI proponents like to augment their case by adding in such claims about pursuing gender justice (something that, admittedly, is not a primary aim of the minimum wage or welfare state). But there are fears that UBI might actually reinforce existing gender roles. This is particularly plausible given that people may adjust their plans to fit prevailing expectations or social norms. If girls are socialized to "prefer" the role of a housewife during adulthood, then a UBI may reinforce this preference by making it a more affordable option. The general point here is that gender roles are complex, and they are sustained by more than just the means through which people gain a monetary income. The tendency for men to be higher paid, though very real, may be a consequence of a subtler and more complex web of conventions that are as old as humanity itself (and thereby older than the labor market as we know it).[17]

Less often discussed are UBIs' potential indirect and long-term effects on births and immigration. Since every citizen is guaranteed some amount of money, any increase in the population will increase the cost to taxpayers. It is probably unlikely that this will lead to something like China's one-child policy for natives, but there is a very good chance that UBI might be used as a justification to severely limit immigration—foreigners will come and "steal our benefits." Many immigration opponents already make similar arguments about the welfare state, but it is likely that the sentiment would get even more extreme under the UBI, even if the reality were that migrants would be willing to work and pay taxes.

[17] A good way to learn more about this issue is to consult Ingrid Robeyns's (2016) article in the Further Reading section. Also relevant is Anne Alstott's shorter piece in the *What's Wrong with a Free Lunch?* collection (van Parijs, Cohen, and Rogers 2001), in this chapter's Further Reading.

## 4. Prevention Is Better Than Cure? Property-Owning Democracy

UBI gives people cash, no questions asked. But why not give people other things as well? Chapter 5 reviewed the socialist concern that market societies involve class distinctions—specifically between a dominant propertied class and a working class. A striking feature of all the proposals discussed so far is that they make no attempt to do anything about this background condition. The minimum wage and the welfare state take it for granted that there will be a large class of unskilled workers needing assistance. UBI proposes to make workers not need to work. But it doesn't propose to give workers the sort of good reserved for the economic elite, namely, capital.

John Rawls—the 20th century's most influential political philosopher—complained that "welfare state capitalism permits a small class to have a near monopoly on the means of production."[18] Rawls believed that the solution was to "disperse the wealth and capital" around the population. This, he thought, would be superior to just compensating workers with modest cash grants. For Rawls, capital ought to be spread around to remove the old division between the propertied and working classes. Rawls referred to this social arrangement as a *property-owning democracy* (POD).

Rawls was convinced that, when large inequalities of wealth were allowed to endure over time, plutocracy would follow. While the rest of the population may retain a right to vote, and possess other political liberties, such as free speech, Rawls thought that these basic freedoms would lack "fair value." He thought that a right to vote is simply not worth much when you can only select between candidates offering policies designed to solicit campaign donations from the wealthy. Dispersing capital, so as to break up wealth inequalities, is supposed to restore the fair value of political liberties. This accounts for the appearance of "democracy" in POD.[19]

It is important to note that POD is not socialism. For one thing, it does not suggest that capital should be passed into state control or any similar sort of collective ownership. Wealth remains owned by private individuals who can still choose to sell their labor. There's nothing strange about individuals owning some piece of capital but selling their labor because they

[18] These remarks come from Rawls's brief but clear and influential remarks about the difference between these two systems, made in his last book *Justice as Fairness: A Restatement* (2001, 139).

[19] If you'd like to read more about the problem of money in politics, try the articles by Cohen (2001) and Christiano (2012).

wish to work on someone else's capital. I might own a hardware store but prefer to work in someone else's fruit store, hiring someone else who wants to work in a hardware store, and so on. Or I might own capital in a larger company and work as an artisan. POD does bear some resemblance, however, to the market socialism advocated by Mill, though Mill apparently assumed that workers would be partial owners of the *same* companies for which they worked. Because it still promotes an idea of free trade between private citizens, POD might even represent the sort of "market paradise" that Adam Smith is sometimes read as envisioning, where everyone has some capital to play with but nobody has a disproportionately large share.

POD seeks to prevent the disease of poverty by providing ex ante capital endowments that either (1) help people acquire skills or (2) enable people to not rely on selling their labor. This may be an advantage of POD or a disadvantage, depending on how easy it is to work out the details. To the frustration of many of his readers, Rawls said almost nothing about what it might mean to actually take a nation's capital and disperse it.

Others have since tried to offer a more developed account of what's involved in the dispersal of ex ante capital endowments rather than ex post cash transfers to labor market losers.[20] There is a strong emphasis on the provision of education at free or highly subsidized levels, and the role of inheritance taxes in preventing wealth concentrations from building up over time. There is also an emphasis on improving people's prospects for home ownership and for starting their own businesses, including worker cooperatives (again, the resemblance with market socialism).

Critics allege that POD's supporters have not yet done enough to explain how their proposal could be implemented and why it is as superior as Rawls said it was. One criticism is that Rawls drew an artificially strong contrast between POD and the welfare state in the first place. Recall that the *classic* welfare state is a system of state-managed unemployment insurance. But, in practice, what countries actually provide under the label of "welfare state" is rather more than just insurance payouts for the unemployed. This point is developed in an important article by Christian Schemmel, who emphasizes that state provision needn't be wholly ex ante or wholly ex post.[21] Many states *do* provide conditional unemployment benefit. But they also provide such

[20] This paragraph summarizes the ideas laid out in the collection edited by O'Neill and Williamson (2012).

[21] His (2015) article.

things as unconditional free (or heavily subsidized) education and healthcare. In addition, states may have various laws in place that aim to prevent plutocracy, depending on what is meant by that term.

POD apparently gives everyone a fair chance to avoid having to sell unskilled labor. One objection is that it overlooks the big financial risks associated with capital ownership in relatively small quantities. Capital can lose its value, often through no fault of the person who owns it. Educational qualifications can become obsolete, as can businesses. Acts of God sometimes intervene, as when an earthquake destroys a corner store. All owners of capital are to some extent exposed to this sort of problem, and only those with very large capital stocks can diversify and spread their risk out somewhat. Indeed, this is precisely what motivates the idea that the state ought to provide some sort of risk pooling through insurance schemes.

Rawls wanted POD to prevent the existence of an underclass of unskilled workers. Giving capital to people may help them, but the worry remains that an underclass nevertheless will emerge, sooner or later, if only because some people will be unlucky. Of course, we can develop insurance schemes for capital depreciation as well as unemployment, but now we're back in the territory of conditional ex post assistance. Many people would rather give up the possibilities of making a fortune as an entrepreneur or whatever (given the likely risk of failure in a competitive economy) for the security of earning a regular salary.

Another objection is that a POD disperses capital at the cost of limiting the total stock of capital. Keeping capital spread around in a roughly equal distribution will indeed stop people from accumulating too much of it. But this may come at the cost of suppressing some productive activity. Further, the effective dispersion of capital places much faith in the state's ability to know how to use it. Here, one might simply recall the Hayekian views outlined in chapter 4. Ultimately, it's just very hard for the state (or anyone else) to absorb and retain information about which person can do the most good with some amount and type of capital.[22] These criticisms are perfectly compatible with the idea that the wider dispersal of wealth and capital would advance economic justice. But saying is one thing; doing is another.

The case for a POD remains worthy of discussion and can compete with the other proposals identified in this chapter. These criticisms remind us that

[22] Criticisms mentioned in this paragraph are developed at greater length by Kevin Vallier in his (2015) article.

sometimes it is better to cure a disease than prevent it. We can prevent an outbreak of flu by quarantining everyone to their homes. While this might stamp out the flu more quickly than anything else we might do, clearly, it's better (on balance) to let people go around infecting each other and do what we can to administer medicines to those who get infected. And even the best preventative measures may require a cure as a back-up plan. Although the slogan might suggest otherwise, there is no principled reason why preventing something is better than removing or mitigating the worst of its effects. But there is a burden of proof.

## 5. Meritocracy

Another alternative to the classic welfare state is some kind of meritocracy. Thomas Mulligan (2017) in his *Justice and the Meritocratic State* develops a defense of a fully meritocratic state as an alternative to the welfare state. He defends his version of meritocracy as morally superior to other systems of economic justice. According to Mulligan, jobs, income, and educational opportunities should be distributed according to merit. Additionally, taxes should be focused on eliminating undeserved wealth and income. David Miller (2001) has also argued for the importance of merit in any system of distributive justice, as have John Kekes (1997) and George Sher (1989).

The problem, they argue, is that the welfare state, UBI, and POD all *ignore* merit. The welfare state insures against bad luck, but it doesn't really discriminate whose bad luck results from reckless conduct from those whose bad luck was wholly unavoidable. The UBI is indiscriminate and pays people regardless of whether they work or decide to surf all day. Property-owning democracy distributes the life blood of the economy, capital, on an arbitrary and equal basis, disregarding the fact that some people are better able to use those resources than others.

Many find the idea of a meritocracy appealing. After all, why reward the undeserving? Nevertheless, "deserving" and "merit" are disputed notions. That is, we don't always (or maybe even often) agree that much about who is deserving or not. Sometimes our intuitions on the matter are downright contradictory. We might say in regards to a basketball game that one team "deserved to win," even if they didn't actually win because they played well or showed a lot of heart. Even so, we still think the team that scored more points in the game "deserves" to get the win on their record. Or following a point made by David Schmidtz (2002), we might think that someone "deserves a chance" on the basis of what we expect them to do, rather than what they have actually done. In one sense, if someone "deserves a chance," they are clearly not deserving in the traditional sense, but we can also make sense of the former idea. Meritocrats have different responses to what makes something more deserving, but it is likely that any of their answers—however sensible—would be controversial in a pluralistic society. What's more, presumably any system that rewarded citizens according to merit would have to scrutinize them to find out who was most (and least) meritorious.

The second problem and, perhaps, the more serious one was raised by F. A. Hayek in his *The Constitution of Liberty*. There he argued against conservatives and socialists alike that markets do not and (more important) cannot reward merit. Markets reward market demand or, to put it another way, the values and interests of those in the market. This is, as Hayek (1960b, 97) argued, a good thing; "we do not wish people to earn a maximum of merit but to achieve a maximum of usefulness at a minimum of pain and sacrifice and therefore a minimum of merit." Markets, as we saw in chapter 4, rely on distributed price signals to direct producers and consumers to where they are most needed at any given time. Any merit-based system would require some kind of guiding force (e.g., a plan or planner) to direct resources to the more deserving rather than the less. Not only would this, according to Hayek, be a severe restriction of freedom, it would also suffer drawbacks of other planned economies like socialism.

Despite these and other problems, the idea of meritocracy has an enduring appeal. This is perhaps nowhere better evinced than in American higher education and in the military. We want the best officers to lead our forces and the best students to get the highest grades. Although in these contexts, merit-based rewards seem uncontroversial (perhaps because merit in narrow contexts parallels usefulness in those contexts), the question remains whether it is possible, wise, or just to run a whole society on that basis.

## 6. Comparing Systems

Ultimately, none of the proposals brought up in this chapter wholly excludes any of the others. Most modern Western democracies practice a mixture of them, though these tend to be restricted to a welfare state and a minimum wage. But though it may be complex, it is not unthinkable for a state to rely on each of these methods at once.

The question of how to regulate a labor market, principally to overcome the persistence of low pay, remains an enduring problem in political economy. Poverty, as we said, is in some ways the biggest problem of economic justice. The wealth of solutions, so to speak, partly reflects this. But it also reflects the reasons *why* the problem has persisted so long—basically, it's hard to solve completely. And it is unlikely to remain so long as markets in unskilled labor remain (which may not, of course, be forever).

## Conclusions

*This chapter has surveyed a variety of proposals aimed at regulating labor markets, with the principal goal of mitigating the persistence of low pay. All of these proposals remain live options, in the sense that versions of them are actually implemented through the labor market laws of many current states, and/or have a following of proponents in the philosophical literature. The comparative evaluation of the ideas discussed here is well worth a more extended discussion than we've given in this chapter. Remember that different policies might work best for different times and places, but also that there are principled disagreements about what range of goals a solution to low wages ought to be aiming at.*

## Study Questions

- We noted that, historically, laws requiring extra pay on Sundays and holidays reflect special difficulties of working on these days, and/or special reasons to want people to have time off at the same time. The strength of these reasons apparently varies with local conditions relating to culture and infrastructure. How strong are these reasons in the 21st century, in the place where you live?
- It is not a conceptual truth that labor markets are subject to a division between a class who sell their labor and a class who own capital and can

therefore employ labor. Are there good reasons to regulate labor markets in ways that seek to erode this distinction, or is it enough to regulate so that neither class has any special power or advantage over the other?

- Which would you prefer—state assistance in starting your own business, or state rescue in the event of becoming unemployed?
- If UBI were implemented, and you preferred to pursue paid work to increase your income, would it bother you if some people did absolutely nothing and simply lived off the tax that the state extracted from your paychecks?
- Have you ever been unemployed? If so, what kind of experience did you endure when receiving any welfare payments from the government? Do your own experiences corroborate the concerns raised by Jonathan Wolff against the classical welfare state?

## Further Reading

*Economics without Illusions* by Joseph Heath (Broadway Books, 2009)

Chapter 10, "Equal Pay" provides much more substance on the themes we've outlined in the first two sections of this chapter, particularly about moral intuitions versus the causes of low pay, and some of the problems associated with minimum wages.

*What's Wrong with a Free Lunch?* edited by Joshua Cohen and Joel Rogers (Beacon Press, 2001)

An excellent collection, though a little old, of very short papers that criticize the basic income proposal as defended by Philippe van Parijs, one of its most influential contemporary proponents.

"Will a Basic Income Do Justice to Women?" by Ingrid Robeyns, *Analyse & Kritik* 23 (2001): 88–105

A very comprehensive discussion of the many ways in which UBI might, or might not, work to address gender injustice both inside and outside the labor market.

*Property-Owning Democracy: Rawls and Beyond*, edited by Martin O'Neill and Thad Williamson (Wiley-Blackwell, 2012)

An important collection of papers that seeks to develop the idea of property-owning democracy beginning with some of John Rawls's thoughts about the shortcomings of welfare state capitalism. Very much the go-to publication for contemporary defenses of POD.

# 8

# We Are the World; or, How I Learned to Stop Worrying and Love Global Trade

*In this chapter, we'll examine some concerns about capitalism with respect to relations between different countries, or people within them. For the most part, we focus on trade across borders and its connection to problems of global justice, such as inequality between rich and poor nations and the abject poverty that continues to afflict such large swathes of the global population. As with many of the themes in this book, we'll show you that early defenses of capitalism from the golden age saw trade as a force for prosperity, and possibly justice. Once again, the reasons behind this view prove useful for evaluating how things have turned out since, and for working out how things might be better. This will help us examine contemporary "economic nationalism," which is a rising force in politics but makes some of the old mistakes addressed during the golden age. We will also identify important questions for pro-trade views, particularly justice in the structure of global institutions.*

## 1. Globalization—The New Common Enemy?

International trade gets a bad rap these days. In the US presidential election in 2016, the candidates of both parties tried their best to distance themselves from various trade deals and railed against the evils of trade generally. The winning candidate, Donald Trump, continued to promote an anti-trade narrative, especially regarding China, after gaining office. The current regime of international trade developed at the end of World War II and accelerated after the collapse of the Soviet bloc in the early 1990s. During this period, as more nations entered the global economy, increasing emphasis was put on reducing impediments to trade. Europe, first under the "common market"

*The Ethics of Capitalism*. Daniel Halliday and John Thrasher, Oxford University Press (2020).

DOI: 10.1093/oso/9780190096205.001.0001

and then under the European Union (EU), became a zone of free movement of goods and people. The North American Free Trade Agreement (NAFTA) opened up trade between Canada, the United States, and Mexico. In addition, the General Agreement on Tariffs and Trade (GATT) and the World Trade Organization (WTO) attempted to implement and regulate an international regime of low tariffs (taxes on imports) and freer trade. Among the criticisms of these institutions and agreements is that they have tended (intentionally or otherwise) to favor rich developed countries over poor ones. We will get to some of these criticisms, but we should note that the current global trading regime has done much to scale up the amount of international trade that now takes place.

This movement to liberalize trade became known as "globalization," and its consequences are still being felt. Globalization is not limited to the movement of goods and capital. It also means the movement of ideas, culture, and people as well. For governments and societies committed to the status quo, globalization was seen as a powerful process of disruption. The tendency of capitalism to disrupt and undermine the status quo is what the economist Joseph Schumpeter called "creative destruction," and it is one of the most powerful forces at play in the world today. Those who oppose increased international trade often fear the results of this revolutionary process. Those who embrace it tend to be more optimistic about globalization and disruption.

In this chapter, we look carefully at the nature of international trade and the negative and positive results of increasing globalization. One theme we will emphasize over and over in this chapter is that international trade should be seen as a fundamentally *revolutionary* process rather than merely the movement of goods and capital. We are living in perhaps the most unsettling period of human history since the invention of agriculture, and this is due in large part to the increasing ability of ideas, goods, people, and everything else to travel very quickly around the world. One of the most serious mistakes in thinking about the ethical implications of capitalism is to misunderstand or downplay the nature of this global revolution. There are reasons to believe that this revolution is ultimately a powerful force for good in the long run, but there are significant ethical issues that we need to consider along the way. In addition, there is an awful lot of misleading political rhetoric about the supposed badness of global trade that, in spite of having little substance, has an increasing power to persuade large bodies of the voting public. We will try to say something about this as well.

## 2. *Homo Mercator*

In chapter II of the *Wealth of Nations*, Adam Smith observed that there is a "propensity in human nature" to "truck, barter, and exchange one thing for another" (WN I.ii.1). In other words, human nature includes a disposition to seek opportunities to trade. He continues: "It [this propensity] is common to all men, and to be found in no other race of animals, which see to know neither this nor any other species of contracts" (WN I.ii.1). According to Smith, trade is what makes humans special. In this way, Smith is subtlety challenging the tradition, going back to at least Aristotle, of regarding *reason* as the defining feature of human beings. On the traditional view, humans are *Homo sapiens*, the "wise" or "thinking" man.[1] Smith is arguing something rather different. Reason and speech may be crucial enablers for our propensity to trade, but it is this propensity that more interestingly distinguishes us. Rather than thinking of ourselves as *Homo sapiens*, we should think of ourselves as *Homo mercator*—"man the trader."

In a comical aside, Smith points out that while one may see animals, specifically dogs, working together to bring down prey, "nobody ever saw a dog make a fair and deliberate exchange of one bone for another with another dog" (WN I.ii2). This example is more important than it may initially seem. Nonhuman animals are not able get what they want through reciprocal trade. Instead, they must depend on the favors of nature or of their benefactors.[2] It is no coincidence that animals are much less productive than humans and don't tend to be very good at increasing or diversifying the stock of resources that make their lives better. The flip side of this, Smith argues, is that nonhuman animals are largely independent of one another. Even pack animals can live on their own if circumstances dictate. Not so for humans. As Smith writes, "in civilized society he stands at all times in need of the co-operation and assistance of great multitudes, while his whole life is scarce sufficient to gain the friendship of a few persons" (WN I.ii.2).

This fact creates a problem. Humans need the help and cooperation of others. But, even in large societies, we can only really form close relationships with a small number of people. Our friends, family, and others probably do

[1] Of course, we mean "man" in the broadest sense that it has traditionally been used in English to include both men and women, that is, humankind as a whole.

[2] This is not entirely true: Since Smith's time biologists have observed examples of behavior that have the appearance at least of cooperative reciprocity in the way that trade does. Most notably, vampire bats seem to engage in blood sharing on a reciprocal basis, and it may be that this practice is more common than was once thought. This does not make Smith's point any less important, however.

not have all the requisite skills and opportunities to supply us with everything we need. Those who do have the skills and materials to supply us with what we need are often not our friends. If we had to rely on gifts and sharing from friends and relatives, we wouldn't be able to get most of what we need. We need to appeal to, not only the benevolence of our fellows, but also their interests. When we do this, we engage in trade. As Smith described it:

> Whoever offers to another a bargain of any kind, proposes to do this: Give me that which I want, and you shall have this which you want, is the meaning of every such offer; and it is in this manner that we obtain from one another the far greater part of those good offices which we stand in need of. It is not from the benevolence of the butcher, the brewer, or the baker, that we expect our dinner, but from their regard to their own interest. We address ourselves, not to their humanity but to their self-love, and never talk to them of our own necessitics but of their advantages. Nobody but a beggar chuses to depend chiefly upon the benevolence of his fellow-citizens. (WN I.ii.2)

Even the beggar, as Smith points out, relies on the trade of others for his charity.

Trade is not only central to our nature, it changes us. We not only expect the butcher and baker to provide us our dinner, we *need* them to. Our society has evolved into a vast network of trade and reciprocity. Without that network, few of us would have the skills to provide even the most minimal conditions for our lives. It is no exaggeration to say that large-scale social life is impossible without trade. But that's only the tip of the iceberg when it comes to what we can learn from the way in which we trade, and the ways in which we might trade more extensively with each other.

## 3. Why Do We Trade Anyway?

Adam Smith argued that trade is psychologically natural for humans, but also that increased trade allows for the division of labor. Here we'll briefly recap the story we first told in chapter 2. When labor is divided, one job is split into multiple smaller jobs. The example used in the *Wealth of Nations* was of pin production. According to Smith, an individual artisan pin maker could make between 1 and 20 pins a day. By increasing the number of people working on making pins and by subdividing each job so that each worker focuses on only one task, Smith argued that that a group of 10 pin makers could make around 48,000 pins per day. There are several reasons that Smith gave for why productivity increases under the division of labor. Workers learn their jobs better by focusing on them. They become more efficient and increasingly skilled. They also don't waste time switching from one task to another constantly. This increased skill and focus also leads to innovations and inventions that the workers will devise tools to make production even smoother.

As Smith saw, however, labor can only be divided to the extent of the market—division won't continue if there's not the demand to be met. If there is no need to produce more than 20 pins a day, no one will bother introducing the division of labor into the manufacturing process to boost production. Only when there is substantial demand and trade can the division of labor take place, and only when the division of labor is in place can surpluses be created for the benefit of trade. Trade allows unconnected groups to pool their web of exchanges, making for greater demand and larger markets, driving further division of labor. This cuts both ways, as specialization will make goods cheaper, enabling yet more trade. Trade and the division of labor are locked into a magnifying feedback loop where the increase of one leads to the increase of the other. Economists call this a "positive returns" situation, but it is one that can only exist in markets of a sufficient size.

Although Adam Smith didn't make the connection directly in the *Wealth of Nations*, his insight about the importance of the division of labor also explains gains from trade more generally. Smith's examples implicitly assume that each party in the enterprise is roughly of equal skill at preforming their tasks. What about when this is not the case, when some people are better than others at some tasks? As David Ricardo argued later, this is actually one of the chief reasons why division of labor and trade create gains. They arise primarily because trade can utilize what we call comparative advantage of productive powers between traders.

We will return to these ideas again and again. It is the basic reason that voluntary trade is not only beneficial, but usually very beneficial for whoever's doing the trading. You'll remember from earlier chapters that voluntary trade or exchange always has the property of being *Pareto* beneficial for both parties. That is, at least one party is better off than they were before, and no party is worse off. This can be proved in a variety of complex ways, but the basic reason is quite simple. No one would engage in exchange if they didn't think it would benefit them. (Unless, of course, they are coerced.) If an exchange or trade looks unfair or unjust, the first step should be to look for coercion of one of the parties.

What Ricardo showed is that *unequal* traders can benefit one another through trade. This is pretty counterintuitive. We tend to think that if a rich nation trades with a poor one, there tends to be some exploitation or injustice involved. As we will see in the next two sections, that can often be the case in practice, but it is not the necessary case.

Ricardo shows this by using a simple example. Imagine that both France and England can produce wine and textiles. Now imagine France is better at producing wine than England, while England is better at producing textiles than France. In that case, it is obviously mutually advantageous for England to focus on producing textiles and France to focus on producing wine and for them to trade.

In Table 8.1, imagine that it takes 1 units of input (labor, capital, rent, etc.) to produce 2 units of wine. In England, it takes 1 unit of input to produce 2 units of textiles and vice versa. This is a case of what Ricardo called *absolute advantage*.

If each country has 4 units of input, we can easily see that it makes sense for them to invest all of their energies in producing what they are best at producing and then trading. This can be seen in Table 8.2.

| | France | England |
|---|---|---|
| Wine | 2 | 1 |
| Textiles | 1 | 2 |

**Table 8.1** Absolute Advantage

| Input Wine | Input Cloth | France | England |
|---|---|---|---|
| 4 | 0 | 8 | 4 |
| 3 | 1 | 7 | 5 |
| 2 | 2 | 6 | 6 |
| 1 | 3 | 5 | 7 |
| 0 | 4 | 4 | 8 |

**Table 8.2** Production in Absolute Advantage

If France specializes in producing wine and England in textiles, their combined output will be 16 (shaded cells). This is the highest possible level of output for both countries. Since there are differential costs in producing each, however, it will be beneficial to specialize in the more productive good (wine for France, textiles for England) and trade. This is the obvious case that everyone seems to understand.

The more interesting case is when one country is better at producing both goods. Say that France, over time, becomes better and better at producing both wine and textiles so that the output ratios look like they do in Table 8.3.

In this case, France is better than England at producing both wine and textiles. Why would France have reason to trade with England? Even though France has an *absolute* advantage at producing both goods, it still has a *comparative* or relative advantage at producing wine. It produces wine better than it produces textiles (see Table 8.4).

If each country focuses all of their inputs on producing what they are comparatively better at producing (wine for France and textiles for England), they can maximize joint production (shaded cells) at 24 units of output. Further, England can only produce 4 units of wine at the maximum of its effort. England, however, can likely trade enough textiles to France to get more wine and textiles than it otherwise would.

In pursuing comparative advantage, countries sometimes do import goods that are inferior to those they can, and perhaps once did, make for

| | France | England |
|---|---|---|
| Wine | 4 | 1 |
| Textiles | 3 | 2 |

**Table 8.3** Comparative Advantage

| Input Wine | Input Cloth | France | England |
|---|---|---|---|
| 4 | 0 | 16 | 4 |
| 3 | 1 | 15 | 5 |
| 2 | 2 | 14 | 6 |
| 1 | 3 | 13 | 7 |
| 0 | 4 | 12 | 8 |

**Table 8.4** Production in Comparative Advantage

themselves. This is sometimes offered as evidence against the benefits of trade. What's almost always overlooked is that, in switching to importing a product, the importing nation has freed up its ability to produce other things at home that are of even higher quality than whatever it stopped making when switching to inferior imports. And it's worth emphasizing that while foreign countries sometimes produce poor goods, the quality almost always improves with time. South Korea first began exporting cars by selling low-quality models to South American countries in the 1970s. The Korean car industry is now globally recognized for its quality.

The truly revolutionary result here is that trade between unequal parties benefits both! This is deeply counterintuitive, but nevertheless true. This idea is also the main reason that the division of labor between countries is so beneficial. We see the idea of comparative advantage at a personal level as well as a national level. Imagine that in a firm one person is both the best salesman and the best accountant, but is a better salesman than an accountant. It makes sense for that person to focus all of his or her efforts on selling and to hire someone else who may be worse at accounting but *even* worse at sales.

By all accounts, LeBron James was the best basketball player and football player at his high school, but he was nevertheless a better basketball player than football player. It made sense for him to focus on his strength (playing basketball) rather than to try to do both. He is the greatest basketball player of all time partly because he has focused all of his attention on perfecting his basketball game at the expense of other possible athletic pursuits. Bo Jackson, on the other hand, played both football and baseball throughout his career. He was a great talent in both, but by splitting his efforts, he was injured more than he should have been and was never truly great at either. We can only wonder at how good Bo would have been had he focused on his comparative advantage and picked a single sport like LeBron.

This is the basic argument for trade. By focusing on comparative advantage and trading for mutual gain, all parties benefit maximally. As we will see in the next several sections, however, there are many ways for this to go wrong. Trade can be forced, ensuring that it is not mutually advantageous, and trade can be restricted in order to supposedly benefit the producers. Both are errors for reasons that Ricardo showed in the 18th century, but these errors are repeated in contemporary populist movements. We will look at these mistakes in later sections, along with problems not foreseen by Smith and Ricardo, having to do with the way in which modern, globalized trade is facilitated by institutions like the WTO.

## 4. The British Empire and the Persistence of Pseudo-Trade

Before applying the Smith/Ricardo view of trade to the real world in the 21st century, we should note first that what is *perceived* as free trade in the real world is often not really free trade at all, or is at best a distorted version of it. Understanding how this is so will put us in a better position to evaluate the benefits of trade as well as many of the injustices of the status quo.

The British sometimes congratulate themselves at having been the pioneers of global free trade during the 19th century, spreading the fruits of the Industrial Revolution to the rest of the world. The reality is a bit more complex, to say the least.[3] During the 19th century, the British had indeed gotten better at producing certain goods thanks to the growth in manufacturing industries. The British were now looking for someone to buy their new widgets. The trouble was that not everyone wanted them. At the same time, Britain's emerging middle class had developed a strong demand for cups of tea. But Britain was not very good at growing tea (it still isn't). So the British were importing tea from China (along with silk and porcelain, the latter still referred to as "china" in the United Kingdom). Frustratingly, for the British, the Chinese were among the nations not particularly interested in buying their widgets. Who needs shiny new knives and forks when chopsticks will do? So the British were forced to run a trade deficit with China—they bought more than they sold, meaning that the more Chinese tea shipped into Britain, the more British gold had to be shipped into China.

The fact that the British were unhappy with this trade deficit was already based on some questionable reasoning, as we will make clear in the next two sections. Finding it hard to get the Chinese hooked on knives and forks, the British decided to try and get them hooked on something more physiologically irresistible, namely opium. Thanks to the British having already colonized other parts of Asia, it was easy for ships heading to pick up tea from China to collect opium on their way over, from Bengal—another British imperial possession. This Indian opium could then be sold to normal Chinese people who were curious to give it a try. Opium being what it is, the Chinese people got addicted. And so, they wanted to buy more. Problem solved! The

[3] For a great analysis of the historical record and for an explanation of why the British drink beer but the French drink wine, see John Nye's (2007) *War, Wine, and Taxes*.

British no longer had a trade deficit. They could simply take opium to China, sell it there, and bring tea back.

Naturally, the Chinese didn't like this and tried to get the British to stop. This led to the series of conflicts called the "Opium Wars" (1839–1842 and 1856–1860). At the time, the Chinese simply didn't have the naval firepower that the British enjoyed and so there was nothing stopping the Royal Navy from simply bombarding Chinese cities until the Chinese agreed to sign a peace treaty. The various treaties that were signed granted Britain the right to sell opium in China, including a small island from which it could direct its business operations in privacy, namely Hong Kong. Hong Kong was returned to the Chinese in 1997, when the lease expired on the "New Territories," which had been added to the colony at the end of the 19th century.[4] By this time Britannia no longer ruled the waves. Whether the handover ends up being good for Hong Kong in the long run remains to be seen.

The behavior of the British was *not* an instance of free trade. It worked only because the British were able to force an addictive product on a consumer and then resort to violence. The business model used by the British is basically the same as that currently used by drug gangs in many 21st-century urban environments. At least most drug cartels nowadays don't pretend they are civilizing barbarous nations by giving them a new way of life.

## 5. The Old Skepticism: Mercantilism and Why the British Empire Was Actually Bad for the British

The British tried to turn the Chinese into drug addicts so as to buy tea with opium rather than with gold. But why? Britain, like other European imperialist states, had quite a fixation with gold and other precious metals. The Spanish were perhaps the most extreme: they killed large numbers of people in Central and South America apparently *just* to get the gold that was located there. What's so good about gold anyway? It doesn't do very much, apart from sit there—remember the example of Smaug the dragon from chapter 2, who just slept on top of his gold. Many of the industrial applications for gold

[4] It is often said, incorrectly, that Hong Kong as a whole was leased. Hong Kong *island* was ceded in perpetuity in the early treaties. The lease pertained to the "New Territories" on the mainland, the subject of a later treaty. Technically, Britain could have kept the island in 1997 so far as the old treaties were concerned, but this was politically unfeasible, given Chinese power by this time (and also economically unfeasible, as much of the colony's crucial infrastructure was in the mainland portion).

(like the conduction of electricity) had not been discovered when these empires began to emerge. It can be (and was) used, however, as a *medium of exchange*—as money. This is thanks to its durability, divisibility, and relative ease of transport. But this is not to say that gold is actually *wealth itself*, just that it can be used to represent wealth. What made it so hard for people to figure out this difference?

By and large, imperial expansions of the 18th and 19th century didn't produce all that much *real* wealth. This was because empires were largely run on what we now call *mercantilist* principles. The goal of empire was to take wealth (or at least resources) from other parts of the world and bring it back to the mother country. More wealth could not really be produced, because wealth *just was* precious metal like gold.[5] In Book IV of *Wealth of Nations*, Adam Smith took it upon himself to explain why mercantilism was a load of rubbish. Here is one representative quote:

> Among the Tartars, as among all other nations of shepherds, who are generally ignorant of the use of money, cattle are the instruments of commerce and the measures of value. Wealth, therefore, according to them, consisted in cattle, as according to the Spaniards it consisted in gold and silver. Of the two, the Tartar notion, perhaps, was the nearest to the truth. (WN IV.i.2)

To repeat, the problem with gold as a measure of wealth is that you can't do much with it. You can't eat it, wear it, or breed it. But with cattle, you can do all three. It is in this sense that the Tartars were onto something when it came to wealth measurement.

As Smith went on to explain, at some point people got confused and took the medium of exchange to be wealth itself, rather than just a proxy. This meant that countries had got stuck into amassing something other than what would benefit their people.

> To attempt to increase the wealth of any country, either by introducing or by detaining in it an unnecessary quantity of gold and silver, is as absurd as it would be to attempt to increase the good cheer of private families by obliging them to keep an unnecessary number of kitchen utensils. (WN IV.i.19)

[5] As we argued in chapter 2, the sophisticated mercantilists like Thomas Mun didn't really believe this, but this is more or less how the doctrine was communicated at the time.

In other words, while *some* gold might put food on the table *so long as it is used to buy food*, gold is not food on the table in itself.[6] Smith's reference to what benefits a family is a common technique he used to illustrate the substance of his points about global trade: often we can figure out what a country does and doesn't need, and thus how much wealth it has, by asking how a family or an individual might trade so as to increase its prosperity. Here is how he puts this point more explicitly, a little later on:

> What is prudence in the conduct of every private family can scarce be folly in that of a great kingdom. If a foreign country can supply us with a commodity cheaper than we ourselves can make it, better buy it of them with some part of the produce of our own industry employed in a way in which we have some advantage. (WN IV.ii.12)

As with all analogies, this one can be overstretched, but it works for trade and the idea that countries, like individuals, should stick to what they're good at and then participate in exchanges. For instance, the French may actually hate wine and love wearing wool. But they may still be better off making wine and swapping it for English wool, rather than attempting to produce wool themselves and restrict imports from England.

Smith was also at great pains to stress the other big problem with mercantilism, namely, its straightforward encouragement of *violence*. Because wealth was seen as fixed in quantity, countries had to find a way to take what their neighbors had without giving anything in return. This meant conquest and slavery, rather than trade and employment. Apart from anything else, this wasted a good opportunity:

> The commodities of Europe were almost all new to America, and many of those of America were new to Europe. A new set of exchanges, therefore, began to take place which had never been thought of before, and which should naturally have proved as advantageous to the new, as it certainly did to the old continent. The savage injustice of the Europeans rendered an event, which ought to have been beneficial to all, ruinous and destructive to several of those unfortunate countries. (WN IV.i.32)

[6] A point that is clearly communicated in the fable about King Midas. The avaricious king gets his wish to make everything he touches turn to gold only to discover—too late—that his food also turns to gold. His confusion of gold with wealth leads him to starve. A point that the Ancient Greeks had appreciated better than civilizations living over two thousand years later.

In other words, any benefits from empire were in fact benefits *in spite of* empire: violent conquest enabled some trading that wouldn't have otherwise occurred and might have occurred on a larger scale if nations had prioritized it over conquest. While there are compelling independent arguments for the injustices of slavery and conquest, it is foregone opportunity that may have made the British, French, and Spanish empires a bad thing for their own people.

Clearly what the rich countries needed to do, Smith thought, was work out how to enter into more mutually advantageous relations with poorer countries. This meant reconceptualizing what wealth actually was and abandoning the idea that it all boiled down to a fixed stock of metal. Because mercantilist empires didn't produce much wealth, their people didn't prosper. Britain was the most successful (in mercantilist terms) of the great empire-building nations of the 19th century, but it didn't do a very good job of enriching its people. Britain did have an emerging middle class in the 19th century, but this was in spite of the empire, not because of it. The Industrial Revolution was, of course, a domestic event in the first place, and enriched some people thanks to the increase in output that it enabled.

While the empire did create some labor market opportunities for the average Brit, like serving in the military (and maybe getting killed), poverty remained pretty rife in Britain throughout its imperial ascendancy. It might be argued, with some plausibility, that imperial Britain simply didn't *try* to benefit its poor people who, after all, could not vote for a change of government. But the fact remains that the British poor stood to gain more once Britain engaged in proper trade with overseas nations, which might result in the import of what its people actually wanted, and the export of what other nations wanted and whose production might employ Britain's poor more productively. This remains true today.

Adam Smith desperately wanted to emphasize that trade was a *peaceful* way for different countries to interact, just like it is a peaceful way for individual people to interact. The biggest problem with mercantilism was, aside from its fixation on erroneous measurement of wealth, that it characterized international relations as essentially antagonistic rather than as having potential for mutually advantageous cooperation. After all, the French need their textiles and the English like their wine. Better to allow each other to grow more and swap it in ways that maximize what's available to all. Much better to do this, at any rate, than to fight wars of conquest in pursuit of the limited amount already produced, killing and enslaving those who get caught up in things.

## 6. The New Skepticism: Populism in the 21st Century

These days, many people are becoming more skeptical about trade and, to be frank, somewhat mercantilist. In today's world, people want to see less global trade and more focus on reviving local industries—a trend sometimes described as "economic nationalism." Such nationalism is based on a variety of mistakes, which, in part, represent a revival of mercantilist thinking (which perhaps never went away).

What are these mistakes? Well, in the first place, voters often decry the "decline" of historically strong industries that have moved overseas. There is also a hostility to the movement of migrant labor from overseas—the common complaint is that migrants "steal jobs." These mistakes are linked insofar as they treat employment as a zero-sum game; that is, that there is only a fixed quantity of jobs to go around in the whole world. When industries leave, and people come in, this reduces the number of jobs while increasing the number of people chasing them. This zero-sum thinking is a version of the old mercantilist fallacy about the prospects for producing wealth. It is, in fact, perfectly possible for some industries to leave and for some workers to show up without the number of jobs going down. Indeed, in the long term, this is always how economies grow.

As we will say in the next section, people are led to these conclusions partly because they detect a worsening in their quality of life, along with their labor market opportunities. This is an accurate sentiment in many respects. The problem is that it is blamed on the wrong factors, which is what populist politicians seek to exploit in ways that mean they're not solving the problems that the voting public need help with. Populism in its current form often fixates on bilateral trade deficits that a nation has with other nations with whom it trades. As we said earlier, a trade deficit occurs when one party buys from another without the other buying something else back to the same degree. This is often thought of as a bad thing. But it's not. Once again, trade gets blamed too hastily.

It is hopeless to fixate on bilateral trading relationships in isolation from each other. Bilateral trades are part of a much larger network of other bilateral exchanges that, very easily, balance each other out. To stick with Smith's method, ask yourself what bilateral trade deals you have. One is with your employer, who buys your labor. Another is with your supermarket, whose groceries *you* buy. Both of these arrangements are highly imbalanced in isolation. You likely never supply the grocery store with produce or hire your employer. But they're part of a larger system that can, and often does, balance itself overall. This is because supermarkets also buy things from other parties—labor from their employees, produce from wholesalers, software from tech firms, and so on. And all of these parties buy from and sell things to yet more parties. Sooner or later, the chain of exchanges will reach as far as the employers of the supermarket's customers.

The authors of this textbook sell their labor to their respective universities and spend (some) of their salaries at the supermarket. This supermarket quite possibly buys software that was developed by research staff at the university. Or maybe it hires consultants who were trained by the university. The chains may be longer than this, but ultimately what goes around, in this case the money transferred when any of these trades occur, comes around. Most important, it goes around in ways that make everyone better off by producing more knowledge, technology, and loaves of bread.

The bilateral trade that we engage in on a daily basis does not just even out in a series of exchanges. Value is actually created at each trade, so, by engaging in trade, we are actually increasing the value or welfare in the world. This is an important point that arises because of the voluntary nature of (free) trade and the subjectivism about value that we discussed in previous chapters. If you buy an avocado from the grocery that is priced at $2, presumably you value the avocado more than the $2. If you didn't, you wouldn't have made the purchase in the first place. Similarly, the shop values the $2 more than the avocado, or they would have upped the price. Once you and the shop trade, you are both better off than you were before, but no new stuff has been created in the world. Trade itself has increased the value or welfare of all involved. Now, take this case and multiply it throughout the economy and apply it to nations. Doing so makes ideas like the "balance of trade" look like accounting notions that are mistaken for morally or economically important measures, while missing the real importance of the interactions involved.

We can use this analysis to explain why populist complaints about trade deficits make no sense at all. Imagine finding someone roaming the supermarket aisles complaining that although they keep going to the supermarket to buy stuff, the supermarket never buys anything from them in return. Imagine this character trying to persuade all the other customers that, because they're all in the same boat, the supermarket is taking them all for a ride and that they need a proper "negotiator" to get tough with the supermarket so that it "plays fair." Anyone going around with such talk would be spouting nonsense. And yet this imagined character is basically the populist politician at the highly localized level where trade deals are concerned. Clearly, this is a hopeless complaint to make about the way in which people do business with supermarkets. And it is hopeless because it overlooks the much larger system of exchanges that make it OK for some individual trading relationships to be completely asymmetric. Deep down we all know this, which is why we don't believe that the supermarket incurs an obligation to buy from us, the more we buy from it.

Trade at the global level can balance out despite comprising largely asymmetric exchanges between isolated pairs of countries. Let's say the United States buys laptops from China and doesn't sell much back. China buys raw materials from Australia and doesn't sell much back. Australia hires university lecturers who wrote their PhD dissertations in the United States on one of these laptops. We're simplifying somewhat, but you can see how the balance can occur. The irony is that the chain of exchanges between countries is often shorter than that between individual people, just because there are far fewer countries in the world than people. In this respect, opposition to bilateral trade deficits is *even more hopeless* than the imagined character walking around the supermarket grumbling about the unfairness of the deal. The fact that populists around the world have managed to persuade a large bloc of voters to accept this view has to do with various differences between the high visibility of local trade in which one participates, and the opaquer nature of trades across long distances between companies, governments, and other large parties. In addition, it's probably easier to persuade American voters that their county can make better cars than Asia than it is to, say, persuade them that they can make better detergent than what they can buy in their supermarkets.

A related fallacy is in the idea that countries are competing with each other, as opposed to swapping stuff. As philosopher Joseph Heath has explained, countries are not really *competing* with each other as much as they think they are.[7] *Businesses* compete for consumers, but countries don't have customers. Instead, they *trade*. It is true that some countries might be *better* at producing some things than others. But still, countries are not

[7] This paragraph is adapted from Heath's (2010) chapter in the Further Reading section.

rivals like supermarket chains trying to sell the same goods to some group of customers. Countries are places where customers live as citizens, and they should try to work out ways to swap what they produce so that their citizens can prosper. Ultimately, there is nothing wrong with America "losing" the competition to produce the best cars and Korea "winning." This is because America is not a corporation whose success depends on its ability to "sell" one thing. It is common, as countries develop, for industries to come and go. Better to let this happen, recognizing that it is part of a process that, if allowed to run properly, can lead to an increase in overall wealth. Americans are often better off driving Hyundais made in 2006 than they would be driving American cars. Many Americans certainly seem to think so since they keep buying these cars. In short, economic nostalgia involves a failure to appreciate that what a country is good at producing can change over time. If countries can trade with each other, then they can basically take turns at producing certain goods in ways that reflect this. But protectionism for the sake of *preventing* a historic industry from leaving, or in the vain hope of bringing it back, is never going to work or indeed bring about the prosperity than trade can bring.

## 7. Trade Justice in the 21st Century

In this chapter, we have tried to defend the case for global trade against the kind of economic nationalism, or "populism" about trade, on which countries should try to keep industries from leaving and try to maintain a balance of exports over imports. This view overlooks the potential for mutual benefit due to comparative advantage, and instead it brings mercantilist thinking back from where it belongs, namely the intellectual dustbin. We should note, however, that the defense of global trade needs to be qualified. Globalization in its status quo incarnation doesn't always live up to its ideal. In one sense, this shouldn't be a surprise. One of the core themes in this book is that we shouldn't equate the status quo with capitalism, and the same can be said about globalization and free trade.

In chapter 3, we reviewed one way in which the thinkers of the golden age may have lacked foresight. In championing the rise of labor markets, Adam Smith had in mind a "nation of shopkeepers" in which people worked as freelancers or were employed in small numbers conducive to a spirit of friendship between workers and bosses. The postindustrial reality saw the rise of large firms, which has made for a rather different labor market than Smith envisaged. Something a bit similar applies to the emergence of global trade in the 20th century. Ricardo's argument about comparative advantage, like Smith on labor markets, basically assumes that trade will be an aggregate of isolated, smooth exchanges between nations. The reality, however, is that trade needs to be facilitated by institutions that set rules and coordinate the nations that agree to trade by these rules (by aligning domestic policies, handling disputes, and much else). In this sense, talk of "free trade" is a bit like talk of the "free market"—it misleads because it conceals the role played by institutions, and hence some degree of restrictions on freedom, in enabling the practice to occur. Globalization may be a spontaneous order, but like any market, it won't flourish by being *unordered.* That said, the regularized rules of the international trading system as it has developed since World War II has led to a substantial increase in trade between nations. Good institutions (as we saw in chapter 4) reduce transactions costs and assure trading partners that everyone is on the level.

International trade is not so much a set of transactions between parties wishing to engage in it as a *regime*—a wider body of treaties, rules, and other institutions, evolving over time, shaping what transactions are possible and how they must occur. Central to the current regime are the multinational institutions mentioned at the beginning of the chapter, these being principally the WTO, along with various more local regimes like NAFTA and the EU. Although nothing like these was anticipated by Ricardo or Smith, they are now central. Also included in the regime are influential associations of producers and consumers (like OPEC [Organization of the Petroleum Exporting Countries], which has great power over crude oil prices), and lending institutions like the International Monetary Fund (IMF) and the World Bank, which do much to shape trade, too. Even seemingly unrelated institutions like NATO and the US Navy play an important role in maintaining peace and enforcing freedom of navigation.

A very familiar example illustrating why oversight by such bodies is important is the simple shipping container. Wherever you go in the world, you'll see the same type of shipping container on trucks, freight trains, and (obviously) container ships. The standardized shipping container has made trade *much* easier, and it is a hallmark of the postwar shift toward globalization. But it did not get here by itself. The shipping container was finally standardized in 1968, because countries abided by a ruling made by the International Organization for Standardization.[8]

Allowing international bodies to set rules is conducive toward trade occurring more readily on a global scale. But this is not to say that the likes of the WTO form rules that are necessarily *fair* or that allow the benefits of trade to fall equally on all countries that participate. There are various reasons for this. One is that while global institutions can, on paper, seek to formulate trade rules in a democratic way, effective participation is often costly in ways that allow richer countries to gain more leverage (this is a bit like rich individuals being able to afford better legal teams when they go to court). Theoretical optimism about trade, and the rejection of economic nationalism, should not detract from appreciating that the status quo trade regimes leave a lot to be desired. Philosophers working on trade justice have been at pains to point this out.[9]

The persistence of global inequality, whereby trade and globalization seem not to have delivered economic development to poor countries, shouldn't be blamed on countries being free to trade more often with each other. Instead, it might be blamed, in large part, on wealthy countries trying to make poor countries trade *in ways that suit the rich countries and preserve their position*. This can encourage the view that "trade" is only benefitting the economic elite. This is true, though, only because we are talking about an artificially constrained trade that is really rigged by government institutions doing favors for cronies. Such practices can actually be quite bad for rich countries in the long run. Back in the 19th century, the British would have done better if they could have worked out how to produce something the Chinese actually needed, while thereby benefitting the Chinese more in the process. But when wealthy countries try to protect their position in the global economic order, they often lose sight of this fact. Trade, as such, is not the enemy. The problem has more to do with how wealthy countries behave when it comes to their view about what might benefit them in the immediate term, and how the wealthier countries come to influence the trade regimes that then emerge.

[8] The humble shipping container is so important here that there's a whole book on the topic—see Levinson (2016).

[9] See especially the new book by Gabriel Wollner and Matthias Risse, in the Further Reading section.

## 8. If Trade Isn't the Enemy, Then What (or Who) Is?

The populist insurgencies promoting economic nationalism in the United States and United Kingdom have succeeded in part by blaming trade (including deals with other countries and the movement of labor) for people's problems. Many of the problems they cite are real, which is why populist politicians have been able to attract votes. But trade has not been to blame for problems in the past, such as the damage done by empires, nor is it to blame for the persistence of poverty at the hands of the global economic order. The argument in favor of trade that began with Smith and was refined by Ricardo defended a model on which countries traded on a voluntary basis according to what they could produce to meet what was demanded elsewhere, while other countries responded in kind. Much of the world's actual economic history does not accord with this model, though there is a strong case for attributing increases in prosperity to periods in which it has been followed.

We would suggest that the short explanation for populism's success owes much to the economic injustices, and problems connected with them, that have been discussed in the earlier chapters of this book.

### A. Protectionism and Subsidizing Failing Industries

Sometimes countries do try hard to keep industries from leaving. This is done by subsidizing them via the taxpayer. The American auto industry is a case in point. Americans might be sad to see the demise of their car industry, and there are costs associated with the job losses that this entails in the short term. But the common practice of bailing out failing companies is not going to help. It makes the general population poorer without necessarily making the saved industry any better. Similar things might be said about bailouts for other industries, such as banking. While it is always going to be difficult to manage the death of any failing industry that employs a lot of people, taxing everyone else to keep it going is, once again, not a way of ensuring any growth in national wealth, rather than prolonging the inevitable in ways that suck up more resources. This point is implicit in the foundational arguments for capitalism that we discussed in chapter 3, namely the importance of allowing competition (between firms) to do its thing. It is also important to see these "subsidies" as what they are: redistribution from the productive members of society to support less productive aspects. If an industry is not competitive, it either needs to change or stop. Dumping taxpayer funds into its lap when things don't go well prevents either from happening. What's more, bailouts have a marked tendency to subsidize executive pay and bonuses. It would be better to let a company fail and then use taxpayer funds to support the workers laid off, which is basically what (noncorporate) welfare aims to do.

## B. Mobility of Capital and Its Impact on Taxation

Globalization isn't just about trade. It's a multifaceted phenomenon that includes things quite distinct from trade. One of these is the mobility of capital. Wealth, in the form of companies or assets, is increasingly able to "move offshore" given improvements in transportation and communication technology. Often this movement occurs merely on paper, as a company that does its real businesses in one country is allowed to domicile itself in a tax haven. The problem here is with countries (or, more accurately, fiscal jurisdictions) having to compete to attract capital. As capital is granted a lower tax burden, the result is some combination of a higher tax burden for labor, which cannot so easily move, and less spending on goods that the state provides for normal working people. Tax competition is now recognized as a serious issue of justice.[10] While this may be a cost of globalization, it has nothing to do with the ability of different countries to *swap* what they have produced. As such, restricting trade has got nothing to do with solving the sort of collective action problem posed by fiscal competition. This is a problem of public finance, not of trade.

## C. Automation

Jobs don't always disappear overseas. Sometimes they disappear, period. This happens, very often, when the labor in question can be taken over by a machine, or when machines enable the same output to be produced with less human labor. This is one of the easiest phenomena for populists to blame on trade, just because it is often very hard for people to tell the difference between when their job has moved overseas to be done by another human and

[10] For a proper philosophical discussion of global tax competition, see Dietsch (2015).

when it has simply been taken over by a machine that is also in a different location (but not necessarily a different country). We'll look more closely at the issue of automation in chapter 10. While it is a difficult problem to solve, solutions have more to do with adjusting the *pace* of automation and creating opportunities for workers to learn more skills. Yet again, this is not a problem that is caused by more trade nor is it a problem that is going to be fixed by restricting trade.

In some respects, these are easy problems to see. Lots of people do see them, which is why they do not vote for populist politicians. But a lot of people don't, or choose not to. As long as this is the case, the case for global trade will have a fight on its hands if it is to get heard. But, in the current climate, it needs to be heard perhaps more than at any time since Smith sought to complain about the injustices of slavery and empire.

## Conclusions

*This chapter has introduced you to the classic argument for global trade, which emphasizes the value of divisions of labor between countries who then swap what each other is better at producing, having produced more of what each other wants than if they tried to be self-sufficient. We've also shown that some of the criticisms of status quo global trade actually target ways in which trade is restricted or distorted, according to this classical justification. There remain important questions about the value of restricting trade in certain circumstances, such as protectionism for developing countries. But dissatisfaction with "globalization," though justified, can be made sense of without the skepticism about trade that typically accompanies it, and more in terms of other injustices that, for various reasons, politicians don't seek to highlight.*

## Study Questions

- Suppose a rich country is in a position to lend money to a poor country. Does the rich country have any right at all to dictate the economic policies of the poor country as a condition of the loan?

- Can you think of any cases where it makes moral sense to "buy local," in spite of the arguments discussed in this chapter? More specifically, can you think of a case where buying a product made in your own country would be better than buying an import? What are the justifications in this case?
- What other populist skepticism have you come across regarding your country's trade relationships with others? How persuasive do you find it?

## Further Reading

"Justice and International Trade" by Helena de Bres *Philosophy Compass* 11 (10) (2016): 570–579

A concise overview of the golden age arguments about comparative advantage, along with a detailed summary of the contemporary philosophical writing on trade and related aspects of globalization and global justice.

*On Trade Justice: A Philosophical Plea for a New Global Deal* by Matthias Risse and Gabriel Wollner (Oxford University Press, 2019)

A comprehensive discussion of global trade and its significance as a topic about economic justice. While containing a useful summary of the theoretical arguments from Smith and Ricardo, the main value of this book is in detailing the history of, and current problems with, the global trade regime and constitutive institutions like the WTO.

*In Defense of Openness: Wy Global Freedom is the Humane Solution to Global Poverty* by Bas Van Der Vossen and Jason Brennan (Oxford University Press, 2018)

An excellent, comprehensive defense of free trade and free movement as a solution to problems of global poverty. The authors articulate and address to most sophisticated and well-developed arguments against trade and free movement.

*Normative Aspects of International Trade Institutions*, special issue of *Moral Philosophy & Politics* 5 (2) (2018), edited by Valentin Beck

Another recent contribution to the newly emerging philosophical literature on global trade justice, dealing with a variety of focused discussions, some going beyond what's been discussed in this chapter.

# 9

# Keeping Up with the Joneses (and the Kardashians)

## Positional Goods and Wars of All against All

*In this chapter, we'll look at the problems posed by positional goods. These are goods that confer relative or "competitive" advantages, and whose supply is therefore limited as a matter of logic. We'll begin by looking at the way in which early theoretical work on positional goods leads to some very general worries about the long-term prospects for capitalism, which contrast with the optimism of figures like Hayek and Smith. We'll then look at some important specific cases, such as education, before ending with a discussion about some proposals for taking the heat out of current positional competition.*

### 1. We Can't All Be Better Than Average

Nobody wants to die in a car crash. But if you *are* in a multivehicle collision, your chances improve if your vehicle is the bigger one. "Safety" is one reason why some people try to buy vehicles that are relatively large and heavy. Of course, whether a vehicle is *relatively* large and heavy depends on what other vehicles are already out on the road. So the more consumers "buy big," the more other consumers have to respond in kind to avoid being left behind. It is common to find four-wheel drives and pickup trucks in suburban streets, even though people use these vehicles mainly for making short journeys that hardly require a vehicle of such size or power.[1] Here, consumers try to out-muscle each other for something that, collectively speaking, they can't

[1] For a more extended analysis of this phenomenon, focusing on the United States, see White (2004).

*The Ethics of Capitalism*. Daniel Halliday and John Thrasher, Oxford University Press (2020).

DOI: 10.1093/oso/9780190096205.001.0001

all obtain at once. When one consumer gets a larger vehicle, they protect themselves at the expense of other people who have not upgraded their vehicle. In the jargon used by economists and philosophers, vehicle size is a *positional* good.

We introduced the problem of positional goods when discussing market failure in chapter 4. Now we're going to look at it more carefully. Competition for positional advantage is often highly undesirable. The example we just gave is a case in point: larger vehicles are more expensive than small cars. They lead to more traffic jams and higher fuel emissions—costs partly absorbed by others, as externalities. Ironically, widespread purchasing of large vehicles may actually *reduce* safety overall. Buying a larger car may only increase your safety *given* a collision with another vehicle. This is logically quite distinct from having protection against getting into a collision in the first place! Large vehicles tend to have poorer sightlines, higher centers of gravity, and longer breaking distances, all of which also increase the risks of single-vehicle accidents *and* multivehicle collisions. So a shift toward purchasing large cars may increase the *frequency* of accidents on the road. This may mean more danger overall, regardless of how well protected people might be on a "per collision" basis.

Positional goods are so-called because they confer relative rather than absolute benefit. But it is worth being more precise than this. We're going to use a definition provided by the philosophers Harry Brighouse and Adam Swift (2006, 472):

> Positional goods . . . are goods with the property that one's relative place in the distribution of the good affects one's absolute position with respect to its value.

In other words, the protective benefit I get from my car depends on my car's position in a ranking of *all* cars on the road, according to size and weight. Shares in the total supply of a positional good amount to *positions* in an ordering. It is, admittedly, a little odd to talk about the "supply" of things like vehicle size, but it makes logical sense: relative size is what consumers are demanding, and the producers of automobiles are producing a certain amount of size and mass as part of the vehicles they manufacture.

Positional competition occurs with respect to services as well as goods. If you visit Disneyland in California (near where one of the authors lives), you can pay a basic entrance fee of around US$100. (The fee varies by the time of year, and children get in for less.) This entitles you to join queues at the various rides and attractions. But Disneyland also offers a VIP ticket to cater for its more queue-averse customers. Prices for this ticket start at $2,400. The ticket is a positional good: it confers the benefit of shorter wait times, relative to other visitors who have only paid the standard admission fee. A similar service can often be purchased in other places where people want to pay for shorter waiting times, like airports.

Many of what we call "luxury" goods are positional. You may have noticed that expensive bottles of whisky are often marketed as "limited edition" or "small batch." This might seem curious. The fact that some whisky has been made in a small quantity is hardly something you can detect in its flavor. So why the higher price? The answer is that there is demand not just for taste, but for exclusivity. And often, exclusivity is desired because it can be made *conspicuous*. Owning a luxury item that is *visibly* expensive represents one way of signaling one's wealth to others.[2] Giving a small-batch whisky as a gift, or bringing it out at one's dinner party, might have a more impressive effect than bringing out one of the more mass-produced brands.

Sellers often need to work hard to preserve a product's "exclusivity." The luxury status of clothing often relies on little more than a designer label, which is easy for someone else to produce (unlike whisky, which is rather hard to produce). One of the authors of this textbook has a friend who once worked for the French fashion house Louis Vuitton. Her job involved monitoring the availability of counterfeit items, sold at a lower price on the internet and in nonmainstream retail outlets. At the time, the author was confused as to why Louis Vuitton was concerned about items being sold to people who were never going to be able to afford the real thing anyway. His friend gave a clear explanation: Louis Vuitton wasn't concerned about *losing* customers *to* the counterfeiters, but to rival fashion houses: a proliferation of visually indistinguishable counterfeits would make Louis Vuitton products lose their air of exclusivity, and hence their power to signal the bearer's wealth. So counterfeits need to be kept down so that consumers who would *never* buy fakes didn't simply switch to Gucci, Prada, or any rival better at keeping supply of *their* fakes under control. Louis Vuitton is fortunate that counterfeiting its products happens to be illegal, because it owns its brand names and is basically entitled to have the scarcity of its product enforced by law. Not all sellers of luxury goods have this luxury. Diamond makers don't

[2] For an excellent overview of signaling theory in general, see Skyrms (2010).

have a property right in the carbon allotrope, and there was industry-wide panic once the synthetic production of diamond became economically feasible, dramatically reducing the scarcity of the substance.

It is often said that when a good is positional, its distribution should be regulated more carefully than if it were nonpositional. But it is not immediately obvious how to defend this claim. It may be very general, that is, that *all* positional goods are morally significant just because of their positionality. Another view is that positionality is important when it comes to the distribution of some goods but not so much others. On this view, there is nothing of *prior* moral importance about the distribution of cars or small-batch whisky. And we might think it's not worth getting too concerned about the distribution of wait times in airports and theme parks. If some people want to spend thousands of dollars to get the most out of a Disneyland visit, then maybe that's OK.

The distribution of some other positional goods seems to be more a matter of justice. One of the most discussed cases is education. As we pointed out in chapter 4, the benefits you get from your education depend highly on how your educational resources and achievements affected your *position* in the overall ranking of students in your peer group. Another potentially morally important positional good is political influence. One reason for treating both education and political influence differently from things like whisky is that we tend to think there are reasons to be concerned when they become distributed unequally in a democratic society. Indeed, philosophers like Brighouse and Swift argue that education's positional character counts strongly in favor of distributing access to educational resources more equally (see later discussion).

Of course, some caveats apply. Schools are not equal in quality. For instance, many private schools are better in all sorts of ways than most government-run schools. The same is true in the United States among public schools. Schools in richer districts tend to be much better than those in poorer districts. While there are certainly important concerns about the justice of forcing children to go to a public school in a poor neighborhood merely because they can't afford to move to a richer neighborhood, the problem here is not really about a need to eliminate positionality.

Introducing choice in the form of allowing students to choose their districts or providing vouchers to attend private schools would alleviate an important form of injustice in unequal access to schooling without eliminating inequality or even positionality. The question then is why is a certain kind of positionality especially important in goods like education? The mere inequality can't be the only reason.

Setting aside questions about specific positional goods, something can be said about the rise of positional consumption as a phase in economic development. Positional goods are a very *modern* problem. Though they existed during the golden age, they were not much discussed. Most of the examples we've listed so far in this chapter have been around only since the 20th century. Indeed, positional goods look, for want of a better expression, very *middle class*. The fact is that poorer people can't afford air travel, trips to Disneyland, expensive cars, and expensive education. In the golden age, almost all people were (very) poor. They struggled to afford basic necessities like food, clothing, and shelter. And these basic necessities are nonpositional goods. For this reason, people didn't have the resources to get stuck into positional competitions with each other. So far as markets were concerned, the sale of positional goods was largely restricted to luxuries reserved for the very wealthy. Adam Smith used this fact to make an important observation about what we now call *conspicuous consumption*, which might ultimately explain why people want to buy limited-edition whisky.[3] One of the consequences of wealthy people buying material things is that other people see them flaunting it. This has an effect on those lower down the totem pole of consumption.

> The poor man's son, whom heaven in its anger has visited with ambition, when he looks around him, admires the condition of the rich. He finds the cottage of his father too small for his accommodation, and fancies he should be lodged more at his ease in a palace (TMS IV.i.8).

This is an important point about the psychology of consumer behavior (the surrounding text in the *Theory of Moral Sentiments* is well worth reading in full). Such behavior has been well studied since Smith's time, particularly by the American sociologist Juliet Schor (2014). Among Schor's findings are that consumption of conspicuous luxuries really took off after the rise of television. It is true that people are, as Smith put it, "enchanted" by wealth once they see it. The rise of positional consumption is in large part due to people wanting to mimic the lifestyles of those at higher economic levels, partly in the hope of being perceived as being closer to that level than they really are. In

[3] The classic theories of conspicuous consumption are found in the work of Thorstein Veblen (1965) and John Kenneth Galbraith (1998).

Schor's terminology, people's "reference points" became much higher, given the tendency of television to depict wealthy individuals in a favorable light.

Keeping up with the Joneses has turned into keeping up with the Kardashians (who are, of course, much harder to keep up with). And yet, unlike the Kardashians, we are not all trying to look richer than everyone else. The philosopher Judith Lichtenberg (1996) has pointed out that "although a person may consume to show that he is better than others, he may also consume to show that he is as good as others." Much of our positional consumption is an attempt to simply not fall *too far behind*.

We've given you a wide range of examples partly because we want to give the impression that different positional goods are important for different reasons. Just as important, there's the fact that the competition for positional goods does not always have the same structure. This is a subtle point that will become clearer later on. Let's start by looking at some general attempts to develop principles for regulating positional goods.

## 2. Zero Sum versus Positive Sum

Brighouse and Swift argue that when goods are positional, justice tends to require a more equal distribution than it does for goods that are nonpositional. This draws on a certain way of thinking about equality and when it can be defended.

A very influential thought in political philosophy is that inequalities can be justified only when they are necessary to benefit the least advantaged. This idea became particularly prominent when developed by John Rawls, as part of his theory of justice. One doesn't need to buy into the other aspects of Rawls's theory in order to endorse this sort of justification for inequalities. As Brighouse and Swift (2006) explain, a more straightforward but similar view is just that justice requires giving priority to the worst-off members of society. It may be that many inequalities can be justified in this way. For example, the worst-off are generally benefitted by state-provided healthcare. But the successful delivery of healthcare involves a number of very demanding tasks, such as surgery. In order to become a surgeon, one must undergo years of difficult training. And the job itself is stressful and comes with a high degree of responsibility. If we make a mistake writing this textbook, at least nobody bleeds to death on an operating table. There may be a strong case for allowing surgeons to be paid relatively large sums of money on grounds that the worst-off (not to mention everyone else) would have less access to good surgery otherwise.

We should point out that this view about permissible inequality is controversial. There are some who deny that *any* inequalities can be permitted in accordance with this sort of reasoning.[4] We'll have to set this disagreement aside. What's important here, though, is that whatever one thinks about *when* it is possible to justify inequalities on grounds that they benefit the least advantaged, such justification apparently cannot *ever* be used to justify inequalities in positional goods.

Why can't inequalities in positional goods raise the position of the least advantaged? Simple: when a positional good is unequally distributed, those who are better off in this distribution are only so in virtue of the fact that others are worse off. This is because distributions of positional goods are "zero sum." If the position of the better off were to be lowered, then the absolute position of the worst off could be raised. This is one reason for making the better off worse off. Brighouse and Swift use this sort of reasoning to argue that, for example, markets in education are unjust. This is because such markets allow the children of wealthier parents to acquire superior educational opportunities just because their parents can afford it. As Swift has said in some solo-authored work, children sent to elite private schools "are jumping the queue for university places and well-paid or interesting jobs." Swift (2003, 24–25) goes on to write that:

> Queues are zero-sum. That's why you don't like it when the woman in front lets her friend in ahead of her. The fact that some children are getting a helping hand disadvantages those who aren't. This is the obvious and standard argument from equality of opportunity against private schools.

Lots could be said about the alleged injustice of private education. We don't have time to review the debate here, which is quite complicated. Even Brighouse and Swift concede that the state shouldn't simply prohibit private education altogether.[5]

[4] G. A. Cohen defends this view, against Rawls, in his (2008) book, *Rescuing Justice and Equality*. One of the authors argues against Cohen's position in several places (Thrasher and Hankins 2015; Thrasher 2018b).

[5] An important more recent article, in which some other aspects of educational justice are made clear, is Brighouse and Swift (2014). See also Brighouse's sole-authored book in the Further Reading section.

One general criticism of the Brighouse/Swift approach can be highlighted here. Talking about the distribution of a positional good being zero sum, such that inequalities always help the better off at the expense of the worse off, is only guaranteed to be true with respect to *the positional good in question*. It is perfectly possible that, by allowing an inequality to form with respect to a positional good, we could promote effects on the distribution of *other* goods. Educational inequalities, for example, might be such that the *education* of better-off people improves in ways that degrade the education of those lower down. But, in principle, giving a superior education to some minority might turn out to benefit the less well educated in some more indirect way.

This may not be *fair* so long as the distribution of educational opportunities is viewed in isolation, but there may be ways of justifying it all things considered. If educational inequalities have the right sort of positive externalities, then they may be compatible with justice. This all depends, of course, on whether there are good reasons for seeking principles that Brighouse and Swift describe as being "specific" to a positional good under examination, and which might therefore ignore what the externalities are. But this has proven to be a controversial claim, whatever positional good it might be applied to.[6]

It is also not true, strictly speaking, that the positional goods are zero sum in a larger sense. Even those at the tail end of the distribution are getting educated, regardless of how those who get better educations fare. To think otherwise might be to have an obsessively comparative analysis of the value of education. Surely students at nonelite schools are being educated and that is certainly of value. If so, they are benefitting from the system of education, and the fact that someone else goes to a "better" school does not make them worse off in *all* the ways that matter.

Brighouse and Swift are focusing largely (although they don't describe it this way) on the *signaling* value of education.[7] This is the quality that your educational credentials indicate to potential employers. They are right that the value of that signal is degraded if a more attractive signal is generated by another candidate, but this is not the whole story. First, there is more to education than signaling. Second, employers look for more than just the signal of a quality education. So the idea of one "job queue" where all applicants are

[6] This paragraph summarizes the discussion in Frieman (2014).

[7] Bryan Caplan (2018) argues that almost all of the value of education is in the signal it sends.

ranked by education alone is a little strange, though there is something to the idea that we should get away from a situation in which the same educational ranking is being used to ration a wide range of jobs (see the remarks on "bottlenecks," later on).

Education's signaling function basically requires that there be educational inequalities of some sort. Employers still need to make distinctions in order to find good candidates to hire. If they can't rely on educational credentials to do so, they will use other factors that they believe will signal quality. Perhaps they will use family connections, religious affiliation, race, or some other feature that distinguishes people. Most of these look worse than educational quality, which is at least somewhat meritocratic.

But, perhaps, meritocracy is the problem. By allowing competition from roughly equal starting points (we can always debate about *how* equal these starting points really are), we will see inequality of outcome. Unless we believe that all people are equal in abilities, egalitarianism about outcomes seems incompatible with meritocratic processes like we find in education. Most people, if pushed, are committed to the basic fairness of meritocratic institutions and would balk at treating individuals unequally or unfairly in order to generate equal outcomes. In any case, this is one of the core problems at the heart of the issue of positional goods.

## 3. Capitalism's Great Disappointment?

We can now say more about how positional goods are a modern, middle-class phenomenon. The term "positional good" was coined in the 1970s, by Fred Hirsch (2005), in his book *Social Limits to Growth*. Hirsch was a throwback to the golden age: he wrote economics in prose, eschewing the technical concepts of the fragmented age. He was interested in the long-run evolution of economic cooperation and whether capitalism could be expected to improve the quality of human life for much longer. Like Marx, though in a very different way, Hirsch was a pessimist. He thought that capitalism was, in his words, set to become "a victim of its own propaganda." Hirsch regarded competition for positional goods as a sign that capitalism had passed its use-by date. The basic idea is that markets are great for increasing the supply of nonpositional goods, like food and shelter (once very scarce). But markets get into trouble once people have had their fill of these goods and start wanting positional goods instead. Hirsch thought that this shift was inevitable, and one that all market economies capable of growth would eventually encounter.

Here's a summary of Hirsch's story. The historic stability of capitalist-leaning economies relies on a popular opinion of markets as gradually raising the standard of living. Since the 19th century, goods that were scarce and expensive gradually became more affordable from one generation to the next, to such an extent that what one generation considered a luxury became taken for granted by subsequent generations. Owning a car in the 1950s was a great way to signal one's wealth. Nowadays, people just assume you already own a car even if you're of quite modest means. Any car would've made your grandparents look well off. The wrong car will make *you* look *poor*.

Here, Hirsch builds on Adam Smith's observation that people's consumer goals will be influenced by a desire to mimic the lifestyles of the wealthy. In the early days, luxuries were often nonpositional goods: glass windows were the height of opulence in the 18th century. But the rise of markets created incentives for people to find cheaper ways of producing glass and bringing it to market. So glass windows became cheaper and eventually proliferated. Nowadays, glass windows are considered a basic necessity—anyone renting a windowless apartment to tenants will probably be breaking the law. Goods like roast chicken, cars, commercial plane tickets, and soap are nowadays nothing special. Go back far enough, often just a few generations, and such goods were symbols of great affluence. At some time they became affordable to people whose parents could not have afforded them. According to Hirsch, capitalism survived based on the promise that this process will continue. Everyone will end up better off, materially speaking, than their parents' generation. Hence, people tolerate market order even if they're not as well rewarded as some of their peers.

This process (Hirsch called it "embourgeoisement") cannot go on forever. Crucially, expansion in the production of luxuries, and the consequent lowering of their price, can only occur so long as the goods in question are nonpositional. Positional goods will remain left over as the luxuries of the very wealthy. Nowadays, the goods associated with wealth are more linked to scarcity than they ever were. Think about top-floor penthouses, private islands, and sports cars (like the Ferrari Enzo) made in small numbers and sold by invitation only. Once the masses possess glass windows, chicken for dinner, and a plane ticket somewhere, they will want positional goods next. But, as Hirsch put it, positional goods are subject to "absolute limits on their supply" (more on this in a moment). This fact doesn't stop consumers from demanding positional goods or from being willing to pay good money for them. But this fact does stop everyone getting what they demand. Hence, embourgeoisement will grind to a halt.

One problem here is that the market couldn't care less about absolute limits on supply, so far as the possibility of continued economic exchange is concerned. This is because markets *can* supply goods and services that pass positional advantage back and forth between consumers. There is no obstacle to the sale of goods and services that *promise* to increase the consumer's positional advantage. It's just that these are available to other consumers and so people will simply have to pay more and/or work harder to "out-consume" each other. Hirsch observed that "in the positional sector, individuals chase each other's tails. The race gets longer for the same prize." So saying that the market "doesn't care" is just a metaphor for the fact that people will keep on paying for positional consumption even when they are cancelling each other out. The market will not "correct" for this by inducing any increase of supply, as per the Hayekian story we told in chapter 4. Hirsch saw the success of the spontaneous order of markets, associated with Smith and Hayek, as a sort of "favorable inaugural condition of liberal capitalism." The spontaneous order of markets may rock on, undisturbed by a revolution, but while it will keep signaling demand to producers, aggregate satisfaction of demand will ebb away.

This cannot end well. Once enough consumers have their nonpositional consumption satisfied, the growth of the positional sector "threatens to displace Smithian harmony with Hobbesian strife." If you've read Thomas Hobbes, you'll appreciate that these are pessimistic sentiments, far darker than anything written by optimists like Adam Smith.[8] Hobbes spoke of a war of all against all that could only be addressed by a highly coercive state (or *Leviathan*). Consumer arms races aren't a war in the traditional sense, but they may be structurally close to it in the Hobbesian sense—a form of conflict in which the weapon is willingness to pay. Again, Hirsch doesn't predict a revolution, just widespread disappointment. Perhaps this is why he lags behind Marx when it comes to inspiring activist movements. That said,

[8] If you've not read Hobbes, don't worry (though he's worth reading sometime if you can). As you may sense, Hobbes worried that society was doomed to internal conflict unless government found a way to do something about it. Hobbes meant well, but was no liberal and may be among the biggest deniers of spontaneous order in the Western political tradition (though he was still a good philosopher, perhaps the greatest political philosopher who wrote in English). Hobbes wrote before the golden age of political economy, but he would have appreciated Hirsch's narrative, we think.

we'd venture that most market societies show more evidence of bearing out Hirsch's forecast than Marx's.

Whether Hirsch was right about capitalism's inevitable and irreversible drift into disappointment, he did much to illuminate the concept of a positional good and the mechanisms by which consumers compete for positional advantage. Hirsch's claim that positional goods are subject to absolute limits on their supply is quite intuitive when applied to specific examples of positional goods, such as educational grades. People generally want "A" grades because they are better than "B" or "C" grades. But if *everyone* got A grades, this would just prevent an A grade from signaling superior educational credentials. Giving an A grade to everyone who wants one would, in effect, not be giving people what they want. Alternatively, imagine what Disneyland be like if everyone in the park had obtained a queue-jumping ticket. It would be full of irritated consumers thinking they'd been conned. Strictly speaking, then, increasing the supply of a positional good is either strictly impossible, or merely results in the devaluing of the existing supply, which is really a way of failing to increase the supply.

Generally speaking, economies will find some other way of coping with consumer demand if the supply of some good or service cannot be increased. In effect, if supply cannot be expanded, then consumers have to be weeded out. Hirsch distinguished here between two allocation mechanisms that operate for positional goods:

- Auctioning: The price of a positional good simply goes up until only some relatively small number of people can afford it.
- Screening: Positional goods are allocated according to some broadly meritocratic criterion other than willingness to pay.

All of the examples we've highlighted involve at least one of these mechanisms at work. In the case of road vehicles, relative size is *auctioned* as heavier, larger cars cost more than smaller ones. In theme parks and airports, shorter wait times are being auctioned in a very obvious fashion. The high cost of luxury goods is another case of auctioning a scarce signal. Education, on the other hand, is supposed to involve *screening*, since students get assigned grades in accordance with how well they perform in exams. The existence of markets in education can make it look like educational credentials are being auctioned. But there is a strong sense in which it is impossible to actually *buy* education. All one can purchase is access to superior educational *resources*, which are really services that assist with the screening process. Top schools may have great teaching, but students still need to work hard. Another sign that we're dealing with screening is that the positional good cannot be transferred—we can't give you our PhD degrees no matter how much you'd be willing to pay us. This means that markets in education, though they may seem objectionable and even unjust under certain conditions, will never be quite like markets in which you can buy the right to jump a queue.

The allocation mechanisms Hirsch identified are important structural elements of positional competition. We can use his framework to grapple more fully with the problems posed by positional goods in our current context.

## 4. Arms Races, Good and Bad

When evaluating competition for positional goods, it is important to consider whether the competition is set up to *escalate*. Some positional competitions are not set up in this way. People are not in airports and theme parks for very long, and they don't get repeated opportunities to make purchases. To this extent, the choice of what sort of theme park ticket to buy is what game theorists call a "one-shot game"—everyone makes a choice once, and they don't have a chance to adjust that choice upon learning what others have chosen. Road usage is different—many people replace their car quite frequently, and many such people use the road every day. Indeed, consumer demand for larger vehicles seems to have become more entrenched in places where driving is a bigger part of life, such as California, compared to regions where public transport is more common, such as Western Europe.[9]

Political influence is another sort of positional good that leads to massive consumer spending. Campaigning for the 2016 US presidential election began in late 2015. Before Christmas, that is, before the election year (i.e., 2016) had even begun, several candidates had already raised more than Barack Obama accumulated over the *entire* election campaign of 2012.[10] This significant growth in spending was not due to any proportionate increase in the overall output of any individual campaigns. Campaigners were

[9] Though there may be other reasons for this difference—for example, older European towns with narrow streets and small parking places make large vehicles inconvenient.

[10] http://www.npr.org/sections/itsallpolitics/2015/08/19/432759311/2016-campaign-tv-ad-spending

competing for better shares in what is a relatively fixed size pie of public attention.[11] The race is not to produce *more* political influence overall, but to gain a larger relative share of a fixed amount of opportunities to exercise such influence.

Education exhibits a similar trend. In many developed countries, the cost of raising a child is increasing. This is not because basic goods of childcare, like food and clothing, are more expensive. It's access to educational resources that is getting pricier. Wealthy parents are spending more on private school fees. Middle-income parents who cannot afford such fees are spending more on supplementary tuition and similar services that augment free state education. Parents are doing what they're doing so that their children don't get left behind. The financial burden on parents is accompanied by the burdens that children must shoulder in order to realize these higher levels of participation. In countries where educational competition is more entrenched, such as South Korea, children work considerably harder, at least in terms of hours spent studying, than in most other countries. While the education systems of these countries are often commended relative to academic criteria, their intensity may be cause for concern.

As you can probably guess, the term "arms race" comes from the example of competition between governments seeking military superiority over each other. These are common throughout history. Most infamous is probably the nuclear arms race that played out in the Cold War between the United States (with its NATO allies, some of which possessed nuclear weapons) and the Soviet Union (with its Warsaw Pact "allies"). The nuclear arms race was, of course, a competition for positional advantage—in this case, having relative superiority in the ability to use deadly force.

Arms races are common outside of markets. In fact, the study of arms races really got going when the tools of game theory were applied to the study of genetics. The Inland Taipan, an Australian snake, has a bite thought to release enough venom to kill seventy adult humans. Intuitively, this seems like sheer overkill. What on earth does a snake need such strong venom for? Since when did snakes have to fight off large groups of human assailants? The answer is that human organisms have got nothing to do with it, which is actually why we're so vulnerable to the venom. At some point in its history, the Taipan, or its genetic ancestor, was frequently biting some prey, or some predator, that gradually evolved resistance to the venom. The Taipan's

[11] We owe this observation to Christiano (2012). Also useful is Cohen (2001).

ancestors "counter-evolved" a stronger venom as a result. Hence, an arms race between different species got played out in ways structurally parallel to the examples involving human consumers and market supply. The Taipan's competitor in this arms race is probably now extinct, which is what makes the Taipan's venom look "unreasonably" potent relative to other creatures, such as humans, which arrived in Australia much more recently in terms of evolutionary history. The good news, for humans, is that Taipans are not very aggressive snakes.

Orthodox treatments of positional goods in market settings often overlook the lesson we can draw from the Taipan case: positional competition tends to occur as a long, drawn-out process. Once we appreciate that the more serious cases of positional competition occur as arms races, it becomes somewhat easier to say what's morally problematic about them.

As arms races progress, they may begin to distort the consumption of *other* goods that are distinct from the relevant positional good, but whose accessibility is causally connected. This is very much true of education. Generally speaking, the term "education" is marred by the fact that education is not really a single good, but a cluster of goods. Not all of these goods are positional. For sure, part of the point of education is to rank students according to academic ability, that is, to enable a sort of screening to be performed. But this is not *all* that education is for. What's problematic is that the "best," or at least the most expensive, forms of education made available by markets often prioritize the positional elements of education at the expense of other things. This was appreciated by John Stuart Mill, who complained about "elite" education in his autobiography.

> Most boys or youths who have had much knowledge drilled into them, have their mental capacities not strengthened, but over-laid by it. They are crammed with mere facts, and with the opinions or phrases of other people, and these are accepted as a substitute for the power to form opinions of their own: and thus the sons of eminent fathers, who have spared no pains in their education, so often grow up mere parroters of what they have learnt, incapable of using their minds except in the furrows traced for them.[12]

[12] Mill makes these remarks in his *Autobiography*, when speaking of his own childhood and education.

Mill wasn't really talking about an educational arms race, which hadn't got going in his time. As per Hirsch's theory, most people in Mill's day were still pining after nonpositional luxuries, like toilets. Mill's point is, however, quite applicable to the problem of arms races: when the delivery of education focuses on ranking students according to exam performance, it's likely that other elements of education get crowded out. One problem with markets in education is that it's easier to sell competitive advantage than the other things that education is for.[13] As a result, there's a danger that markets in education will take this sort of distortion to a particularly extreme level.

The question of exactly what goals education should pursue is a very difficult one, and we don't have space to get into it properly (but see Harry Brighouse's book in this chapter's Further Reading section). While there are disagreements among philosophers about what education is really all about, most agree with Mill that there's more to it than ranking young people according to their ability to regurgitate information in exams. Mill's wisdom is sound: disagreeing with other philosophers, and working out how to *defend* those disagreements, is good for you (especially if you do the second thing as well as the first thing!).

Being sensitive to how arms races actually play out can also accommodate the possibility that they start off as relatively benign, and become cause for concern only when they reach a certain point of escalation. Children in South Korea may nowadays be quite overworked. But the rise of Korea's demanding education system may have done much to bring about the country's rapid industrialization and associated prosperity. In the 1950s, South Korea was a war-ravaged, peasant economy. Possessing little by way of natural resources, Korea had to get ahead by developing its human capital. A few decades later, Korea had become a world leader in several industries, with household names like Hyundai, Samsung, and Psy. Not all of these valuable industries may be due to an intensive education system, but at least the first two probably owe something to it.[14]

To summarize: positional arms races are potentially quite undesirable things. And Hirsch was probably right to suggest that they'll become more prominent as market economies mature over time. But it remains an open question as to precisely when an arms race is cause for moral concern. This could depend on what sort of good is being distributed, and whether an

[13] One of the authors has defended this point at greater length elsewhere—see Halliday (2016).
[14] For an economic history of South Korea since the 1950s, see John Lie's (2000) book.

arms race might be undercutting the supply of some distinct good or creating inequalities that should not obtain for the positional good in question. There is also a serious question about the entitlements of the participants—we might think that children should be protected from an overly demanding educational experience, even if we do not say this about consumers engaging in other arms races as adults. Overall, there's much work to be done before we have a general theory that can equip us to distinguish different positional goods according to their moral seriousness.

## 5. Peace Treaties and Finish Lines

Irrespective of when and why positional competition is cause for concern, there is a fairly constant set of regulatory methods for addressing it. Broadly speaking, we can pursue preventions or cures. We'll look at some examples of each category in turn.

One approach might be to stop positional competition before it starts. For many years, university education in New Zealand was pretty much open to anyone who wanted it. So long as you had actually *finished* high school, you could just turn up to university—*any* university you liked—and enroll there. In Hirsch's terminology, there was no screening. This reduced the intensity of high school education. Of course, New Zealand had to sort out which students could be granted admission to the more demanding and/or popular degree programs, like law and medicine, but this was determined by exams that students took *after* enrolment at university. It is sometimes said that an arms race has no finish line. But some arms races do have a clear *start line*, and education is one of these. In effect, New Zealand's solution was to move this start line back by delaying screening.

Various lessons can be drawn from this case. Admittedly, New Zealand's small size probably helped. Since there are only a handful of universities and not much variation in quality, there was little prospect of one university being completely swamped. Things are different in countries like the United States. If people could simply show up at any college they liked, it's likely that those with the greatest reputations would be overwhelmed. That being said, most countries could do something to move the start line back when it comes to educational screening, for example by delaying the age at which students begin undergoing tests.

Another approach is to make positional goods redundant. Generally speaking, positional goods ration access to some other good that simply happens to be scarce. Vehicle size, for example, rations access to the nonpositional good of safety. In principle, vehicles could be made safer without being made bigger. Technology such as airbags and crumpling car bodies represent ways of increasing the overall supply of safety in ways that may relieve the pressure for people to compete with each other. Small cars may eventually become so safe that there is simply no need to fear being in a crash. When it comes to designing policy, the vehicular arms race might fizzle out if safety can be enhanced in any of these other ways.

Positional goods often ration access to several goods at once. Education is a case in point. The fact is that most people don't want the same things out of life. If you're a student reading this textbook for a university class, it's very likely that your ambitions for postuniversity life differ from those of the other students enrolled in the class. So why are you all showing up in the same institution competing for the same scarce supply of grades? The short answer is that *you have to, given the way that labor markets have been arranged*. Generally speaking, developed societies use the same screening criteria (university education) to allocate scarce positions across highly diverse categories of adult employment. Accordingly, the successful pursuit of your own particular ambitions requires you to compete alongside other students who may not be "natural" competitors, insofar as they are not trying to get the same outcome as you. This is by no means necessary. And yet the dependence on universities as sort of universal screening device is quite widespread.

One philosopher who develops this evaluation is Joseph Fishkin (2014). He has argued that society suffers from too many of what he calls "bottlenecks," by which he means roughly what we've described earlier—arenas of competition where people must fight for positional advantage even though they're trying to pursue different and ultimately quite compatible life plans. Fishkin's solution is to propose what he calls "opportunity pluralism." What this means in practice is something like the creation of a variety of smaller competitive arenas, each of which may be less intense than the one big arena through which everyone must currently squeeze. This might involve the fragmentation of education, particularly higher education, into a variety of different credentialing systems. There is room for debate about how to design this approach for effective use in practice, but the basic formal point may be quite compelling. By making positional goods less multipurpose as screening devices, the competition for them will become less intense.

The aforementioned approaches all try to address the causes of positional competition by reducing *demand* for positional consumption. Other approaches differ by making positional consumption more *difficult* instead. Perhaps the most extreme way of doing this is to prohibit certain sorts of positional consumption altogether. Most countries actually have laws that limit the amount of time that children spend in school, by way of legally mandated school holidays and rules about the start and end of the school day. Markets in education have somewhat circumvented these rules, for example by providing supplementary tuition outside of these mandated periods. It is difficult for governments to police this. South Korea, for example, has at times sought to prohibit the supply of private tutors, but with limited success.

A less extreme approach is to impose taxation on the economic exchanges that enable competition to escalate. This approach may be especially effective in cases where wealthy consumers set reference points that inflate the consumption goals of less wealthy consumers. Focusing on conspicuous luxury goods, Robert Frank (2012) has offered such a defense of consumption taxes in a series of recent writings. Here the point is to cut off what Frank calls "expenditure cascades," where the big spending of a rich celebrity sets off a domino effect. In short, keeping up with the Kardashians would be less difficult if some control could be put on the Kardashians' spending so that they just wouldn't flaunt it so much.

These are just a few proposals. It is likely that the heterogeneous nature of positional competition means that different solutions will work for different positional goods. Serious study of positional competition is only a recent addition to work in political economy. The challenge is likely to get harder before it gets easier. Positional competition remains set to pose one of the bigger issues in the future study of political economy. Any set of moral foundations for capitalism will remain incomplete so long as it says nothing about it.

## Conclusions

*This chapter has shown that positional goods pose a distinctive, if somewhat varied, challenge. Once this has been appreciated, attention needs to be paid to the ways in which not all positional goods are alike. While there may be some truth to Fred Hirsch's contention that positional competition represents an inevitable problem for market order, taking it seriously may mean applying a variety of localized solutions.*

## Study Questions

- Can you think of an example of conspicuous consumption engaged in by members of a certain industry or profession? How plausible is it that consumers in this example are merely responding to pressures whose existence they might greatly regret?
- According to sociologists like Juliet Schor, we set our "consumption goals" according to "reference points" such as the depiction of certain lifestyles by the media. Do you find this plausible? Are there moral reasons for regulating these ways in which reference points get fixed?
- Study of markets in education tends to focus on financial costs to parents. You're probably a university student who had to study hard at high school to gain admission. Do you think that you were a victim of an educational arms race? If so, what was the (nonfinancial) cost to your childhood?

## Further Reading

"Consuming Because Others Consume" by Judith Lichtenberg, *Social Theory and Practice* 22 (3): 273–297

A very concise explanation of why we might regard competitive consumption as driven by external social pressures rather than vanity or any other internal commitment to a materialistic view of the good life. Plenty of helpful references to Adam Smith's views, along with a case for updating them.

*Social Limits to Growth* by Fred Hirsch (Routledge, 2005)

The classic text on positional goods. It's old, but it hasn't really dated. Most of the basics have been covered in this chapter, so read the full text only if you want a deeper grasp of why Hirsch thought capitalism had a sell-by date.

*On Education* by Harry Brighouse (Routledge, 2006)

A philosophically sophisticated but highly accessible examination of some central philosophical questions about the purpose of education. Overall, the view defended is that education should (ideally) equip young people with the ability to flourish as autonomous adults. Although Brighouse has done important work on positionality, there's more going on in this book.

*The Darwin Economy: Liberty, Competition, and the Common Good* by Robert Frank (Princeton University Press, 2012)

One in a series of books in which Frank examines the problem of competitive consumption. This book stands out for its engagement with Adam Smith, whom Frank seeks to compare with Charles Darwin. As with much of Frank's writing, the focus is very much on cases of *conspicuous* consumption that is motivated by a desire to signal wealth, such as luxury goods.

# 10

# Why Are We Still Working So Hard?

*In this chapter, we'll discuss various questions about how a market society might develop, such that its citizens spend less time in paid employment. This can occur by way of an increased displacement of labor by technology or "automation" in the production process and/or by government regulation that limits the amount of time that people spend working. This enables us to grapple with some interesting questions about the place of technology in labor markets (particularly whether it should be feared), the value of leisure time, and the overall future of work (including whether work even has a future).*

## 1. Keynes and the 15-Hour Week

In the early days of the Industrial Revolution, English textile workers became alarmed by the rise of mechanization in their industry. Artisan weavers, who worked by hand in their cottages, were being displaced by large cotton mills. One group of workers resorted to sabotaging machinery in the new mills. They became known as the Luddites (named after Ned Ludd, who is supposed to have instigated the sabotage movement). The term "luddite" nowadays lives on as a label for someone who is somewhat technophobic, though usually not to the extent that they'll resort to smashing things up in a desire to find old-fashioned employment. The original Luddites caused a great deal of trouble, and it took military force to finally put down their activities.

Fear of losing one's job to automation has a perennial presence. And yet there is also something odd about why this fear should remain. Broadly speaking, machines work so that we don't have to. Surely, that's a good thing? Who wants to do boring, dangerous, or dirty work when a machine can do it instead, particularly if the machine can do it better? The answer, of course, is that people have no other source of money. If machines put people out of work, then it's no help pointing out that the machines are more productive if

*The Ethics of Capitalism.* Daniel Halliday and John Thrasher, Oxford University Press (2020).

DOI: 10.1093/oso/9780190096205.001.0001

people can't afford to buy whatever's being produced. And yet it is still true that automation has the *potential* to make everyone much better off. The Luddites understandably didn't want to lose their jobs. But we should all be glad that their sabotage didn't stop the Industrial Revolution. Imagine what the textile industry would be like today if it still involved artisan weavers turning out a few shirts per week.

So the automation of labor introduces benefits and burdens. These are not evenly spread over the workers immediately affected by any particular introduction of labor-saving technology, nor are they spread evenly over time. The beneficiaries of automation are, in the short term, the owners of the means of production and the consumers of its output. This is because automation basically lowers production costs, lowering prices and/or raising profits. Eventually, a shift to machine labor will create benefits elsewhere (i.e., positive externalities), but this takes time. These facts raise important questions about how the automation process ought (or ought not) to be regulated.

The mechanization process is not as straightforward as machines coming along and destroying human jobs. The more historically accurate description is that machines destroy some jobs while creating others. Before the Industrial Revolution, working hours were limited by the availability of natural light. Nobody could work the fields when it was pitch dark outside. Temperature was another factor. In many countries, the ground freezes in winter. For these reasons, people didn't work very many hours during the agrarian era. The Industrial Revolution, with artificial lighting and the movement of labor indoors, saw the working week lengthen dramatically. The subsequent rise of the labor movement led to collective bargaining and unions that, among other things, brought about a reduction in working hours. In the 20th century, it became normal for workers to receive leisure time. Many countries have employment law that gives workers an entitlement to a certain number of days off each year, without losing any pay. These general historical trends show that mechanization isn't simply about the *displacement* of human labor. Machines do much to enable human labor that wasn't possible before the introduction of certain sorts of technology.

We might wonder why the gradual reduction of working hours came to a halt so early. Indeed, economists writing shortly after the rise of the labor movement did predict that this trend was bound to continue. In his 1930 essay, "Economic Possibilities for Our Grandchildren," John Maynard Keynes forecasted that the working week would decline to 15 hours within the next 100 years. There are still a few years left for Keynes's forecast to come true. But a lot would have to happen for him to be proven right. Keynes's essay doesn't really suggest a causal mechanism that might bring about the reduction in working hours. Insofar as Keynes makes any case at all, it consists in some scattered remarks about the rate of production having been increased so that work is becoming less necessary. Keynes evidently had a sort of disdain for people who would rather work than engage in intellectual pursuits. He talks about the "love of money" being "one of those semi-criminal, semi-pathological propensities which one hands over with a shudder to the specialists in mental disease."[1] Even if this is right, it hardly helps us figure out how to reduce work for everyone.

Why was Keynes (probably) wrong? The answer can't be that we haven't yet designed sophisticated enough machines. It is true that many unskilled and undesirable jobs, like cleaning toilets, are still performed almost entirely by human labor. But machines have replaced humans in far more difficult tasks. Robots can now perform such complex tasks as the disposal of bombs. Surely, then, a robot could be developed to clean a toilet. The reason this hasn't happened isn't to do with the technological challenges, but rather the difficulty of finding humans willing to perform bomb disposal work, along with the various political considerations that make governments want to minimize deaths of military personnel. A toilet-cleaning robot would be especially welcome in parts of the world where the production of latrines is held back by social norms stigmatizing whoever cleans toilets. The result, in such countries, is the enduring practice of open defecation that does much to spread infectious disease. Once again, we should note that social norms die hard. Creating the right robot (which will not worry about stigma) might be easier than bringing about a shift in traditions.[2]

The more general reasons for why the machines haven't taken over, in spite of increased levels of production, may be quite numerous. Let's quickly review some of the more plausible ones.

One explanation for why working hours haven't declined is our disposition to compete for various forms of positional advantage. Keynes seemed to appreciate this, distinguishing explicitly between our satiable need for absolute goods and our need for "superiority" that might be "insatiable." But rather than see this as a factor that might keep people working long hours, Keynes seemed to think that overcoming the desire for status (or at least

[1] The essay is reprinted as Keynes (2010). The quote is at p. 84.

[2] There's a book-length treatment of this problem, focusing on India, where open defecation has persisted in spite of other economic development—see Coffey and Spears (2017)

status gained through working for more income) required only "the readjustment of the habits and instincts of the ordinary man, bred into him for countless generations." As we saw in chapter 9, positional competition is sufficiently entrenched that its displacement probably requires more than a "readjustment of habits."[3]

Another reason is that the output of human labor often has higher exchange value than similar output provided by machines. This is especially true in the service sector. Waiter-service restaurants are still popular, though more expensive than vending machines or self-service cafes. One may try to explain this on grounds that the food is better, but this would be a strange coincidence given that food quality has little to do with the person who takes your order and brings the dish to your table. A more plausible explanation is that people willing to pay for better food are often willing to pay for other luxuries at the same time, human service being one of these. More important may be that machines are often bad at handling slight changes in the tasks they're asked to perform. This is a major obstacle for most service provision, which is more subject to variations in consumer needs than the provision of goods. Supermarkets have recently shifted from staffed checkouts to mechanized, self-service checkouts. The first mechanized checkouts were awful. Machines kept failing to scan items, giving rise to repeated utterances of jarring phrases like "unexpected item in bagging area," which became an internet meme in Britain. For similar reasons, it is always preferable to talk to a human, rather than a system of automated prompts, when phoning up a company or institution with which one has to do some business. Most of us dread having to phone the bank, electricity company, or other business, knowing that such technology will be encountered.

Mechanization may also be slowed when consumer preference seems to err toward the human touch in the production of *goods*, too. Walk past a bakery or gift shop and you might see signage emphasizing the "handmade" or traditional nature of what's on sale. No hospital, on the other hand, would boast about having handmade surgical equipment or rustic operating rooms. This suggests that while goods benefit from the human touch in their production process, machines help provide assurances about standardization—desirable when consumers want to know exactly what they're getting and dislike surprises. This makes it hard to generalize about how far technology

[3] Keynes (2015: 81–82)

improves the quality of what was previously produced by human labor, as opposed to simply lowering the costs of its production.

There's room for debate about which of these explanations is the most compelling, and they do not really compete with each other. We will come back to the fact that the machines are owned by a few and what might be achieved by changing this. But we've said enough to get a sense of what sort of problem is presented by the status quo. The process of automation is not going to stop. But the process of people needing to consume necessities is not going to stop either. So people will always have reasons to try and get jobs so long as they are not among the few that own substantial capital. And so we are left in a sort of bind—machines work harder so that human labor is no longer required by producers, and yet humans who provide such labor still need to find ways to sell it. Something needs to give.

## 2. What Jobs Are Machines "Stealing" and How?

As we've said, the apparent problem with machines is that they *destroy jobs*. Although automation is often presented as a new or future problem, it is in fact one of the oldest trends in the production process. Labor-saving technology has been pursued in some form or another for as long as labor has carried nontrivial running costs. On the whole, many machines are cheaper to run than human workers. And even if a machine does a worse job, reduced production costs may make up for this: mass-produced goods are often of poorer quality than handmade versions of the same thing, but their lower price often means consumers prefer them. David Ricardo wrote in 1817 that "the substitution of machinery for human labor is often very injurious to the interests of the class of laborers."[4] Ricardo was around in England at the same time as the Luddites, so it is natural that he was drawn to this question. Again, what's important is not *that* mechanization is occurring in the production of goods and services, but what *kind* of mechanization is occurring, and whether there might be reasons to alter it in some way.

Contemporary economists disagree about whether the status quo mechanization process should be viewed, on balance, as a bad thing. The economist Robert Reich is particularly impressed by the recent acceleration in the

[4] See chapter 31 of his *Principles of Political Economy and Taxation*. Like the rest of this book, the reasoning in this chapter is remarkably concise.

automation of service-sector jobs.[5] Classically, automation has been about getting machines to provide brute power that exceeds what humans can do. This is manifest in many great technological innovations of past centuries, such as the Archimedean screw, the steam engine, and the nuclear reactor. These have great ability to do things to or with physical objects. But they are not particularly clever—they don't do anything with information or have much ability to *change* what they're doing without some human controller taking over. As noted earlier, service work has long been a holdout of human labor due to the tendency of machines to be pretty inflexible. But, according to Reich, machines are finally starting to get "smart." Much automation now comes in the form of technology whose impact on production comes by way of artificial intelligence, rather than brute force. This likely changes the sort of challenge that automation represents.

Smarter machines are finally beginning to storm the services bastion. Supermarket automated checkouts have improved their expectations of what might be put in front of them. The internet continues to remove human labor from the retail sector, as websites make it less necessary for customers to go to a store where other humans can be given jobs. Autonomous vehicles—aka driverless cars—are now on the horizon (figuratively speaking) and may mean the end of the road for human labor in the public transport and freight haulage industries.

Reich argues that the only solution is to treat technology as the 21st-century equivalent of agricultural land in the preindustrial era: essential for the goods and services that we expect to consume, but likely to be controlled by some small economic elite. Labor-saving technology will make a great deal of money for whomever happens to own it (assuming, at least, that there are any consumers left to pay for the machines' output). If we can't create jobs, we should simply tax the income gained by the owners of all this lucrative technology and redistribute it to everyone else. What this means, for Reich, is that the continued rise of technology seals the case for a universal basic income, or perhaps a stakeholder grant, of the sort that was discussed earlier in chapter 6. Reich believes we have passed the point at which workers can still stay ahead of technology simply by getting more education. Robots will "supplant the middle class."

Another economist, Tyler Cowen, takes a different view.[6] In effect, he rejects Reich's claim that humans can't still find ways to work with machines,

[5] Here we're drawing on chapters 22 and 23 of his (2016) book, *Saving Capitalism*.
[6] He we draw on various elements of Cowen's (2013) book, *Average Is Over*.

so as to augment their labor. Here is the truth in Cowen's claim: almost all of us work in jobs that did not exist, or which were much less efficient, 100 years ago. And the reason for this is that most of us now work with machines that were not around until relatively recently. Indeed, most jobs that currently exist, including (in fact, especially) the very high paid ones, tend to involve a human working in a "team" with a machine or some form of machine-supported resource. It would have been very hard for us to write this book without the help of computer technology that enabled us to draft and redraft the chapters much more quickly than if it had been hand-written. The internet helped us do the necessary research and to communicate with each other when necessary. It helped both of us write while in geographical locations extremely far from any university library, and indeed from each other. For any coauthored book written a few decades ago, such lack of proximity between coauthors would have been unthinkable, much less a complex product like Google or a Hollywood film.

For these reasons, Cowen thinks that the right response to technology is to embrace it and to concentrate on identifying opportunities to create more forms of paid work given the latest developments in technology. At the same time, Cowen seems to acknowledge some of Reich's worries. He admits that technology may result in greater "labor market polarization" (recall chapter 6), where those with the skills to work with machines have good earning prospects, while an underclass remains of those who pick up what's left of unskilled work or have to rely on benefits. Cowen notes that the underclass will still have some goods that technology has made cheaper, such as the internet. But this may be cold comfort. Today's poor have access to the luxuries of Ricardo's day, like electricity, but nobody takes this to be evidence that poverty has been eliminated.

What should we conclude? A key variable is the *speed* with which technology replaces human labor, which itself depends on the speed with which new technology is designed and brought to market. On the whole, jobs take more time to create than to destroy. So, if machines replace labor quickly, the consequences may be worse than if labor is replaced slowly. Ricardo saw things more or less this way. He explicitly discouraged "the inference that machinery should not be encouraged," explaining that "I have been supposing that improved machinery is suddenly discovered and extensively used; but the truth is that these discoveries are gradual." This may have been the right assessment in the 19th century, but things have gathered pace since then.

So the disagreement between Reich and Cowen may hinge largely on the *rate* of automation. If the pace is low enough, then we may be able to embrace the benefits of increased output while finding ways for workers to add value through the right sort of skills. But if machines are taking over too fast, the more plausible option might be to just let them get on with it and agree to share the wealth. In short, perhaps machines affect labor markets like weightlifting affects muscle growth: there is tremendous potential on offer, but too much too soon may be a bad thing. It's not clear we could or should slow down the pace of change even if we wanted to, however.

So far as justice is concerned, perhaps the most important consideration is whether automation is, on balance, creating opportunities or removing them. If the latter, then there may be a case for regulating labor markets in ways that help with education and perhaps soften the blow for workers who lose their jobs to machines. But if things reach the point at which workers are being asked to fight a losing battle, the case for basic income may become particularly strong. As always, there is room for further disagreement and reflection about this topic. We need to remember that political economy is not all about timeless principles, but about principles that can be updated according to changes in economic conditions.

## 3. More on Machine Misbehavior

There's more to automation than what to do about the destruction of jobs. There's also the question of what sort of things the machines might get up to once they start processing information. There was never much cause to worry about the behavior of ploughs and jet engines, or other "dumb" technology. (Of course, there have always been worries about pollution, which we'll come to in chapter 11.) But artificial intelligence raises serious concerns about the impact of continued automation on our lives. This goes beyond the question of justice with respect to the labor market, but some of the questions that arise are very much about justice in other respects, notably whether machines are disposed to treat people fairly.

Since when were people treated unfairly by machines? Well, since such a time as machines started being used to make decisions about whether a human being was likely to default on a mortgage, or reoffend if given a short prison sentence, or whether they might be a terrorist seeking to blow up the plane they've bought a ticket to fly on. Such decisions need to be made somehow. But historically, it was human beings who judged whether some other person could be trusted to pay back a loan or was likely to commit crimes. Nowadays, these decisions are increasingly being made by technology. Even if a human being still needs to "rubber stamp" a prison sentence or a loan approval, they are increasingly being influenced by "recommendations" made by computers. This may be cause for concern.

Broadly speaking, artificial intelligence works in two ways. First, it enables the gathering and storing of large amounts of information (or "big data," as the current buzzword goes). Second, it enables these large data sets to be processed into predictions about what will happen next. This second aspect of artificial intelligence relies on algorithms—basically procedures for converting one set of information into another set of judgments or conclusions. We use algorithms all the time, but we are limited by our cognitive processing capacities. Machines make it possible to run algorithms based on *much* larger pools of data, and involving more complicated calculations on such data. There is nothing wrong, in principle, with making use of the impressive powers of technology when it comes to storage and processing. What we need to remember is that such power comes with certain limitations and hazards.

First, there is the fact that artificial intelligence is only as good as the algorithms that it uses. Algorithms are still the product of human labor, and their design has all the fallibilities of human labor. But the use of technology is often naïve about this fact. For example, consider the fact that many humans have the same name. Other humans realize that there are multiple persons in the world with any particular name. Machines often "forget" this. Indeed, there are numerous cases of automated processes mixing up the identities of different people.

Perhaps the most compelling (and yet ridiculous) piece of evidence comes from the California government's attempt to develop a database of known gang members. When this database, "CalGang," was audited in 2016, it was found to contain forty-two gang members under the age of 1 year. Of these gangster babies, twenty-eight were listed as having already confessed to authorities that they held gang membership. Obviously, this is absurd. But how did it happen? Ultimately, it's hard to know (which is a problem in itself—see later), but very likely the technology just got names mixed up. It is worth emphasizing that CalGang was in use for over 10 years before this audit occurred. It is anybody's guess how many other mistakes it made. And it is only when such a profoundly ludicrous error gets revealed that a compelling case can be made for the technology's fallibility. All sorts of mistakes might get made, with huge costs to the individuals concerned, without anyone ever being able to prove this, and many parties (not least those with a stake in the machine's success) continuing to insist that "computers don't lie."

Second, there is the fact that not all data are alike. Machines tend to be good at storing and processing quantitative data that exhibit patterns. They tend to be less good at processing data that are less pattern oriented. A good example comes from the use of algorithms in policing. Generally speaking, police forces want to reduce crime. Technology now exists that stores information about where and when crimes have been committed. This technology can guide decisions as to where to send police officers on patrol. But such technology has, in practice, tended to result in the police targeting so-called nuisance crimes, such as vagrancy and aggressive begging, while not targeting more serious crimes like burglary and murder. The explanation is simple: vagrancy and begging tend to keep occurring in the same places. Burglaries and murders do not. By its very nature, burglary moves around from place to place. Murder, though less by nature, tends to do the same. This means that algorithms aimed at helping the police "fight crime" might divert police attention to less serious crimes, just because it is easier for computers to crunch data so as to predict where these might next occur.

Third, it may be difficult to ensure that machines have an effective human boss to keep them in line. The global financial crisis of 2008 took hold after many American homebuyers had been lent what came to be known as "subprime" mortgages. These were loans given out to hordes of people who could not afford to pay them. Once people started defaulting on loans, the banks could not cope and were forced to repossess houses. Those who did not lose homes lost a good deal of the value on them as the market was flooded with homes from which people had been evicted, which banks wanted to sell. Why did this happen? Any plausible answer will be complex, but much has been attributed to the use of computers to assess homebuyers based on poor (human-designed) algorithms that, thanks to the processing power of computers, began to be used on a massive scale. And because all of the "thinking" was being done by machines, the humans who were (nominally) in charge of it all were not keeping an eye on things. After all, the machines were being used because the processing power of the humans was too weak to get the job done. By the time humans realized what was going on, it was too late to stop the crisis. Had lending been carried out in the traditional way, with human minds more involved in individual decisions about whether to grant mortgages to other humans, things may well have gotten less out of hand. Again, though, the problem was not so much with fallibility in the artificial intelligence being used, but with inability of human intelligence to both program and oversee the technology in question.

Fourth, there is the fact that machines do not always protect the data they are given. It's no great exaggeration to say that big companies like Facebook and Amazon store more information about the citizens of developed countries than was ever possessed by the secret police of the communist bloc in the 20th century.[7] It is one question as to what Facebook and Amazon will do with this data (perhaps, sell it to other companies willing to pay for it). It is another question what might be done with this data by others who manage to *steal* it. One problem with "big data" is that machines never forget, even if they do sometimes lie. When information was retained by human minds, or even just written down, it could easily be destroyed, and some degree of information would inevitably be lost upon the death of any human whose brain held it. In addition, data stored on paper, rather than electronically, cannot be accessed from a geographically remote location. But times have changed, and it might be easier to get data out of machines than out of human brains. Hacking data sets may happen without anyone noticing. There have already been several high-profile cases of datasets being stolen after being stored electronically and used for ill purposes.

One notorious case is that of the company Ashley Madison, which branded itself as a social networking service to connect people seeking extramarital affairs. In 2015, a hacker group called "The Impact Team" managed to steal Ashley Madison's data and used it to blackmail some of its users. Such a data breach would have been unfeasible had the information in question not been stored in one single place that was accessible remotely, as in the old days of printed paper in filing cabinets. Incidentally, the Ashley Madison hack revealed that the greater majority of Ashley Madison users were men, and that the minority of female users largely comprised sex workers looking to solicit clients. This indicates that data theft can sometimes reveal that a product didn't do what it said on the tin—a silver lining of sorts.

Much more could be added to these concerns (take a look at Cathy O'Neil's book in the Further Reading section). But here's the general point: The question, when it comes to labor-saving technology, isn't really whether we should be concerned about machines taking things over. The more pressing

[7] Although perhaps not as much as possessed by the NSA.

question attends to what *types* of labor are being taken over by new technology and which are not. The power of technology to process and store information may be exceeding the prospects for keeping machines on task and under control. If so, then we should try and slow down automation until such a time (if it ever arrives) at which artificial intelligence is able to work in a more balanced and self-correcting way.

## 4. The (Moral) Importance of Leisure Time

Keynes believed that it was good for us to have time off. Many of us share this view, and labor law often confers entitlements to paid leave from one's job. But what case can be made for this view? *Should* we be working less hard? And if so, how might governments go about designing the relevant laws and policies?

Political philosophy, and indeed political economy, has devoted enormous attention to the distribution of income and wealth, and the associated distributions of wages and capital. While much has been said about ensuring that people have enough of their own money, less has been said about ensuring that people have enough of their own time—that is, time that is *discretionary*. Some have argued that in order to be genuinely discretionary, such time needs to be protected by legislation that prevents workers from agreeing to surrender it as part of the time they spend working for their employers. According to the political philosopher Julie Rose (2014, 2016), this failure to connect leisure time with questions of economic justice is a major theoretical shortcoming. This is because leisure time is a basic good, like food or housing. Goods are basic in Rose's sense when they cannot be replaced by other goods without some sort of negative impact on a person's wellbeing. If you suffer a lack of one of these goods, then you'll be very badly off as a result, even if you get an abundant quantity of other basic goods.

Rose points out that leisure time, properly speaking, isn't just any time left over after one has stopped performing paid work. A lot of this time is spent doing things that are not really "discretionary." This includes, at least, time spent sleeping, performing household chores, commuting, caring for relatives, and various other unpaid tasks that cannot reasonably be avoided. How far to extend any such list would be controversial, but it's uncontroversial that life does not divide perfectly into periods of work and periods of recreation. Leisure time, then, is not simply time out of work but time when one can *really* choose what one does.

Another background point is that the borderline between leisure and nonleisure time might be vague. Commuting is a good example. Some of us travel to and from work on crowded trains or buses, which can be stressful and tiring. Some of us may enjoy a pleasant drive listening to music or podcasts, which may be considered quasi-leisure, insofar as there is a degree of discretion as to what one does in this time and a relative lack of burden associated with the other task one is performing, that is, driving.

Childcare is unpaid work but involves building personal relationships and comes with other pleasures at the same time. Vagueness also exists regarding the sorts of work that, the saying goes, you always bring home with you. Some forms of paid labor involve interaction with physical capital that stays at the workplace. Bus drivers, coal miners, and waiters literally can't take their work home with them. But other jobs, particularly those involving work with information instead of physical objects, are different. If it's your job to write and teach philosophy, you're probably thinking about it pretty much all the time (or else thinking that you *ought* to be thinking about it). The authors can assure you that this has consequences for domestic life. Passing laws that say we must stop working for some number of days each year do not solve this problem all by themselves, if it is indeed a problem at all.

Such complexities aside, there's a real question here about why leisure time is important in ways that warrant calling it a basic good, and hence there being a case for protecting workers' entitlement to time off with relevant labor law. Rose's project is in trying to work out how to answer this question. To measure the strength of the case for leisure time, we can distinguish justifications that focus on the individual worker from justifications that focus on community.

To see the individual benefits of leisure time, we need only recall the problem of alienated labor that was discussed back in chapter 6. Many jobs are, quite simply, mind-numbingly boring, monotonous to the point of psychological damage, devoid of any creativity, or just take the fun out of an activity. Whatever one's theory of alienated labor, possessing discretionary time can make up for whatever is alienating about the job. Broadly speaking, leisure time is an opportunity to do nice things that can't be done at work. Leisure is about being an individual again, whether this means being creative, developing personal relationships, or simply being free.

These considerations lend some support to providing people with periods of paid leave per year, that is, periods of time that employees can fail to show up for work and yet still be paid. There may need to be constraints on this entitlement, such as requiring workers to inform their employers in advance as to when they will take the leave. But people can generally take it when they want. This, however, may fall short of what is desirable about having discretionary time. Part of the value of giving people time off is that they will spend it *with each other*. Not just with friends and family, but with the wider community. Crucially, this requires some overlap in when people take their leisure time. In order for valuable community events to occur, some critical mass of the population must take their leisure time *simultaneously*.

Most societies have a history of restricting labor markets to preserve time for shared religious worship. This is one way of ensuring that a community of people do something together outside of work. But there is no reason why this practice cannot be given a secular justification. One reason for having regular shared time, for example by restricting work on Sundays, is so that all sorts of community-oriented events might spring up, some on a larger scale than others. According to Julie Rose, this makes for a very strong liberal, secular justification for restricting work on a particular day of the week.

These are all forceful considerations in favor of legally mandated leisure time. Still, there may be other considerations that complicate the case for enforcing discretionary time through labor market regulation. First of all, should everyone get the same amount of discretionary time? What about the fact that some people have really boring monotonous jobs, while others don't? While we don't wish to speak for the rest of the academic profession, we (the authors) are happy to admit that our jobs give us a lot of autonomy, creative opportunity, and are generally not alienating. Though we are given, along with other workers, a certain allowance of days paid leave per year, we often spend much of it just doing more reading and writing. Is this evidence that our jobs have been arranged such that the law doesn't succeed in giving us the discretionary time to which we're entitled, or merely that our jobs are already so discretionary that it is hard to notice any difference?

What about the case for shared time, as enforced by public holidays and restrictions on working on a specific day of the week? Public holidays are often assigned to days with some national, cultural, or religious significance. This may end up discriminating against certain groups whose culture or religious practices do not align with those chosen by the state. State selection of public holidays may also be at some risk of being used by the state to promote certain forms of propaganda.

In Australia, everyone gets a day off on Anzac Day, which falls each year on April 25. This is the date when Australian and New Zealand forces attempted an amphibious landing in Gallipoli, Turkey, as part of a major military offensive in World War I. The engagement went badly, with many Anzac soldiers being killed. In Australia, the current practice of commemorating Anzac Day is seen by some as recognition of a day on which Australia began to forge its own distinctive identity, and for reflection about the great loss of life. Critics complain that there is little to celebrate in an event of sending young men to be slaughtered on behalf of the British Empire. We do not want to push a particular line about Anzac Day in this textbook, but the example usefully illustrates the hazards associated with selecting certain days to declare as national public holidays in order to promote certain values associated with community. At the same time, Anzac Day is marked by parades and a dawn service. As such, it is not simply about giving everyone a day to do whatever they feel like: perhaps the case for shared time off from work is not *wholly* about increasing everyone's discretionary time after all.

The enforcement of shared time might be particularly detrimental to persons who are self-employed. Legally mandated public holidays often put these people out of a day's work. This is because, for anyone self-employed, "paid leave" is a misnomer. Some self-employed workers can still make money during public holidays, especially if they provide services that others consume as part of enjoying their leisure. But others are not so fortunate. If you're a self-employed worker who sells services to companies only on days that their offices are open, then you may have no one to sell to when all the offices are closed. And it's unclear what a legal entitlement means to workers who can't easily leave the work "in the office." (Coincidentally, this section of the chapter was first drafted on Anzac Day in 2017.) Even if the government has declared that everyone should put down tools for the day, it doesn't mean everyone easily can, particularly if they have annual targets to meet.

Generally speaking, the enforcement of paid leave most easily benefits workers who (1) cannot work when not physically in the vicinity of some form of capital, like an office or a piece of machinery, and (2) workers who are paid by some employer who will not lower the annual pay if the worker takes the amount of leisure time to which they're entitled. Not all workers fit into both of these categories, and some fit into neither (e.g., a self-employed journalist). The more workers that can't easily benefit from legislation guaranteeing discretionary time, the more complicated the case for *enforcing* leisure time might become, irrespective of its value. This is particularly true for the enforcement of *shared* leisure time. None of this is meant to assemble a strong case against the value of discretionary time, just to note that labor markets are sufficiently complex that careful thought is required when designing ways to enforce the requirement that people take time off.

## 5. The End of Work?

Keynes was convinced that at some point in the future we would live in a society of such plenty that the need for work and thrift would be greatly reduced. In this way, he shares, in outline, the dreams of the utopian socialists of the 19th century (recall chapter 5)—a dream that was incorporated by Marx into his version of socialism.

Interestingly, this vision was not shared by most of the economists of the golden age. Instead, they saw the progress of economic history as leading toward disaster rather than utopia. They feared that the logic of economic development would lead to what they called the "stationary state." This refers to a scenario in which all of the possibilities for increasing profits in production have been exhausted and, hence, it is impossible for wages to continue to rise. For the economists of the golden age, wages were a function of *average* growth. As population increased and growth slowed, wages would necessarily also stagnate until population exceeded economic growth when growth reaches zero in the stationary state.

This is a terrifying vision of the future, one that many of the classical economists were keen to put off for as long as possible. But there were a few dissenters. Interestingly, Adam Smith did not share this vision of the stationary state because he did not believe that rates of return on capital would ever reach zero—Smith didn't equate capital as directly with labor and land as Ricardo and Malthus later did. Smith also argued that wages were a function of *aggregate* economic growth rather than average growth. We can think of the difference between Smith and the other golden age economists as Smith believed that something like total GDP determined wages, whereas Ricardo believed that wages were determined by something like per capita GDP. In the latter approach, if GDP is fixed and population continues to grow, average wages will shrink.

John Stuart Mill dissented in a different way. He agreed with Ricardo and Malthus that the stationary state was inevitable, but he disagreed that it would necessarily be a bad thing. Mill was influenced by European romantic thinkers and by many of the socialist thinkers of his time. He believed that we could learn to live with and even benefit from a no-growth society. Instead of focusing on economic gain, we would be free, in the stationary state, to focus on noneconomic pursuits like poetry and literature.

Mill devoted a short chapter of his epic *Principles* to defending this outlook. In it, Mill suggests that our current lot—competition for wages—may prove to be a transitional phase that will eventually get us to something more desirable.

> I confess I am not charmed with the ideal of life held out by those who think that the normal state of human beings is that of struggling to get on; that the trampling, crushing, elbowing, and treading on each other's heels, which form the existing type of social life, are the most desirable lot of human kind, or anything but the disagreeable symptoms of one of the phases of industrial progress. It may be a necessary stage in the progress of civilization . . . But it is not a kind of social perfection. (PPE IV.vi.5)

Might Mill have been right to encourage our embracing the stationary state? Possibly so, but the harder question may be whether we can find an effective means of transitioning to a stationary state in ways that free people from the need to sell their labor. Failure to do this will either make the stationary state less likely to occur or worse for most people if and when it does occur. So the real problem remains the one to which we have given most prominence in this chapter—that of finding a way to arrange the economy so that it really is better for everyone if the machines work so we don't have to.

## Conclusions

*This chapter has explored a variety of questions about human labor and machine labor. The classical question of whether machines steal jobs needs to be assessed carefully, depending on the rate at which human labor is displaced by technology and what, if anything, might be done about it. We have also explored some fallibilities and hazards associated with relying on technology to get work done for us, particularly when it comes to the storage of "big data" associated with artificial intelligence. Finally, there is much that can still be said on why human workers may have an entitlement to leisure time, and how this entitlement is to be best understood.*

## Study Questions

- Is there some amount of annual salary that you would accept in return for not having any days off? What does your answer suggest about the importance of leisure time?
- Do you think that there is something morally desirable about performing *paid* labor, as opposed to engaging in merely *productive* labor or leisure activity? Many people feel pride in bringing home a paycheck. Is this just an instance of what Keynes described as "habits and instincts that have been bred into the ordinary man for decades"?
- If we choose to supply personal information to some computerized service, should we do so at our own risk? Does it make a difference whether I am (say) giving information to a company that offers to help me cheat on my spouse, or giving financial information to my bank? If so, what sort of difference do we have here? What about some other cases?
- Do you think that there is any moral problem with the sort of historical occasions that your country's government has decided to use when identifying which days to make public holidays?

## Further Reading

*Average Is Over* by Tyler Cowen (Dutton Press, 2013)

Makes many predictions about the way in which labor markets will be transformed by the rise of ever more powerful forms of technology, including consequences for education, economic inequality, and migration. Exhibits a certain pessimism but does not call for any redistributive intervention.

*Saving Capitalism: For the Many, Not the Few* by Robert Reich (Knopf Press, 2015)

A comprehensive book focused on what the author regards as many moral ills of contemporary capitalism. Later chapters focus on the rise of machines and make explicit comparison with the work of Thomas Paine in arguing for a universal basic income.

*Free Time* by Julie Rose (Princeton University Press, 2017)

A philosophical account of the importance of leisure time. Very accessible and one of the first book-length treatments of the topic's moral significance to have ever been written.

*Weapons of Math Destruction: How Big Data Increases Inequality and Threatens Democracy* by Cathy O'Neil (Allen Lane, 2016)

A very comprehensive discussion of the perils of the new dependence on algorithms, discussed in section 3. Written by a mathematician who experienced the global financial crises from within the hedge fund industry.

# 11

# Do Markets Wreck the Planet?

*In this chapter, we'll look at some ways in which capitalism impacts on the natural world. While capitalism and markets can never be solely to blame in general for environmental harms, there are some specific objections to markets that we shall seek to explore in some detail. We might also distinguish between the role of markets in causing environmentally destructive human conduct, and the role that markets could and, in a few cases, might already be playing in bringing about a constructive response. There's no getting away from the fact that an effective global response to climate change is both urgently needed and distressingly hard to achieve. Our goal here is to help you avoid distracting conclusions about what's to blame for this and to acquaint you better with a more robust approach to the problem as one of political economy.*

## 1. Stories of Destruction

If there's one thing that the early proponents of capitalism did not appreciate, it was the capacity of industrial production to deliver catastrophic environmental harms. The thinkers of the golden age knew that production involved exploiting environmental resources, and they appreciated that such resources had limits. Land, especially, was always understood to be limited in its quantity and, more important, quality. But it was generally not suspected that land might become damaged or depleted when employed as a factor of production.[1] The environment was thought to be limited in its geographic extent and productive potential, but it was also considered largely indestructible.

Nowadays, of course, we know better. Humans have done all sorts of environmental damage and are showing few signs of stopping. Emissions of

[1] See especially Mill's claims in PPE II.xii.

*The Ethics of Capitalism.* Daniel Halliday and John Thrasher, Oxford University Press (2020).

DOI: 10.1093/oso/9780190096205.001.0001

greenhouse gases (such as carbon dioxide and methane) are behind recent and still developing changes to the earth's climate. These changes are predicted to create considerable problems in the relatively near future, such as an increased geographical range of tropical diseases, less predictable weather patterns, and rising sea levels. In large part, these emissions have come about through pursuit of goods and services such as vehicular transportation, generation of electricity, and the rearing of animals for food. Other environmental damage has resulted from the gathering of raw materials serving as inputs into many of these production processes. The mining industry, for example, has done substantial ecological damage in regions with substantial mineral deposits. Disasters associated with the transportation of raw materials, notably the contamination of marine ecosystems with crude oil, are also familiar.

Prior to the 20th century, the chemical and biological sciences were not advanced enough for anybody to appreciate what sort of effect human activity might have on the planet's atmosphere. To be fair, while the golden age thinkers generally couldn't grasp the macro-level effects of humans' impact on the environment, they did have some grasp of these effects at the micro level. In some respects, pollution was more evident back then than it is to us now (at least in developed countries). Until the invention of automobiles, streets and sewers were clogged with horse manure and other forms of biological waste. Clean water was rare. Over the period of 1832–1849 in London, around 14,000 people died from cholera. It wasn't until 1854 that John Snow eventually showed that the sewage system was contaminating the water supply.[2] This discovery not only helped prevent future cholera outbreaks, it was decisive evidence in favor of the germ theory of disease.

All the same, the golden age thinkers cared, in their own way, about the environment. John Stuart Mill, for example, lamented the way in which the growth of industry and agriculture would jeopardize natural beauty and the great "pleasantness" of the earth. Mill worried that, left unchecked, industrial progress would result in a world with "scarcely a place left where a wild shrub or flower could grow."[3] This was largely an aesthetic concern. Indeed, Mill thought that the value of biodiversity came from its enablement of good "solitude in the presence of natural beauty and grandeur." As with aesthetic judgments generally, there is room for disagreement. After all, some people

[2] There are several good books on this topic. The most interesting perhaps being Steven Johnson's (2007) book *Ghost Map*.

[3] PPE IV.vi.8.

find heavy industry quite beautiful to behold, and don't really care about national parks or wildflowers. While some people lament the extinction of the Thylacine (the Tasmanian Tiger), others lament the passing of steam trains, which are much worse for the environment than any number of Thylacines.

It is worth considering, yourself, whether your concerns about the environment are similarly aesthetic or existential. People are bothered about the impending extinction of the black rhinoceros (more on this later), and they are bothered about rising sea levels. But these concerns are unlikely to have much in common. To be brutally honest, we could probably get along fine without black rhinos in the world, apart from the fact that we'd be deprived of the spectacle they provide (again, that's aesthetics). But if sea levels were to substantially rise and certain diseases were to spread, the cost in human lives lost would be profound.

There is a deep philosophical question as to whether the environment matters simply because the well-being of humans (and at least some other creatures) depends on it, or whether the environment has some special moral importance in its own right.[4] This most extreme version of the second view is known as "deep ecology," a term owed to the Norwegian philosopher (and accomplished mountaineer) Arne Næss.[5] Many find it intuitively compelling, although it is somewhat hard to explain why such things as trees, mountains, and the like are valuable simply because of what they are. Would it be worse to kill 30,000 polar bears than 30,000 black bears, given that these acts would wipe out the remaining polar bear population but make only a small dent in the abundant black bear population? If we think that biodiversity matters intrinsically, then the answer is probably that losing the polar bears would be the greater tragedy. But if we think that what matters is ultimately the well-being of sentient creatures, then the answer is less obvious.

What's all this got to do with capitalism and the case for or against it? In a recent book about climate change, the Canadian journalist Naomi Klein writes that "market fundamentalism has, from the very first moments, systematically sabotaged our collective response to climate change."[6] It's tempting to agree. After all, most of the problems we've been talking about came into existence, or at least became *big* problems, only after the rise of markets and the

[4] A good overview of many of these topics can be found in David Schmidtz and Elizabeth Willott's (2011) book *Environmental Ethics: What Really Matters, What Really Works*.
[5] See especially his short (1973) article, which is now a classic of environmental ethics.
[6] See her (2014) book *This Changes Everything*.

associated spike in material production. But it would be a mistake to think that capitalism as such is the cause of environmental damage. Let us now highlight some qualifications about the relationship between capitalism and the environment

## A. Markets Aren't the Only Culprits

Governments have proven to be terrible stewards of the environment. This is largely because governments possess massive power and often lack oversight, especially when they are the sort of government that doesn't need to worry about re-election. In countries that industrialized in the absence of markets (e.g., in the Soviet Union or Communist China), environmental damage was even worse than in countries that relied on markets and were therefore closer to the capitalist ideal.

One very compelling example of this is the case of what the Soviet government did to the Aral Sea. This sea, or what's left of it, lies between what is now Uzbekistan and Kazakhstan, former constituent republics of the USSR. In the 1960s, the Soviet government decided to divert the rivers flowing into the Aral for crop irrigation further upstream. Deprived of its major inflow of water, the Aral started to dry up. Although it was once the fourth largest lake in the world, it's now all but disappeared. Apart from the death of the local fishing and tourist industries, the Aral's shrinkage has resulted in enormous ecological problems. The evaporating water has left behind large deposits of salt that have been blown around the region and destroyed agriculture. Although there are now efforts to redirect river water to help the sea recover, the human cost has been huge.

This is just one case of environmental catastrophe that has nothing to do with markets and everything to do with bad governmental decisions backed up by the ability of the state to impose its plans on its citizens. Other examples of destructive governmental actions include nuclear weapons testing and the damming of rivers, which aren't the sort of acts that occur as market transactions. One of the worst examples also happened in the Soviet Union, namely the Chernobyl nuclear disaster in 1986. This meltdown caused dangerous radiation to travel throughout the western Soviet Union and Europe, causing unknown deaths and disease. One of the authors vividly remembers not being allowed to play outside as a child growing up in Germany in 1986 because of Chernobyl.

In some respects, the environment has improved from the industrial era in capitalist countries. This is partly because market providers have reasons to reduce at least some of the environmental harms they might cause and governments often don't. Businesses that produce a lot of pollution are often less efficient than they might otherwise be. Over time, businesses have found cheaper and more efficient ways to reduce their pollution. The legal system in capitalist countries has also developed better ways to hold polluters accountable for the damages they cause, making them liable to lawsuits by those they harm, or in some cases to special taxes. This creates even more incentive to create cleaner ways of doing business. Of course, government can play a role in helping this to happen, as the incentives faced by businesses are largely a product not just of what their consumers want but of what governments make easy and difficult for them, but governments tend to be more effective at this in democratic and capitalist societies rather than nonmarket, authoritarian ones.

We are not suggesting that all environmental harms should be blamed on government agency and never on markets. Often governments are influenced by corporate lobbying in ways that lead to environmental harm (though this may be a sign of an uncompetitive market order). Really, the subject matter is too complicated for it to make much sense trying to work out whether blame should generally be directed one way or the other. Instead, we should approach the problem equipped with the sense that our environment is vulnerable to harms from several different directions at once, some due to markets, some due to governments, and some due to the way in which the two interact. Causes of environmental harm are as diverse as the harms themselves. However much we might want to draw grand conclusions, we should instead be open to drawing specific conclusions about specific ways in which the environment gets damaged. Some of these will have much to do with the way markets work, but others will not.

## B. Resources Often Get Consumed More Readily Than Conserved

Contemporary production wastes a great deal of what gets extracted from the world. Parts of the planet (typically poorer parts—see later) are littered with consumer goods that have been cast aside as consumers replace them with a newer model. Just think about the last time you had to replace your laptop or desktop computer. We're willing to bet that when your computer broke down, probably just one small part or component broke. You probably replaced your laptop simply because *this was cheaper* than getting it repaired. And your discarded laptop added to the growing pile of physical waste needing to be put somewhere.

We all throw out things that are maybe 99% OK, just because of the difficulties of getting them fixed. Why is this so? A common answer gestures at some sort of human desire to have things constantly new and shiny. But this answer is not satisfactory. For one thing, it doesn't explain why, in the past, it was often easier to get things repaired than replaced. The authors are both old enough to remember a time when shoe repair shops (cobblers) were a common presence on major shopping streets. But times have changed—cobblers have disappeared, whereas shoe shops, selling new shoes without offering a repair service for old ones, remain very common.

While we do tend to value novelty, the greater factor is that as an economy develops over time, the production of *goods* gets cheaper while *services* get more expensive. The production of new things is subject to different constraints from the repairing of existing things. Generally speaking, goods come in the form of physical objects, whereas services involve the provision of human labor time. As economies develop, human labor becomes more expensive. This is evident in the fact that countries with high inequality, that is, where there are lots of poor people but also rich people to employ them, tend to have lots of servants.

Another constraint is that the repair industry is not amenable to economies of scale in the way that the production industry is. When it comes to producing new goods, what's usually required is some method of producing large numbers of the *same* thing. This is highly amenable to mechanization. When it comes to repairing things, however, there is much more of a tendency for the task to vary from one unit to the next—laptops, for example, typically do not break in the same way as each other. In addition, production can generally take place on the same site. All laptops might be assembled in the same factory. But they will typically need to be repaired across a variety of locations, as their owners are spread around, and laptops will break at different times. All of these facts make it difficult to take human labor out of the repair industry compared to the ease of taking it out of the production industry. Finally, there is the fact that production involves transactions more easily carried out at a distance. To buy a new laptop, you only need to go online and order it, and then it will come to you. To repair a laptop, you have to take it somewhere or arrange for some human to come and visit you.

All in all, then, we tend to consume new stuff rather than repair existing stuff simply because this becomes easier over time, regardless of the waste it causes. This has nothing to do with any sort of consumption-oriented psychology. You should keep this in mind when you encounter rhetoric about how we have become "addicted" to consumption. (There does remain the important and different question of whether your laptop broke down *earlier than it should have*. We'll come back to this question later.)

## C. Resources Aren't Intrinsically Limited

We're told that the earth is running out of oil. This is true, but misleading. At any given time, resources are, indeed, limited. But what *counts* as a resource changes over time, too. There was a time when fossil oil was worthless. In these times, coal and wood were the primary energy sources, and whale oil was used to power lamps. This led to massive whale hunting all over the world, severely depleting whale populations. Eventually, whale hunting (aside from the Japanese and some Scandinavian countries) dramatically declined. The reason is not because of some moral or environmental outrage about whaling, though outrage does exist, but rather the discovery of how to harness oil in the ground. Pumping oil was much cheaper and more efficient than whaling, and the whale industry got displaced.[7]

At some point in the future, burning oil will no longer be our chief way of creating energy. Reaching this point may be postponed by the efforts of the oil industry to suppress the emergence of often "greener" industries that might replace it, but that's another story—we'll get to it later. But once we've "got off oil," we won't consider it a resource in the same way, much like we no longer consider oak trees an important raw material (before the Industrial Revolution, they were important in the construction of ships, and many were chopped down in England). It might be that we will always be able to transition to new resources through changing production techniques or maybe not. The point is only that we should think of the most important resource that we have as human intelligence and ingenuity. The more that we can

[7] An excellent book on the whaling economy and its ultimate destruction by the discovery of oil from fossil fuels is Eric Jay Dolin's (2007) book, *Leviathan*.

harness and free that resource, the more likely we will be able to solve other resource problems through substitution and change.

## 2. Why Is the Environment So Vulnerable? Collective Action Problems and the Distribution of Incentives

Everyone (individuals, companies, and governments) has an interest in keeping the planet in good condition. Given this, why has it proven so hard to avoid doing the opposite? We'll use this section to get clearer on some of the answers to this question.

According to the political philosopher Stephen M. Gardiner, climate change represents "a perfect moral storm."[8] His point is that climate change is subject to a convergence of several factors. Each has independent moral significance and poses a serious challenge on its own, but their co-occurrence makes climate change especially fiendish. Roughly, the elements of the storm begin with the fact that any human activity impact on the climate cannot be contained within the country where it occurs. The problem needs to be addressed with global cooperation between countries that have different payoffs from the success or failure of such cooperation. Gardiner calls this the "global storm."

Next is the "intergenerational storm." This is basically the fact that addressing climate change means one generation incurring costs while the benefits only start accruing to later generations. Last, there is what Gardiner calls the "theoretical storm," which is the absence of a developed moral theory with any applicability to climate matters. This may account for the fact that attempts to reach agreement on climate policy frequently descend into shouting matches, as do arguments about climate between individual people. Those who deny climate change often see the environmentalist movement as some sort of Marxist conspiracy to install a world government. In the other direction, climate change is sometimes blamed on a sort of free market ideology that represents pure greed and a desire to dominate or destroy nature. Neither side's view of the other is really correct, but they may endure in part because of a regrettable but real human tendency to take a suspicious view of one's opponent in such cases.

[8] See his (2011) book, in this chapter's Further Reading section.

The perfect moral storm metaphor promotes a serious effort to understand the nature of the problem, rather than engage in the blame game. We have already mentioned some reasons for thinking that the relationship between capitalism and environmental degradation is more complex than sometimes suggested. We have also suggested that in parts of the world that are very rich and have well-developed capitalist societies, the local environment is getting better and better by most measures. There is, however, one important sense in which this is not true, namely with regards to $CO_2$ and its effect on global warming. Global warming is increasingly becoming a serious problem and one that is directly related to economic activity.

The countries most responsible for continuing to pump carbon into the atmosphere are, like China, not capitalist societies in any straightforward sense. Of course, the point is not to *blame* China and other states with polluting industries. After all, in large part these countries are just producing what people in the rich countries want to buy. Pollution has decreased in developed countries in part because globalization has enabled the world's wealthy nations to "outsource" the dirty industries on which their consumption depends to countries in which labor is still cheap and political obstacles to pollution are minimal. The point is just that effective popular opposition to pollution might owe something to the freedoms associated with market society. If all societies were free, there might be less outsourcing of dirty industry from one society to another.

Global warming presents unique challenges. We will investigate some of these here, mainly the sort of problems that Gardiner associates with the global and intergenerational storms. We can think of the ways of responding to global warming as falling into two broad categories: prevention and alleviation. These categories are not mutually exclusive, but each has its own challenges and strengths.

## A. Prevention

When we think of "solutions" to climate change, we tend to think of reducing the world output of greenhouse gases. There are two main limitations with this strategy. The first is whether there is *already* too much carbon in the atmosphere to prevent some of the worst effects of warming. The concern here is that prevention may be impossible since we have already gone over the so-called warming cliff. Some estimates suggest that, whatever we do, some warming is assured, along with some of its harmful consequences.

The second problem is the reason why not very much has been done to reduce carbon output so far. This is the collective action problem of warming. This collective action problem has the logic of many environmental problems that can be described as "common pool resource" problem. We owe the idea to Elinor Ostrom, the first—and at the time of this writing, the only—woman to win the Nobel Prize in Economics. We mentioned her work in connection with market failures in chapter 4. Ostrom argues that many tricky resource and environmental problems are characterized by open access (any one can access the resource) and diminishing returns (the more someone uses the resource the less there is for others).

These are "commons" problems, and they have a peculiar logic. Imagine that you are in charge of your country. You can decide to either reduce pollution in an attempt to stem climate change, or you can decide to continue to pollute and reap the economic benefits of doing so. You also know that all the other countries in the world are faced with a similar choice. They can either continue to pollute or stop. Their situation is identical to yours. If they stop polluting *and* you do, too, collectively you may be able to prevent warming. If nobody stops polluting, warming will be assured. If, however, they stop polluting and you don't or vice versa, the polluters will continue to reap the economic benefits of pollution, "free-riding" on the costs of those that stopped polluting. This is the worst outcome for everyone involved. Even though everyone would like to prevent warming, they would rather do so if they can avoid bearing the costs. The logical structure of this situation is represented in Figure 11.1.

| | **Everybody Else** | | |
|---|---|---|---|
| | | *Stop Polluting* | *Continue Polluting* |
| | *Stop Polluting* | Prevent Warming | Costs for your Country, Benefits for Everyone Else |
| **Your Country** | *Continue Polluting* | Benefits for your Country, Costs for Everyone Else | Warming |

**Figure 11.1** Pollution "Tragedy of the Commons"

One thing to note about this kind of collective action problem is that it does not require anyone involved to have base or greedy motives. What each country needs is *assurance* that each other country will do its part in reducing warming. This can be done in a variety of ways. The most familiar approach is a treaty of some sort, but these need nontrivial enforcement mechanisms. This closely resembles the problem of international tax competition mentioned in chapter 8. Global warming prevention is a huge (global) collective action problem with no known solution.

## B. Alleviation

Alleviation, as opposed to prevention, focuses on mitigating or reducing the negative effects of global warming. Unlike prevention, alleviation is able to harness some of the unique strengths of capitalist economies. The strategies fall into two basic categories: technological and economic.

Many technological solutions are still speculative at this point, but they include various geo-engineering approaches as well as techniques for increasing farm yields and providing clean water to areas that will need them. The idea is to use as many strategies as possible to insulate individuals and nations from the negative effects of warming. As with most other technological issues, we don't know what many of these solutions will be or even if there will be solutions in certain cases. We do know, however, that richer and more open societies tend to be more innovative and dynamic. We also know that many potentially great minds are being wasted because of the crushing poverty that much of the world lives in. If this alleviation strategy is viable, development is, in effect, a global warming strategy. Now, more than ever, we need to develop our greatest resource, human intelligence and ingenuity, in order to solve one of the biggest problems the world has faced. We can't do this without helping to bring more of the world out of poverty.

The second approach is economic. Richer societies deal with calamities better than poorer ones. A hurricane that hits the United States is usually substantially less devastating in human terms than a cyclone that hits, say, the Philippines. This is not only because of relief resources; it is also because of better infrastructure. It is easier to get clean water and medicine to people who need them when the roads are good and the power grid comes back into action quickly once the storm has passed. Similarly, medical facilities and building structures tend to be better in richer countries than poorer countries. The basic point is that whatever the results of global warming, richer people will be better able to live with them than poorer people. Again, development and more economic freedom seem to be the solution, not less.

Of course, growing in ways that are environmentally less damaging is always better (and is *logically* possible, since growth can occur in so many ways). But, in the case of the world's poor, sometimes this fact needs to be balanced against the long-term benefits of greater development. This is especially important since the two largest increasing carbon producers are and will continue to be India and China. By developing, these two countries have and are lifting the greatest number of people out of poverty in human history. Perhaps, therefore, they have at least a temporary entitlement to pollute more than countries who have already benefitted from development. We need to think carefully about how our policies would affect the global poor in the short and long term, and how growth might be pursued in ways that are less at the environment's expense. There is now a large literature on how to justly distribute the harms of climate change, and the costs of addressing these harms. Here, philosophers are doing what they can to fight the theoretical storm, though there is still no consensus on how to think about these questions.[9]

In the remaining sections, we will look at some more focused concerns about the relation between environmental harms and specific aspects of market (as opposed to governmental) activity.

## 3. If It Ain't Broke Don't Sell It? Planned Obsolescence

Earlier in this chapter, we explained that the growing tendency to throw out only slightly broken goods owes much to replacement being cheaper than repair. What we didn't comment on was how *quickly* items wear out in the first place. Producers have an interest in selling us products that we like, but whose life cycle is short so that we soon come back for more. Consequently, producers have an incentive to make a product wear out more quickly than it has to. This gives rise to the method commonly known as "planned obsolescence."

The classic case of planned obsolescence goes back to the 1920s and the rivalry between the great American car manufacturers, Ford and General

[9] Two good entry points into the literature on climate change justice are recent articles by Caney (2018) and Moellendorf (2015).

Motors. During this period, the automobile market reached saturation—pretty much every person who could afford a car had bought one. This posed a problem for car manufacturers, who still had to sell cars. General Motors decided to make minor changes to the styling of their cars each year, so that owners of older cars would begin to feel like their models were out of date. The strategy worked. Ford didn't do the same thing, and General Motors gained the larger market share in the 1930s.

This is now common practice. Try comparing clothing styles from the 1780s and the 1790s. Then compare the 1980s and the 1990s. You'll see a bigger difference. This is partly because people in the 20th century had larger disposable incomes, which may have accelerated the mysterious but very real process of changing fashions. But it was also a consequence of advertising campaigns telling consumers that what they were wearing was now out of date and that they had better buy something new this year.

In the technology industries, the tactics are perhaps the most ingenious—or underhand, depending on how we want to look at it. Smartphone producers have been criticized for making it extremely difficult to replace a phone's battery, meaning a whole phone becomes unusable once a battery expires. The consumer has "no choice" but to buy a wholly new phone. Smartphone manufacturers also go in for such tactics as using special screws, which make it harder to get the phone opened up to repair or replace internal components, while making no contribution whatsoever to the phone's performance.

People don't always notice when planned obsolescence is at work. This is because producers work very hard to convince consumers that the obsolescence is not actually planned. Like General Motors, smartphone producers are constantly releasing slightly different models with incremental improvements (or alleged improvements) so that consumers simply accept that they have independent reason to buy a new phone even if they could keep using their old one indefinitely. An important question about planned obsolescence is how much the incremental improvement is real and how much it is just marketing.[10]

Planned obsolescence might not always be a bad thing—incremental improvements may count for something in the long run. If cars lasted as long as houses, then it might be that we would all still be driving cars like

[10] Apple recently admitted that the batteries in IPhones are designed to slow down after a certain life-span; see http://www.independent.co.uk/infact/iphone-slow-apple-battery-replacement-cost-price-how-to-explained-latest-a8159826.html

those from the mid-20th century, which we might have inherited from our parents. These cars would have been less fuel efficient and therefore worse at polluting, and definitely less safe. All of the innovations that now make cars safer and more pleasant to use have occurred largely because producers are in a position to *sell* new cars and reinvest at least part of the revenues into further research and development.

Whether such observations can be made about a wide range of other products is an interesting question. Office printers, for example, are not much like cars. Although they are subject to planned obsolescence, it's not clear that they've gotten better over the last few decades. Printers seem to break down way more often than cars. This sort of difference may have something to do with the sorts of tactics that producers can use to trigger obsolescence. Indeed, printers have even been fitted with microchips that count the number of times a printer has been used and simply trigger an on-screen warning that the printer "has reached the end of its useful life and must be replaced." There may in fact be nothing wrong with the printer apart from the programming that prevents a user from sending further documents to be printed. But users don't know any better and don't think to look online for downloadable programs that can override the printer's chip. Similarly, an item of clothing goes out of fashion usually long before it becomes unwearable in any physical sense. So perhaps we just need to be highly sensitive to differences between different industries. Maybe cars and clothes are at different ends of a spectrum, with smartphones somewhere in the middle.

Assuming that planned obsolescence is indeed an inefficiency in many cases, the question is what to do about it. One common solution is to make producers legally obliged to replace a broken product, for free, within a certain time span. This will cost producers money, unless of course they design their products so that they don't wear out within the warranty period. This approach may be quite effective for products that are highly resistant to the feeling that they have gone out of fashion. For some reason, nobody feels that their printer is "so last season" in the way that many people feel about their clothing. But the flipside of this observation is that it would be *pointless* to create laws that required clothing retailers to replace clothes that wear out, since consumers are already motivated to replace them long before this happens. Might it be defensible, then, to regulate advertising so that the consumer motive was not so bent on keeping up with what the industry says is the latest thing? Or should consumers just wise up?

It may be that planned obsolescence is most cause for concern when it leads to great amounts of physical waste, as in the case of electrical goods. Planned obsolescence in this industry creates serious environmental harms, mainly because all the old devices have to get dumped somewhere. Currently, much electronics waste gets dumped on the coast of west Africa, particularly Ghana, where it causes lasting environmental damage. There may be a case for developing legislation preventing the exporting of waste. If wealthy countries had to dump their old printers and phones on their own territory, then they may find ways to reduce planned obsolescence or promote recycling over simply throwing things out.

Planned obsolescence is one of the topics in this textbook that could use more philosophical research. While there are plenty of documentaries and journalistic coverage relating to it, we could use some more sustained discussions of its moral significance.[11]

## 4. Who Wants to Shoot a Rhino? Markets and Conservation

We'll now make a positive point about how markets might, perhaps surprisingly, play a role in enabling the conservation of our environment rather than its destruction.

There are two species of African rhinos—the black rhino and the white rhino. Both are seriously threatened with extinction. One of the principal causes of this is poaching—rhinos are killed for their horns and to satisfy some people's desire to shoot a big animal. Poaching threatens the numbers of elephants and lions, too.

In developed countries, it is easy to find campaigns seeking money to protect the remaining populations of these creatures. These campaigns, at least historically, have been associated with efforts to fight poaching and to punish those who engage in it. Often, the concerns that motivate these campaigns are developed from a limited perspective. It's easy for us all to lament the decline of Africa's great mammals from the comfort of, well, countries outside of Africa, but keeping these animals alive comes at a cost. Think about it: if you needed to grow crops to make a living, would you want to have elephants and rhinos stomping around? These are huge animals that roam long

[11] Joseph Guiltinan's (2009) article is something of an exception.

distances. They can be stopped only by very expensive fencing or by being shot. Lions also prey on cattle, another source of livelihood for many in sub-Saharan Africa. Most of us who feel bad about the extinction of majestic big mammals would happily exterminate a rat population if it entered our own home or business, even though rats are unlikely to destroy our source of income, and aren't nearly as scary as lions.

On the whole, political philosophy has not had much to say about hunting animals, or indeed about the economic problems of Africa. But one philosopher who has explored this problem is David Schmidtz. He draws a distinction between what he calls "preservationism" and "conservationism." According to Schmidtz, preservationism is the fairly one-dimensional view that rhinos and elephants are, like many other natural wonders, precious things whose destruction is always a bad thing and must therefore be stopped, by force if necessary. Conservationism, on the other hand, is a view that grants similar importance to these creatures but is more open to compromise. For Schmidtz, conservationism is the more plausible approach, and key to its potential is the role it might assign to markets.

Here is some of what Schmidtz has to say:

> Like us, the people of Africa care for their natural heritage when they can afford to do so, when rewards for doing so go to them and not just to others, and when they know how to do so . . . When we try to impose our preservationist ideals on local villagers who have to live with wildlife, we risk starting a war between locals and wildlife, a war that both sides lose. The problem is that preservation ethics does not allow the local people to profit from wildlife, and not allowing people to profit from wildlife effectively pits people against wildlife, which is bad for wildlife as well as the local people.[12]

A conservationist approach work might recommend legalization of hunting. This sounds odd. If we are trying to conserve an endangered species, why on earth would we let people pay to kill its members? The answer is that legalized, controlled hunting introduces discrimination in ways that poaching doesn't. Using their expertise, the organizers of such markets ensure that the animals killed are those that are no longer involved in breeding. When a bull rhino reaches postreproductive age, it often begins to pose a threat to the surrounding rhino population, by killing younger males that it sees as rivals.

[12] From his (1997, 331) article. Schmidtz's article is in the Further Reading section of this chapter.

Rhinos don't, unfortunately, figure out when they have become too old to father babies. Killing them *discriminately* might be a second-best option: by issuing permits to shoot old, aggressive, but postreproductive males, regulated markets can discriminate.

There's an important generalization here: sometimes it is possible to design a market so that the demand can be absorbed in ways that *increase supply*. This is what can be achieved by selling the right to kill *specific* animals, combined with a prohibition against killing any others. Hunter conservation markets are also a clear case of a highly regulated market rather than a "free market." If anything, an uncontrolled market in rhino hunting bears a closer resemblance to indiscriminate poaching than the sort of case we're discussing here. This should remind us that the idea of a "free" market actually does a disservice to markets.

What's more, a legalized market is one where control might be exercised over where the revenues go. Recall that the tolerance of poaching has much to do with the way in which "big game" animals are large pests so far as local farmers are concerned. If revenues from hunting are redistributed around the population, then there is scope for compensating those who, as Schmidtz puts it, aren't actually rewarded for the more punitive preservationist attempts to simply put a stop to poaching.

Markets in hunter permits remain morally controversial. For some, a source of opposition may simply be that they find hunting morally objectionable. We do not want to dismiss the question of whether it is wrong to kill an animal for personal enjoyment. This question has much philosophical substance, as do related questions about whether it is wrong to pay someone else to kill an animal in ways that contribute to one's personal enjoyment, which is what the rest of us do when we buy food or clothing made from animals. Ultimately, however, these are questions about the moral status of animals, and what that status implies for how we may treat them, inside or outside of markets.

What we can say is that when it comes to killing big animals in Africa, this occurs through different methods and due to different motivations. It is worth examining why we have an aversion to the hunting of rhinos and elephants, but not rats. It is possible that our judgment is being augmented, if not distorted, by a certain perception of who goes hunting and why they do it. We often hear, for example, that demand for rhino horn is rooted in strange customs in east Asia, where the horn of a rhino is regarded as having unlikely medical powers. But this is only converted into poaching given the cooperation of local people. An Asian consumer who is willing to pay good money for a rhino's horn is usually not in a position to go and hunt a rhino in Botswana. They will typically pay someone else to do so.

There are, we should say, a number of wealthy individuals who want to hunt elephants, rhinos, and lions for the fun of it. Often these individuals engage in what industry insiders describe as "canned" hunting. This involves specially bred animals kept in large pens that are easy to hunt by wealthy but decidedly unskilled consumers. Efforts to suppress poaching in national parks typically have no effect against this—they will tend, instead, to target poachers who are actually local Africans with few other options when it comes to making a living. So, while hunting may often be morally objectionable, there may be much variation across cases and practices. What we should do, perhaps, is think about how a conservationist approach might prioritize the methods of hunting that are, on reflection, not as objectionable as some others.

At the time of writing, the Namibian government offers permits to shoot individual black and white rhinos when a postreproductive bull is identified. But you'll have to pay a lot more money than you paid for this textbook or (we daresay) for most of the other things you own. And that's probably a good thing.

## Conclusions

*This chapter has shown that the planet gets wrecked in more ways than one. Some of these are due to features of markets, perhaps most notably the way in which market providers have incentives to design products in ways that lead to more waste than is necessary. But there are also ways in which markets might aid certain efforts to conserve what's valuable about the environment. As always, the important task is to work out what kind of case we're dealing with when considering a specific instance of the many environmental harms that we should want to address.*

## Study Questions

- Do you think that nature has intrinsic value, or is it valuable only to humans and whatever other creatures stand to gain or lose from how it changes? How much difference do you think this question makes when it comes to regulating markets?

- Can you think of an example of where you have ended up making large expenditures due to the planned obsolescence of a product that you consume? Do you think that, on balance, the planned obsolescence was objectionable? If so, what might be done about it?
- If killing animals for fun is morally objectionable, how should this be weighed against the possibility that a regulated hunting market might bring economic prosperity to some parts of Africa?

## Further Reading

*A Perfect Moral Storm: The Ethical Tragedy of Climate Change* by Stephen Gardiner (Oxford University Press, 2011)

While this is not really a work in political economy, it provides a very thorough evaluation of what is at stake and why the challenge is so immense.

*Governing the Commons* by Eleanor Ostrom (Cambridge University Press, 1990)

The classic statement of how commons problems arise with respect to the management of environmental resources, and what prospects there are for overcoming them.

"When Preservation Doesn't Preserve" by David Schmidtz, in *Environmental Values* 6 (3) (1997): 327–339

A short but very concise statement of the theoretical foundations for a defensible market in hunting, based on the problems typically facing those who stand to win or lose from the environmental impact of large African mammals.

# 12

# Boldly Going Where No Market Has Gone Before—Should Some Things Not Be for Sale?

*Many of the questions covered in earlier chapters of this textbook have been undergoing philosophical and economic analysis for decades or centuries. In this chapter, we're examining questions that have arisen more recently, though the philosophical literature on them is already very lively. More specifically, we're interested in the sorts of exchanges that might be "off limits" to markets. This will give us a chance to look at some very interesting specific cases, and to consider the intuitive reactions that many people find they have toward them.*

## 1. Kidneys, Used Underwear, and Tossed Dwarfs: Intuitive Discomfort about Commodification

How much money would you accept for one of your kidneys? If you're willing to sell, there are many who are willing to pay. Healthy human kidneys are a scarce good that can save lives, and many people are desperate for one. Because healthy people have two kidneys and can survive with just one, there is a very large supply of transferable kidneys—almost as many as people.

Most of us, however, are unwilling to donate a kidney for free. Although "altruistic" (i.e., unpaid) kidney donations do occur, these are uncommon, and usually happen when donors and recipients are related. Consequently, most of the potential supply of kidneys has not been converted into actual supply. In the United States, more than 4,000 people die while waiting for a kidney donor every year. But if people *were* allowed to charge for a kidney

*The Ethics of Capitalism*. Daniel Halliday and John Thrasher, Oxford University Press (2020).

DOI: 10.1093/oso/9780190096205.001.0001

donation, then it's almost certain that more would be willing to donate, and thus more people would be able to get off kidney dialysis, or even avoid death.

Most countries prohibit markets in kidneys and only allow altruistic donation.[1] In practice, illegal "black markets" make up (to a limited extent) for government restrictions. There are reports of people in developed countries paying hundreds of thousands of dollars to receive kidneys sourced from overseas through criminal channels. From what we can gather, the going rate for a kidney in world markets is around US$200,000. Black markets source most of their kidneys from "donors" in Eastern Europe and South Asia.

In spite of the high price paid by the consumers, relatively little is paid to the donors, most being taken by the brokers and surgeons who arrange the deals. There is little oversight of surgery conducted within the illegal organ trade. If a desperate consumer pays huge sums for a transplant, there is little they can do if the broker just runs off with the money. There is evidence that many donors do not really know what they are getting into. In India, where donors are disproportionately female, many are coerced by their husbands or fathers.[2] Nevertheless, many people retain a kind of intuitive discomfort at the prospect of a legalized kidney trade. For many, this intuitive discomfort is interpreted as a sign that there's something *morally* wrong with allowing kidneys to be bought and sold.

Intuitive discomfort also attaches to markets in goods whose supply is not a matter of life or death. It's quite easy, nowadays, to buy someone else's used underwear, thanks to the internet and websites like EBay. We don't know of any scholarly work on this kind of market, but some interesting investigative journalism has been done.[3] So far as we know, there are no legal prohibitions on this market. But, anecdotally, we find that people express a certain discomfort, even disgust, when made aware of it. This tends to be accompanied by the thought that there must be *something* morally amiss about these exchanges, consensual though they are.

Here's a third example. When the English rugby team was participating in the 2011 World Cup, some players went out drinking. Photos were later published showing the players in a bar that offered patrons the chance to engage in "dwarf tossing." In this market, people pay to see how far they can

[1] Iran is a notable exception. They have had a market in kidneys since the 1980s and are one of the few countries without a kidney shortage (Ghods and Savaj 2006).

[2] Some reference to these facts is made by Debra Satz (2010, 195–197), whose work we mention later in this chapter.

[3] We've relied mainly on the following story by E. J. Dickson: http://www.dailydot.com/irl/used-panties-reddit-ama/

throw a (living, human) dwarf. Again, there's not too much scholarship on this.[4] It's unclear whether any England rugby players tossed dwarves on the occasion in question. But the story was newsworthy largely because of the dwarf-tossing element. This reflects the fact that people find something intuitively objectionable about dwarf tossing, making it somewhat scandalous for the England rugby team to be caught enjoying it.

In 1991, Michel Wackhenheim, a French dwarf, was banned by the mayor of Morsang-sur-Orge from being tossed. Wackenheim disputed the ban, and his case was eventually heard before the Conseil D'Etat, the supreme court of France. The court upheld the original ban, arguing that although it prevented Wackenheim from earning a living in the way he chose, dwarf throwing undermined his dignity. Part of the decision reads:

> In deciding the case in question, the court of appeal was of the opinion that the entertainment of "dwarf throwing," consisting of the throwing of a dwarf by members of the public, leads to using a person affected by a physical handicap and presented as such as a projectile. An attraction of this sort was regarded as infringing the dignity of the human person in its very objective. Its prohibition was thus legal, even in the absence of particular local circumstances.[5]

Wackenheim appealed the decision to the Human Rights Committee of the United Nations, citing the 1966 International Covenant on Civil and Political Rights. His appeal was rejected in 2002.

We've chosen to begin with these three examples because they share something in common, namely, having something to do with human bodies. There's something about the human body, many of us feel, that makes it or its parts (or objects closely associated with it or its parts) an inappropriate object for market transactions.

Philosophers have discussed kidney markets at some length, along with markets in reproductive labor and in sexual services.[6] It is widely felt that there is something wrong with paying a woman to gestate, and give birth to, a baby that she is then contractually obliged to hand over to some other couple

[4] Although, see the cleverly titled "Nobody Tosses a Dwarf!" (Leget, Borry, and De Vries 2009) and "If Dwarf Tossing Is Outlawed, Only Outlaws Will Toss Dwarves" (McGee 1993).

[5] Quoted in Rosen (2012, 86).

[6] There have even been some interesting philosophical experiments on this topic; see Freiman and Lerner (2015).

who will raise it as legal parents. Elizabeth Anderson (1990) has argued that markets in reproductive labor treat a woman's reproductive organs as something akin to "rented plumbing" and that they wrongly alienate a woman from the child she brings to term only to surrender to someone else. And it is widely felt that there is something wrong with paying someone just to have sex with them, irrespective of whether babies get created. Such intuitions are, as before, reflected in the law: many countries ban commercial surrogacy, and most countries ban, or at least heavily restrict, sex work, that is, markets in sex.

But it's not obvious why these markets must be wrong (if indeed they are wrong) just because they involve transactions or the use of body parts. As Debra Satz points out (more on her views later), there are plenty of well-established markets that seem to share this property without us having any intuitive discomfort. Supermodels are paid basically because of how their bodies look, and athletes are paid because of how they can use their bodies. It is relatively rare to find people who have a problem with this as a matter of principle. If a tall person can be paid to jump long distances, why can't a short person be paid to be thrown long distances? Furthermore, people have sex with each other for all kinds of reasons and, so long as there is consent, we don't really interrogate their motives too much. Why should introducing money into the mix change things?

Another problem is that intuitive discomfort also attaches to certain transactions whose object has little or nothing to do with human bodies. There is a traditional disapproval of "mercenaries"—people who use their military expertise to fight in wars purely for commercial gain (as opposed to a desire to protect their country's interests). A modern version of this view allows that soldiers can be paid, but that they should only be employed by their own country's military services, which are state owned. This was a salient complaint in the 1970s when the United States moved away from an all-voluntary military force. The political economist Milton Friedman was responsible for making the intellectual case that convinced the Nixon administration to end military conscription and move to an all-voluntary force, which the United States still has. At the time, General William Westmoreland objected to Friedman's proposal, arguing that he didn't want to command an army of mercenaries. Friedman replied, "Would you rather command an army of slaves?"

Similar things have been said about the criminal justice system. Generalizing, some philosophers have argued that the state ought to have a monopoly on whatever actions are meant to be done "in the name" of the citizenry, which may apply to national defense and the treatment of criminals. This idea has something in it, but again it is not really about the introduction of cash as corrupting an otherwise neutral activity.[7]

To pick yet another example, some people feel that it's wrong for their government to put citizenship up for sale. This is reflected in common practices of making migrants wait many years before they can qualify for citizenship, and making qualification conditional upon taking a test purporting to measure whether the candidate has the right attitude to qualify as a citizen. There is often controversy about which "values" people need to demonstrate in order to qualify for citizenship, but we suspect that there would be even greater opposition if governments simply offered citizenship based on no other criteria besides paying a fee.[8]

To generalize, then, the claim seems to be that a market in *X* is morally objectionable when subjecting *X* to market supply (i.e., allowing it to be traded for cash) is distinctively wrong. What we mean by this description is that there is something wrong about subjecting *X* to market supply even though there is nothing wrong, or nothing nearly as wrong, with cases where *X* is supplied for free, or according to some mechanism not involving material exchange (as in citizenship tests). We will follow other philosophers in describing this concern as one about *commodification*. To say that it is wrong to "commodify" some good or service *X* is just to say that allowing it to be traded for cash is to somehow *introduce* some wrong treatment of *X* and/or either of the parties trading it.

This abstract description does seem to capture many of the anti-commodification intuitions triggered by many of the examples in this section. It is often said that sex work degrades women, though this is less often said about sex exchanged for free. Paying to toss a dwarf strikes many as expressing disrespect toward dwarves. Similarly, citizenship is often described as something that must be *earned*, in a sense of "earning" not like earning an income (i.e., selling labor).

Our task in this chapter is to see how much we can make sense of this sort of anti-commodification worry, and of what prospects there are for vindicating the intuitive responses (and associated legal prohibitions in the real world) that we've just listed.

[7] See the work of Avihay Dorfman and Alon Harel (2013, 2016).
[8] Javier Hidalgo (2016) is one philosopher who has defended the practice of selling citizenship.

## 2. The Moral Downsides of Prohibition

However strong it proves to be, the case for prohibiting commodification has to deal with one consistent problem: legal prohibition almost always has a moral downside when applied to exchanges that are consensual and *mutually advantageous*. If there is something wrong with commodification, then it will need to be something that established the wrongness of buying and selling certain goods and services *in spite* of such transactions being mutually advantageous.

To describe exchanges as mutually advantageous does not simply presuppose that anti-commodification views are wholly wrong. It might be true that markets in reproductive labor treat women as mere objects, or at least disrespect women in ways that altruistic surrogacy does not. But it does not *follow* that individual exchanges can't yet benefit both transacting parties. The fact remains that people have to earn a living. A woman who can do so by selling her reproductive labor is, strictly speaking, made better off by being paid to do so—it might make the difference between whether she can afford food or not. (It is almost certainly an injustice that a woman is in the position of having to make this choice in the first place, but again that does not establish that her being paid is the injustice.) Our point is not that one of these considerations outweighs the other, but rather that they are independent: we cannot make an inference from the claim that a market exchange in *X* treats *X* in the wrong way, to the claim that this exchange cannot benefit the parties between whom *X* is being exchanged.

To be compelling, any commodification-based argument for prohibition needs to invoke reasons that outweigh the reasons derived from whatever benefits would be realized for the transacting parties by the allegedly commodifying exchange. These benefits are likely to be higher in some cases than others (compare surrogacy and kidneys with dwarf tossing), but in principle they can be large in all cases.

Prohibition has other costly externalities. This is particularly notable when it comes to recreational drugs.[9] Here are two facts that are often used in everyday debates about the case against legalizing drugs. First, many drug dealers, or agents further up the supply chain, are involved in highly

[9] Some of these considerations apply to pharmaceutical drugs as well; see Jessica Flanigan's (2017) book *Pharmaceutical Freedom: Why Patients Have a Right to Self Medicate*.

objectionable enterprises, such as extortion, human trafficking, and other activities associated with organized crime. By purchasing drugs from these suppliers, consumers provide revenue that supports these other heinous acts. Another common argument against buying recreational drugs is that suppliers routinely cut the product with impurities so that they can sell larger quantities of it. Heroin is routinely mixed with substances such as brick dust (similar color), ground glass, and floor cleaner. None of these substances will do you any good if you ingest them.

Both of these considerations represent genuine reasons for not buying recreational drugs (the first is a moral reason, the second prudential). But that's because they are reasons to not buy a good *from a criminal supplier*. This does not make them reasons to *criminalize the supply* of that good. This distinction is easily confused. Many objectionable features of markets in drugs are not consequences of market exchange per se, but consequences of its legal prohibition. The same goes for kidney markets—there's no substance to the claim that kidney markets should remain prohibited because of all the harm done by underground surgery.

It is worth adding that, partly for these reasons, we can't defend the illegality of certain markets just by appealing to that illegality itself. We'll take it for granted that the current legal prohibition of an act is not, by itself, reason to consider that act wrong. There may be general reasons for obeying the law, but these attach to the way we think about law as a whole, and don't have much to do with the status of particular act types that might be legally prohibited, such as certain types of market transaction.

Legalizing a market will usually decrease criminal supply of the good or service in question. This is partly because consumers don't like dealing with criminals, who can be intimidating even when offering a mutually advantageous exchange. A legalized market enables oversight, so consumers know what they are getting—if supermarkets were caught selling instant coffee cut with rat poison, they would be in lots of trouble. As well as improving the product, legalization often lowers the price. This is because legal sellers don't have to worry about being imprisoned or having their staff imprisoned, not to mention the running costs associated with smuggling and having one's product sometimes confiscated by a successful police operation. Easier (and legal) conditions will also tend to attract more sellers, creating more competition. There are other problems with criminalization that go beyond the market itself, such as the sheer cost of putting people in prison and running the court system. These costs are not just financial, and some philosophical opposition to prevailing drug laws relies heavily on these costs alone.[10]

So, whatever the case for restricting a market on anti-commodification grounds, we can't lose sight of the costs of prohibition. None of the points made in this section is decisive, but they should remind us that prohibiting something comes with negative consequences to be weighed against whatever negative consequences may flow from permitting it.

## 3. Are Some Things "Beyond Price"?

A simple way to express the anti-commodification objection to various markets is that the good or service in question ought not to be given a cash value. This is not really an argument for the anti-commodification view, more a restatement of it. So we might begin by registering some arguments against it. First of all, we might wonder why the introduction of a cash price is, on its own, a morally objectionable way of treating what might be exchanged in return. It is sometimes suggested that offering cash for some good or service expresses disrespect in itself. This is a likely reaction one will find when making someone an unsolicited offer of cash for sex, for example. One question is whether this should be explained by facts to do with the exchange being offered, or facts about how the parties are related to each other.

If the case for commodification is going to rely on the view that some goods or services are of a special status, such that offering cash is disrespectful, then there will be counterexamples. Debra Satz points out that even religious labor is paid for: priests, rabbis, and imams typically draw a salary. Religious ceremonies like baptisms and funerals have a price. And yet putting a cash value on doing God's work has long been socially accepted. We might note that clergy typically have rather low salaries and some religious orders, like the Franciscans, take a "vow of poverty" and live a very simple lifestyle. Still, these cases all put pressure on commodification objections made elsewhere.

Nevertheless, it is possible to come up with more plausible groundings for the anti-commodification concern. Following Jason Brennan and Peter Jaworski, we might suggest that offers of cash have a particular signaling effect in certain contexts.[11] Sometimes, offering cash might signal an inappropriate

[10] Especially Douglas Husak (1992, 2002).

[11] In this section, we draw on their (2015b) article. Brennan and Jaworski develop their views further in their (2015a) book—see the Further Reading section.

attitude toward the party with whom you're seeking to transact. This is especially plausible in cases where the parties have some prior relationship that comes with certain norms or expectations. Romantic and professional relationships are cases in point. When you're in relationships like these, certain cash offers are inappropriate. It would be inappropriate for me to ask my spouse to wash the car for $25 if I don't have time to do it myself, but probably appropriate to offer the same deal to my neighbor's 11-year-old son. And it might be perfectly appropriate for me to politely *ask* my spouse to wash the car for free if I don't have the time to do it myself, so long as I'm happy to accept her refusal if she doesn't have time either. It's hard to say exactly which contexts trigger these requirements or how demanding they are. Nobody thinks it should be *illegal* for my spouse and I to make a cash trade so that one of us washes the car while the other gets to do something else. So it's unclear what this example shows about any of the other markets we've mentioned, though we'll look at some similar views about the relationship between cash and interpersonal relationships in the next section.

Ultimately, the norms and expectations emanating from prior relationships are the products of deeper, cultural practices. Yet again, we should remember that the evaluation of markets should pay some attention to prevailing social norms. Importantly, they vary across cultures. Brennan and Jaworski note several examples of exchanges that trigger anti-commodification intuitions in some cultures but not others. For example, Western cultures would frown at the idea of paying strangers to attend a funeral or wedding. Other cultures have developed quite contrary norms. This leads Brennan and Jaworski to suggest that whether a market should be prohibited (on anti-commodification grounds) depends in large part on whether the anti-commodification intuition is grounded in a practice or cultural norm that is worth having. Suppose (simplifying perhaps) that Western norms say that sex should not be exchanged for cash. If exchanging sex for cash would erode these norms *and* that would be a bad thing, then there is a case for prohibiting markets in sexual labor. But this case is defeasible—the benefits of preserving these norms need to be weighed against the costs of allowing them to erode, and indeed against ways of preserving them that might exist other than continuing to prohibit sex work.[12]

[12] Evaluating norms across countries is a tricky business. One of the authors discusses this issue in Thrasher (2018a).

All of this suggests that anti-commodification views about specific exchanges reflect little more than preoccupations of contemporary "Western" culture. As such, they are the consequence of cultural evolution, which is a haphazard process and known not to necessarily aim at morally desirable outcomes. In light of this, Brennan and Jaworski go on to suggest that we should refrain from letting anti-commodification intuitions guide too many of our decisions about market regulation. Instead, we should be open to questioning whatever social norms might be triggering these intuitions, and revising these intuitions where appropriate.

Eventually, Brennan and Jaworski defend the principle that a market in some specific good or service should be prohibited only if there is sufficient reason to prohibit *free exchange* of whatever is being traded (i.e., giving the thing for free). If it is right to prohibit free exchange, it is probably also right to prohibit *prior possession*. This condition has the advantage of upholding legal prohibition of markets in such things as child pornography, since the material being exchanged is already wrong to possess or pass around for free. But the point, as Brennan and Jaworski emphasize, has got nothing to do with markets. Again, it is mysterious to think that the *introduction* of cash has some power to convert a permissible exchange into an impermissible one. Accordingly, Brennan and Jaworski's condition favors permitting some of the morally controversial exchanges we've highlighted. Nobody would claim that it's morally wrong to possess used underwear. Indeed, possession of such a thing is an unavoidable consequence of a normal lifestyle. So, it's OK to sell it, too. Similar things can be said about markets in kidneys, and reproductive and sexual labor.

Critics of Brennan and Jaworski have suggested that their focus on undermining tradition is just the easy bit.[13] Defending a market may require positive arguments as well, as there are likely to be difficult questions about how to design and regulate institutions associated with a market in, say, kidneys. If the hazards associated with a legalized market are substantial, then the disutility associated with the social norm against any sort of market may not prove to be comparatively great. That said, much of the hard work on designing these markets has not been done because of the norms against them.

[13] See for example Moriarty (2017).

## 4. Markets as Hierarchy Reinforcers

The example of offering cash to one's spouse in return for household chores is just one example of a cash exchange that might be judged in light of background social relationships. Spousal relationships are not the only social relationships that might bear on the permissibility of market transactions. Most societies have (indeed, suffer from) various sorts of social hierarchy. These are constituted by relationships between large groups rather than pairs of individuals. Here we have in mind familiar cases where people are treated or viewed in ways influenced by their gender, race, social class, religion, or other type of group membership. One set of examples concerns the way in which people's behavior gets interpreted—frequency of sexual partnerships often gains social esteem (of a certain sort) for men, but opprobrium for women.

A related manifestation is the phenomenon commonly known as "victim blaming." If a woman is the victim of a sexual assault on a college campus, the official response is sometimes along the lines of encouraging female students to dress less provocatively and stay sober at parties, rather than impressing on male students the fact that it is wrong to commit sexual assault or rape. Social hierarchies also have influence when it comes to predicting behavior as well as interpreting it. The most familiar cases involve stereotyping, which occurs when we expect someone to behave in a certain way just because we attribute certain characteristic to some group they're in. This can be positive or negative: if you show up for a job interview dressed in an expensive-looking suit and talking with an educated accent, people on the panel will tend to draw more favorable conclusions about your suitability for the job. Sadly, the panelists may draw less positive conclusions if you have a certain skin color.[14]

Social hierarchies that lead to treatment based purely on group membership tend to be both unfortunate and unjust. This is basically because they lead to some groups being treated worse than, or as inferior to, other groups. Much more could be said about them than we have space for right here. We want to focus on the way in which market transactions might be part of what enables oppressive social hierarchies to endure, when certain goods or

[14] Much has been written on how social hierarchy is oppressive in ways related to how an individual's group membership influences prediction and interpretation of their conduct. A classic work is Iris Young's (1990) book. Also worth consulting is Elizabeth Anderson's (2012) article.

services are being exchanged. The most plausible object of such reinforcement might be hierarchies associated with gender.

The philosopher Debra Satz (2010, 146) writes that "if prostitution is wrong it is because of its effects on how men perceive women and on how women perceive themselves." And she suggests that, in practice, this is what markets in sexual labor tend to do: sex work encourages the view that a woman's role is largely about servicing male desires. Satz takes this to be causally connected with the high frequency of violence against female sex workers (at the hands of clients, but also pimps). Satz says that sex work is a "theater of inequality"—a sphere of activity where individual men and women interact in ways entrenching the status hierarchy between the two groups more broadly. It is these facts that constitute the moral case against markets in women's sexual labor.

One advantage of Satz's position is that it allows distinctions to be drawn between different types of exchanges. Worries about markets in sexual labor often focus on the purchase of sex by men, from women. Satz may be able justify the special concern attached to these exchanges over the lower level of concern typically voiced about male sex work. The case for this justification may be that it is the selling of sex by women to men that does the most to reinforce social hierarchies between men and women. Satz's view may be the only version of the anti-commodification view that can do this in a coherent way. If selling sex is "just wrong," then it would seem, inflexibly, that all cases of markets in sexual labor would have to be on a par.

Satz makes it clear that her case for viewing sex work as objectionable may not establish a decisive case for its illegality, for reasons similar to ones that we reported in section 2 of this chapter. For example, sex workers' exposure to violence is maintained in part by the fact that they cannot seek help from the police without revealing themselves as having engaged in criminal activity. This may suggest that any legal restriction on markets in sexual labor ought to avoid criminalizing the women who sell it.

Satz applies a similar perspective to markets in reproductive labor. Commercial surrogacy, she says, may reinforce the view that the proper role for women in society is in making babies, as opposed to pursuing a wider set of labor market alternatives. But she rejects Anderson's view, mentioned earlier, that commercial surrogacy corrupts something special about the relationship between mother and child. Anderson's view makes it hard to explain why commercial surrogacy is wrong at the same time as abortion is morally permissible, since both acts disrupt the biological relationship between a woman and the child she is gestating. This criticism parallels Satz's rejection of the view that sex work should be seen as wrong just because there is something wrong per se with selling sexual labor.

Does Satz's position generalize to markets other than those in sexual labor? This is a difficult question. In this section, we've only talked about gender hierarchy. It is unclear which, if any, markets might reinforce hierarchies having to do with race, religion, social class, or any other kind of important group difference. Satz suggests kidney markets may compound the difficulties faced by members of poor or lower class groups. One reason for this may be that lenders may be able to demand someone's kidney as collateral before agreeing to loan any cash. This is unlikely to affect wealthy or middle-class borrowers, who can typically offer other things as collateral, assuming they need to borrow at all. Satz does not apply her approach to any markets connected with hierarchies in race or religion.

Satz is clear that the case she makes is defeasible: if a market in *X* reinforces a social hierarchy between those who might purchase *X* and those who typically supply *X*, then this is unlikely to be a matter of conceptual truth, or even to apply to all exchanges of *X* that might be going on around the world. But the lesson here may be that markets are not really what's to blame. Instead, markets merely compound the injustice of certain background conditions, including the social norms and poverty that structure the opportunities available to people in markets. This does not show that markets don't matter, or that specific markets should never be restricted. But that can never be the whole story.

Indeed, some feminist scholars argue that the rise in markets has, historically, played an important role in the emancipation of women.[15] It may still be true that women remain oppressed in certain important respects that continue to be compounded by the way in which certain markets operate.[16] But that conclusion is not the same as one that says market exchange has some corrupting effect when people carry out exchanges that we tend to see as unproblematic when no money changes hands.

In short, if we're going to liberate ourselves from the oppressive forces of certain markets, we'll have to find a way to liberate ourselves from the more ultimate causes of the sort of oppressive hierarchies we're talking about. This

[15] A useful discussion of this controversial claim can be found in the volume coauthored by Ann Cudd and Nancy Holstrom (2011), included in this chapter's Further Reading section.

[16] See, for example, Serene Khader's (2014) discussion of microcredit and women's empowerment.

might require some continued prohibition of the markets in question, but this is just addressing the symptom. More will need to be done to address the cause.

## 5. Maybe It's Just All Too Much? Privacy and the Need for (Any Kind of) Market-Free Zone

So far, we've looked at intuitively objectionable market exchanges concerning some specific good or service. Here's one other example of an intuitively questionable type of market exchange, which may challenge the assumption that so much depends on *what* is being exchanged. We owe this idea to the political philosopher Jonathan Wolff.[17]

Imagine you are on a crowded commuter train, but lucky enough to have a seat while many others are left standing. One of the standing passengers offers you five dollars for your seat. Would you find this strange? Probably you would. The selling of seats (from one passenger to another) doesn't usually happen on commuter trains. This is in spite of the fact that such exchanges would often be mutually advantageous: people standing up after a hard day at work often really want a seat when they still have a long journey home. And at least some of the seated passengers would probably prefer a few dollars to keeping their seat. This case is not one that would stimulate moral outrage of the sort sometimes directed at markets in sex work and human kidneys. And yet there seems to be something morally significant at play. Describing the example himself, Wolff says that "one can almost hear the murmurs of disapproval going round the carriage."

Wolff's example is interesting for several reasons. There is surely nothing sacred about seats on trains. In any case, train travel is subject to market exchange in the first place: the operating company sells tickets and has given them a price already! Why would a problem arise just as soon as they are given a price for a *second* time, when customers exchange seats among themselves? This is worth trying to explain.

Wolff's explanation begins with the observation that seat allocation already has a well-established rule, which people have been generally socialized to follow. Generally speaking, seats on commuter trains are allocated on

[17] In an unpublished lecture titled "Moral Limits of the Market," available on Wolff's webpage: www.homepages.ucl.ac.uk/~uctyjow/MLM.doc

the basis of "first come first served." Like many other conventions, this one is defeasible: it's customary for an able-bodied person to give up their seat for a passenger who is pregnant, elderly, or has a physical disability. (Though again, it would be frowned upon to ask for a few dollars in exchange, even for an elderly passenger who's visibly very wealthy!) This explanation remains compatible with the fact that seats are sold by the train company, given that tickets on commuter trains are typically not for specific seats, but are rather a license to board a train and then claim a seat if there are any left.

Now, we want to make it clear that just because a convention is established in ways that elicit disapproval when it is broken, it does not follow that the convention is morally important (recall the view of Brennan and Jaworski described earlier). Disapproval at the flouting of conventions can be plausibly explained in terms of our sensitivity to the way in which conventions *of some kind* are important for getting things done. But, again, this does not mean that any established convention must be preserved. The crucial question is whether a convention driving nonmarket allocation is better than some form of market rule. In the case of allocating a scarce good such as seats on a train, "first come first served" is unlikely to be efficient. This is precisely why a market exchange would be mutually advantageous—the people who get seats may well be less tired, and more in need of some quick cash, than those who board later.

Wolff makes an interesting further suggestion, which is that human interaction will be of a higher quality if we are not engaging in market exchanges all of the time. Wolff suggests that "there should be a rather large non-market sphere. But . . . it may not matter so much what is in the market sphere and what is not." It is worth considering whether the intuitive reaction to markets in this or that thing is merely a reflection of a social practice that ultimately has quite a randomizing aspect. We've reflected at several points in this book that market forces and incentives are almost always present. It is the norms and institutions of market societies that transform these forces into mutually beneficial "invisible hands" rather than perverse patterns of trade. Wolff may not like the idea of exchange at all, but it is probably more likely that he is opposed to the perversities of markets that don't create beneficial "invisible hands." Banning exchange, as we have emphasized at many points in this chapter, is not always the best way to deal with these situations.

## Conclusions

*This chapter has considered a wide range of specific market exchanges for which there is some intuitive unease, if not outright opposition. We have tried to show that there is a somewhat corresponding variety of possible justifications for intuitive opposition to various markets, but that the opposition is unlikely to be vindicated across the board and is certainly somewhat piecemeal. The most promising arguments draw on the possibility of specific markets being causally connected with certain prevailing sociological harms and on the view that certain services ought not to be provided without a certain moral authority that can be possessed only by the state.*

## Study Questions

- Why might it be wrong for the state to privatize the supply of judges and soldiers, but not the supply of food or uniforms issued to judges and soldiers? What explains the difference (if any)?
- Imagine a company that sold opportunities to toss dwarfs broadened its product base by offering specific opportunities to toss (say) Jewish dwarfs or homosexual dwarfs. Would this make a moral difference?
- What sort of test (if any) do you think foreigners should have to pass in order to become citizens of your country? Why would such a test be a more appropriate gateway than a cash fee of any magnitude?
- Can you think of a market exchange that might reinforce or exacerbate a kind of social hierarchy other than the cases discussed in this chapter? Do you think, in this case, that banning the market would be necessary or sufficient for mitigating or removing the hierarchy you've identified?
- If it is permissible to take cash to gestate a baby for another couple, why shouldn't it be permissible to just sell a baby after having given birth?

## Further Reading

*Why Some Things Should Not Be for Sale: The Moral Limits of Markets* by Debra Satz (Oxford University Press, 2010)

Develops a sophisticated perspective on why many of the markets in this chapter are cause for special concern. The focus in this book is on going beyond intuitive opposition to commodification by focusing on the structural harms that might result from markets in sexual labor, reproductive labor, and human organs.

*Markets without Limits: Moral Virtues and Commercial Interests* by Peter Jaworski and Jason Brennan (Routledge, 2016)

A comprehensive attempt to dismantle the wide range of intuitive opposition that people have to markets in particular goods and services. Builds on the shorter article (concerning semiotic objections to markets) that we discussed in this chapter.

*Capitalism: For and Against—A Feminist Debate* by Ann E. Cudd and Nancy Holmstrom (Cambridge University Press, 2011)

Essential reading if you want a fuller sense of the variety of feminist perspectives on the morality of capitalism. Although this book forms part of a series oriented around various points of philosophical disagreement, Cudd and Holmstrom differ more in their points of emphasis than deep theoretical disagreement. Both show how the economic status quo is in various ways bad for women while being often superior to the treatment of women in pre-capitalist societies. Cudd is more optimistic that the treatment of women can be improved in ways that retain core elements of what might be seen as a capitalist economic system.

*Legalize This! The Case for Decriminalizing Drugs* by Douglas Husak (Verso, 2012)

A short book by a leading legal philosopher, which will give you a good sense of the moral case against criminalizing recreational drug use. It's now a little old, but the war on drugs hasn't changed much since its publication.

# References


Acemoglu, Daron, and James Robinson. 2012. *Why Nations Fail: The Origins of Power, Prosperity, and Poverty*. New York: Crown Business.

Admati, Anat, and Martin Hellwig. 2013. *The Bankers' New Clothes: What's Wrong with Banking and What to Do about It*. 2nd edition. Princeton, NJ: Princeton University Press.

Alstott, Anne, and Bruce A. Ackerman. 2000. *The Stakeholder Society*. New Haven, CT: Yale University Press.

Anderson, Elizabeth. 2015. "Thomas Paine's 'Agrarian Justice' and the Origins of Social Insurance." In *Ten Neglected Classics of Philosophy*, edited by Eric Schliesser, 55–83. New York: Oxford University Press.

Anderson, Elizabeth. 2017. *Private Government: How Employers Rule Our Lives*. Princeton, NJ: Princeton University Press.

Anderson, Elizabeth S. 1990. "Is Women's Labor a Commodity?" *Philosophy & Public Affairs* 19 (1): 71–92.

Anomaly, Jonny. 2015. "Public Goods and Government Action." *Politics, Philosophy and Economics* 14 (2): 109–128.

Anomaly, Jonny, and Geoffrey Brennan. 2014. "Social Norms, the Invisible Hand, and the Law Special Issue for Suri Ratnapala." *University of Queensland Law Journal* 33: 263–284.

Anthony, David W. 2007. *The Horse, the Wheel, and Language: How Bronze-Age Riders from the Eurasian Steppes Shaped the Modern World*. Princeton, NJ: Princeton University Press.

Applebaum, Anne. 2017. *Red Famine: Stalin's War on Ukraine*. London: Penguin.

Arnold, Scott. 1994. *The Philosophy and Economics of Market Socialism*. New York: Oxford University Press.

Beck, Valentin, ed. 2018. "Normative Aspects of International Trade Institutions." Special issue of *Moral Philosophy & Politics* 5 (2): 173–303.

Beckert, Jens. 2008. *Inherited Wealth*. Princeton, NJ: Princeton University Press.

Beito, David T. 2000. *From Mutual Aid to the Welfare State: Fraternal Societies and Social Services, 1890–1967*. Chapel Hill: The University of North Carolina Press.

Belfield, Chris, Richard Blundell, Jonathan Cribb, Andrew Hood, and Robert Joyce. 2017. "Two Decades of Income Inequality in Britain: The Role of Wages, Household Earnings and Redistribution." *Economica* 84 (334): 157–179. https://doi.org/10.1111/ecca.12220.

Brennan, Jason. 2014. *Why Not Capitalism?* 1st ed. New York: Routledge.

Brennan, Jason, and Peter Jaworski. 2015a. *Markets without Limits: Moral Virtues and Commercial Interests*. New York: Routledge.

Brennan, Jason, and Peter Martin Jaworski. 2015b. "Markets without Symbolic Limits." *Ethics* 125 (4): 1053–1077. https://doi.org/10.1086/680907.

de Bres, Helena. 2016. "Justice and International Trade." *Philosophy Compass* 11 (1): 570–579.
Brighouse, Harry. 2006. *On Education*. London: Routledge.
Brighouse, Harry, and Adam Swift. 2006. "Equality, Priority, and Positional Goods." *Ethics* 116: 471–497.
Brouwer, Huub, and Thomas Mulligan, eds. 2018. "On the Very Idea of a Just Wage." Special issue of *Erasmus Journal for Philosophy & Economics* 11 (2): 1–244.
Caney, Simon. 2018. "Climate Change." In *The Oxford Handbook of Distributive Justice*, edited by Serena Olsaretti, 664–688. New York: Oxford University Press.
Caplan, Bryan. 2018. *The Case against Education: Why the Education System Is a Waste of Time and Money*. Princeton, NJ: Princeton University Press.
Chang, Ha-Joon. 2010. *23 Things They Don't Tell You About Capitalism*. London: Penguin Books.
Christiano, Thomas. 2012. "Money in Politics." In *The Oxford Handbook of Political Philosophy*, edited by David Estlund, 241–257. New York: Oxford University Press.
Clavell, James. 1962/2006. *King Rat*. London: Hoddder & Stoughton.
Coase, Ronald. 1937. "The Nature of the Firm." *Economica* 4 (16): 386–405.
Cohen, G. A. 1989. "On the Currency of Egalitarian Justice." *Ethics* 99 (4): 906–944.
Cohen, G. A. 2008. *Rescuing Justice and Equality*. Cambridge, MA: Harvard University Press.
Cohen, G. A. 2009. *Why Not Socialism?* Princeton, NJ: Princeton University Press.
Cohen, Joshua. 2001. "Money, Politics, Political Equality." In *Fact and Value: Essays on Ethics and Metaphysics for Judith Jarvis Thomson*, edited by Alex Byrne, Robert Stalnaker, and Ralph Wedgwood, 47–80. Cambridge, MA: MIT Press.
Coffey, Diane, and Dean Spears. 2017 *Where India Goes: Abandoned Toilets, Stunted Development and the Costs of Caste*. New York: Harper Collins.
Conquest, Robert. 1987. *The Harvest of Sorrow: Soviet Collectivization and the Terror-Famine*. New York: Oxford University Press.
Cowen, Tyler. 2013. *Average Is Over: Powering America beyond the Age of the Great Stagnation*. 1st ed. New York: Dutton.
Cowen, Tyler. 2019. *Big Business: A Love Letter to an American Anti-Hero*. New York: St. Martin's Press.
Cudd, Ann E., and Nancy Holmstrom. 2011. *Capitalism, For and Against: A Feminist Debate*. Cambridge, UK: Cambridge University Press.
Deaton, Angus. 2013. *The Great Escape: Health, Wealth, and the Origins of Inequality*. Princeton, NJ: Princeton University Press.
Dehaene, Stanislas. 2011. *The Number Sense: How the Mind Creates Mathematics, Revised and Updated Edition*. New York: Oxford University Press.
Dietsch, Peter. 2015. *Catching Capital: The Ethics of Tax Competition*. New York: Oxford University Press.
Dolin, Eric Jay. 2007. *Leviathan—The History of Whaling in America*. New York: W. W. Norton & Company.
Dorfman, Avihay, and Alon Harel. 2013. "The Case Against Privatization." *Philosophy & Public Affairs* 41 (1): 67–102. https://doi.org/10.1111/papa.12007.
Dorfman, Avihay, and Alon Harel. 2016. "Against Privatisation as Such." *Oxford Journal of Legal Studies* 36 (2): 400–427. https://doi.org/10.1093/ojls/gqv029.
Durlauf, Steven N. 2012. "Complexity, Economics, and Public Policy." *Politics, Philosophy & Economics* 11 (1): 45–75. https://doi.org/10.1177/1470594X11434625.

Ellsberg, Daniel. 2017. *The Doomsday Machine: Confessions of a Nuclear War Planner*. New York: Bloomsbury.

Elster, Jon. 1985. *Making Sense of Marx*. Cambridge, UK: Cambridge University Press.

Ferguson, Adam. 1767. *An Essay on the History of Civil Society*. Cambridge Texts in the History of Political Thought. Cambridge: Cambridge University Press.

Fishkin, Joseph. 2014. *Bottlenecks: A New Theory of Equal Opportunity*. New York: Oxford University Press.

Flanigan, Jessica. 2017. *Pharmaceutical Freedom: Why Patients Have a Right to Self Medicate*. 1st ed. New York: Oxford University Press.

Fleischacker, Samuel. 2004. *On Adam Smith's Wealth of Nations: A Philosophical Companion*. Princeton, NJ: Princeton University Press.

Frank, Robert H. 2012. *The Darwin Economy: Liberty, Competition, and the Common Good*. Princeton, NJ: Princeton University Press.

Frank, Robert H., and Philip J. Cook. 2010. *The Winner-Take-All Society: Why the Few at the Top Get So Much More Than the Rest of Us*. New York: Random House.

Freeman, Samuel. 2001. "Illiberal Libertarians: Why Libertarianism Is Not a Liberal View." *Philosophy and Public Affairs*, April, 105–151.

Frega, Roberto, Lisa Herzog, and Christian Neuhäuser. 2019. "Workplace Democracy: The Recent Debate." *Philosophy Compass* 14 (4): e12574.

Freiman, Christopher. 2014. "Priority and Position." *Philosophical Studies* 167 (2): 341–360. https://doi.org/10.1007/s11098-013-0099-5.

Freiman, Christopher, and Adam Lerner. 2015. "Self-Ownership and Disgust: Why Compulsory Body Part Redistribution Gets Under Our Skin." *Philosophical Studies* 172 (12): 3167–3190.

Friedman, Milton. 2002. *Capitalism and Freedom: Fortieth Anniversary Edition*. Chicago: University of Chicago Press.

Fukuyama, Francis. 2011. *The Origins of Political Order: From Prehuman Times to the French Revolution*. London: Profile Books.

Galbraith, John Kenneth. 1998. *The Affluent Society*. New York: Houghton Mifflin Harcourt.

Gardiner, Stephen M. 2011. *A Perfect Moral Storm: The Ethical Tragedy of Climate Change*. New York: Oxford University Press.

Gheaus, Anca, and Lisa Herzog. "The Goods of Work (Other Than Money!)." *Journal of Social Philosophy* 47 (1): 70–89.

Ghods, Ahad J., and Shekoufeh Savaj. 2006. "Iranian Model of Paid and Regulated Living-Unrelated Kidney Donation." *Clinical Journal of the American Society of Nephrology* 1 (6): 1136–1145. https://doi.org/10.2215/CJN.00700206.

Goodin, Robert E. 1988. *Reasons for Welfare: The Political Theory of the Welfare State*. Princeton, NJ: Princeton University Press.

Guiltinan, Joseph. 2009. "Creative Destruction and Destructive Creations: Environmental Ethics and Planned Obsolescence." *Journal of Business Ethics* 89 (1): 19–28. https://doi.org/10.1007/s10551-008-9907-9.

Halliday, Daniel. 2016. "Private Education, Positional Goods, and the Arms Race Problem." *Politics, Philosophy & Economics* 15 (2): 150–169. https://doi.org/10.1177/1470594X15603717.

Halliday, Daniel. 2018. *The Inheritance of Wealth: Justice, Equality, and the Right to Bequeath*. New York: Oxford University Press.

Hart, Oliver, and John Moore. 1988. "Incomplete Contracts and Renegotiation." *Econometrica* 56 (4): 755–785. https://doi.org/10.2307/1912698.
Hart, Oliver, and John Moore.1990. "Property Rights and the Nature of the Firm." *Journal of Political Economy* 98 (6): 1119–1158. https://doi.org/10.1086/261729.
Hayek, F. A. 1940. "Socialist Calculation: The Competitive `Solution.'" *Economica* 7 (26): 125–149. https://doi.org/10.2307/2548692.
Hayek, F. A. 1945. "The Use of Knowledge in Society." *American Economic Review* 25 (4): 519–530.
Hayek, F. A. 1960a. *The Constitution of Liberty: The Definitive Edition*. Edited by Ronald Hamowy. Chicago: University of Chicago Press.
Hayek, F. A. 1960b. *The Constitution of Liberty*. Edited by Ronald Hamowy. Chicago: University of Chicago Press.
Heath, Joseph. 2010. *Economics Without Illusions: Debunking the Myths of Modern Capitalism*. 1st ed. New York: Crown Business.
Heilbroner, Robert. *The Worldly Philosophers: The Life, Times, and Ideas of the Great Economic Thinkers*. 7th ed. New York: Penguin Books.
Herzog, Lisa, ed. 2017. *Just Financial Markets? Finance in a Just Society*. New York: Oxford University Press.
Hidalgo, Javier. 2016. "Selling Citizenship: A Defence." *Journal of Applied Philosophy* 33 (3): 223–239. https://doi.org/10.1111/japp.12117.
Hirsch, Fred. 2005. *Social Limits to Growth*. London: Routledge.
Hirst, John. 2014. *Australian History in 7 Questions*. Melbourne: Black Inc.
Husak, Douglas N. 1992. *Drugs and Rights*. Cambridge, UK: Cambridge University Press.
Husak, Douglas N. 2002. *Legalize This!: The Case for Decriminalizing Drugs*. London: Verso.
Ismael, Jennan. 2016. *How Pysics Sets Us Free*. Oxford: Oxford University Press.
Jennings, Chris. 2016. *Paradise Now: The Story of American Utopianism*. New York: Random House.
Johnson, Steven. 2007. *Ghost Map*. Reprint edition. London: Riverhead Books.
Kekes, John. 1997. *Against Liberalism*. Ithaca, NY: Cornell University Press.
Keynes, John Maynard. 2015. "Economic Possibilities for Our Grandchildren." In *The Essential Keynes*, 75–86. London: Penguin.
Khader, Serene. 2014. "Empowerment Through Self-Subordination? Microcredit and Women's Agency." In *Poverty, Agency and Human Rights*, edited by Diana Meyers, 223–248. New York: Oxford University Press.
Kishtainy, Niall. 2017. *A Little History of Economics*. New Haven, CT: Yale University Press.
Klein, Naomi. 2014. *This Changes Everything: Capitalism vs. The Climate*. New York: Simon and Schuster.
Kolakowski, Leszek. 2008. *Main Currents of Marxism: The Founders—The Golden Age—The Breakdown*. Translated by P. S. Falla. 1st ed. New York: W. W. Norton & Company.
Leeson, Peter T. 2009. *The Invisible Hook: The Hidden Economics of Pirates*. Princeton, NJ: Princeton University Press.
Leget, Carlo, Pascal Borry, and Raymond De Vries. 2009. "'Nobody Tosses a Dwarf!' The Relation between the Empirical and the Normative Reexamined." *Bioethics* 23 (4): 226–235. https://doi.org/10.1111/j.1467-8519.2009.01711.x.
Levinson, Marc. 2016. *The Box: How the Shipping Container Made the World Smaller and the World Economy Bigger*. 2nd edition. Princeton, NJ: Princeton University Press.

Lichtenberg, Judith. 1996. "Consuming Because Others Consume." *Social Theory and Practice* 22 (3): 273–297.
Lie, John. 2000. *Han Unbound: The Political Economy of South Korea*. Stanford, CA: Stanford University Press.
Malthus, Thomas. 1992. *An Essay on the Principle of Population*. New York: Cambridge University Press.
Mandela, Nelson. 1956. "Freedom in Our Lifetime." *Liberation*.
Mandela, Nelson. 2013. *Long Walk To Freedom*. London: Hachette.
Mazzucato, Mariana. 2015. *The Entrepreneurial State: Debunking Public vs. Private Sector Myths*. Revised edition. New York: PublicAffairs.
McGee, Robert W. 1993. "If Dwarf Tossing Is Outlawed, Only Outlaws Will Toss Dwarfs: Is Dwarf Tossing a Victimless Crime." *American Journal of Jurisprudence* 38: 335–358.
Medema, Stephen, and Warrn Samuels. 2013. *The History of Economic Thought: A Reader*. 2nd ed. London: Routledge.
Meyer, Kirsten. 2014. *Education, Justice and the Human Good: Fairness and Equality in the Education System*. London: Routledge.
Miller, David. 2001. *Principles of Social Justice*. Cambridge, MA: Harvard University Press.
Moellendorf, Darrel. 2015. "Climate Change Justice." *Philosophy Compass* 10 (3): 173–186.
Montes, Leonidas. 2016. "Adam Smith: Self-Interest and The Virtues." In *Adam Smith: His Life, Thought and Legacy*, edited by Ryan Hanley, 138–156. Princeton, NJ: Princeton University Press.
Moriarty, Jeffrey. 2009. "How Much Compensation Can CEOs Permissibly Accept?" *Business Ethics Quarterly* 19 (2): 235–250. https://doi.org/10.5840/beq200919212.
Moriarty, Jeffrey. 2017. "Wanted: Positive Arguments for Markets." *Journal of Value Inquiry* 51 (4): 641–645.
Mulligan, Thomas. 2017. *Justice and the Meritocratic State*. 1st ed. New York: Routledge.
Munger, Michael. 2018. *Tomorrow 3.0: Transaction Costs and The Sharing Economy*. Cambridge: Cambridge University Press.
Murray, Charles. 2015. *Losing Ground: American Social Policy, 1950–1980*. New York: Basic Books.
Murray, Charles. 2016. *In Our Hands: A Plan to Replace the Welfare State*. Revised, updated ed. Washington, DC: Aei Press.
Naess, Arne. 1973. "The Shallow and the Deep, Long-Range Ecology Movement: A Summary." *Inquiry* 16 (1–4): 95–100. https://doi.org/10.1080/00201747308601682.
North, Douglass C., John Joseph Wallis, and Barry R. Weingast. 2009. *Violence and Social Orders: A Conceptual Framework for Interpreting Recorded Human History*. 1st ed. Cambridge, UK: Cambridge University Press.
Nozick, Robert. 1974. *Anarchy, State, and Utopia*. New York: Basic Books.
Nye, John V. C. 2007. *War, Wine, and Taxes: The Political Economy of Anglo-French Trade, 1689–1900*. Princeton, NJ: Princeton University Press.
Olson, Mancur. (1965) 1971. *The Logic of Collective Action*. Cambridge, MA: Harvard University Press.
O' Neill, Cathy. 2016. *Weapons of Math Destruction: How Big Data Increases Inequality and Threatens Democracy*. New York: Penguin Books.
O'Neill, Martin. 2012. *Property-Owning Democracy: Rawls and Beyond*. 1st ed. Malden, MA: Wiley-Blackwell.
Ostrom, Elinor. 1990. *Governing the Commons: The Evolution of Institutions for Collective Action*. New York: Cambridge University Press.

Otteson, James. 2014. *The End of Socialism*. 1st ed. New York: Cambridge University Press.
Packer, George. 2014. *The Unwinding: An Inner History of the New America*. Reprint ed. New York: Farrar, Straus and Giroux.
Page, Scott. 2011. *Diversity and Complexity*. Princeton, NJ: Princeton University Press.
Panné, Jean-Louis, Andrzej Paczkowski, Karel Bartosek, Jean-Louis Margolin, Nicolas Werth, and Stéphane Courtois. 1999. *The Black Book of Communism: Crimes, Terror, Repression*. Edited by Mark Kramer. Translated by Jonathan Murphy. Cambridge, MA: Harvard University Press.
Parijs, Philippe Van. 1998. *Real Freedom for All: What (If Anything) Can Justify Capitalism*. Oxford: Clarendon Press.
Parijs, Philippe van, Joshua Cohen, and Joel Rogers. 2001. *What's Wrong With a Free Lunch?* 1st ed. Boston: Beacon Press.
Pettit, Philip. 1999. *Republicanism: A Theory of Freedom and Government*. Oxford: Oxford University Press.
Piketty, Thomas. 2014. *Capital in the Twenty-First Century*. Cambridge, MA: Harvard University Press.
Posner, Eric A., and E. Glen Weyl. 2018. *Radical Markets: Uprooting Capitalism and Democracy for a Just Society*. Princeton, NJ: Princeton University Press.
Rawls, John. 1999. *A Theory of Justice*. Revised ed. Cmabridge, MA: Belknap Press.
Rawls, John. 2001. *Justice as Fairness: A Restatement*. Edited by Erin Kelly. Cambridge, MA: Harvard University Press.
Reich, Robert. 2016. *Saving Capitalism: For The Many, Not The Few*. New York: Knopf.
Robeyns, Ingrid. 2016. "Will a Basic Income Do Justice to Women?" *Analyse & Kritik* 23 (1): 88–105. https://doi.org/10.1515/auk-2001-0108.
Robbins, Lionel. 2000. *A History of Economic Thought: The LSE Lectures*. Princeton, NJ: Princeton University Press.
Roemer, John E. 1985. "Should Marxists Be Interested in Exploitation?" *Philosophy & Public Affairs* 14 (1): 30–65.
Ronzoni, Miriam. 2012. "Life Is Not a Camping Trip—On the Desirability of Cohenite Socialism." *Politics, Philosophy & Economics* 11 (2): 171–185. https://doi.org/10.1177/1470594X11417239.
Rose, Julie L. 2014. "Money Does Not Guarantee Time: Discretionary Time as a Distinct Object of Distributive Justice." *Journal of Political Philosophy* 22 (4): 438–457. https://doi.org/10.1111/jopp.12021.
Rose, Julie L. 2016. *Free Time*. Princeton, NJ: Princeton University Press.
Rosen, Michael. 2012. *Dignity: Its History and Meaning*. Cambridge, MA: Harvard University Press.
Roser, Max. 2020. "Economic Growth." Published online at OurWorldInData.org. Retrieved from: https://ourworldindata.org/economic-growth.
Sample, Ruth J. 2003. *Exploitation: What It Is and Why It's Wrong*. Lanham, MD: Rowman & Littlefield.
Satz, Debra. 2010. *Why Some Things Should Not Be for Sale: The Moral Limits of Markets*. New York: Oxford University Press.
Schemmel, Christian. 2015. "How (Not) to Criticise the Welfare State." *Journal of Applied Philosophy* 32 (4): 393–409. https://doi.org/10.1111/japp.12131.
Schmidtz, David. 1991. *The Limits of Government: An Essay on the Public Goods Argument*. Boulder, CO: Westview.
Schmidtz, David. 1997. "When Preservationism Doesn't Preserve." *Environmental Values* 6 (3): 327–339. https://doi.org/10.3197/096327197776679103.

Schmidtz, David. 2002. "How to Deserve." *Political Theory*, December, 774–799.

Schmidtz, David, and Robert E. Goodin. 1998. *Social Welfare and Individual Responsibility*. Cambridge, UK: Cambridge University Press.

Schmidtz, David, and Elizabeth Willott, eds. 2011. *Environmental Ethics: What Really Matters, What Really Works*. 2nd ed. Oxford: Oxford University Press.

Schor, Juliet B. 2014. *Born to Buy: The Commercialized Child and the New Consumer Cult*. New York: Simon and Schuster.

Schumpeter, Joseph. 1994. *Capitalism, Socialism and Democracy*. 5th rev. ed. London: Routledge.

Sher, George. 1989. *Desert*. Princeton, NJ: Princeton University Press.

Skyrms, Brian. 2010. *Signals: Evolution, Learning, and Information*. New York: Oxford University Press.

Slezkine, Yuri. 2017. *The House of Government: A Saga of the Russian Revolution*. 1st ed. Princeton, NJ: Princeton University Press.

Smith, Adam. 1976. *The Theory of Moral Sentiments*. The Glasgow Edition of the Works and Correspondence of Adam Smith. Indianapolis: Liberty Fund Inc.

Smith, Adam. 1982. *An Inquiry into the Nature and Causes of the Wealth of Nations*. The Glasgow Edition of the Works & Correspondence of Adam Smith. Indianapolis: Liberty Fund.

Sutch, Richard. 2017. "The One Percent across Two Centuries: A Replication of Thomas Piketty's Data on the Concentration of Wealth in the United States." *Social Science History* 41 (4): 587–613.

Swift, Adam. 2003. *How Not to Be a Hypocrite: School Choice for the Morally Perplexed Parent*. New York: Psychology Press.

Taylor, Robert S. 2013. "Market Freedom as Antipower." *American Political Science Review* 107 (3): 593–602. https://doi.org/10.1017/S0003055413000300.

Taylor, Robert S. 2017. *Exit Left: Markets and Mobility in Republican Thought*. New York: Oxford University Press.

Thrasher, John. 2018a. "Evaluating Bad Norms." *Social Philosophy & Policy* 35 (1): 196–216.

Thrasher, John. 2018b. "When Equality Matters." In *The Palgrave Handbook of Philosophy and Public Policy*, edited by David Boonin, 409–420. Cham, Switzerland: Palgrave Macmillan.

Thrasher, John, and Keith Hankins. 2015. "When Justice Demands Inequality." *Journal of Moral Philosophy* 12 (2): 172–194.

Tomasi, John. 2012. *Free Market Fairness*. Princeton, NJ: Princeton University Press.

Van Der Vossen, Bas, and Jason Brennan. 2018. *In Defense of Openness: Why Global Freedom is the Humane Solution to Global Poverty*. Oxford: Oxford University Press.

Vallier, Kevin. 2015. "A Moral and Economic Critique of the New Property-Owning Democrats: On Behalf of a Rawlsian Welfare State." *Philosophical Studies* 172 (2): 283–304. https://doi.org/10.1007/s11098-014-0303-2.

Veblen, Thorstein. 1965. *The Theory of the Leisure Class*. London: Penguin.

Veltman, Andrea. 2016. *Meaningful Work*. New York: Oxford University Press.

Weitzman, Susan. 2008. *Not To People Like Us: Hidden Abuse In Upscale Marriages*. New York: Basic Books.

Wertheimer, Alan. 1999. *Exploitation*. Princeton, NJ: Princeton University Press.

White, Michelle J. 2004. "The 'Arms Race' on American Roads: The Effect of Sport Utility Vehicles and Pickup Trucks on Traffic Safety." *The Journal of Law and Economics* 47 (2): 333–355. https://doi.org/10.1086/422979.

Williamson, Oliver E. 1983. *Markets and Hierarchies: Analysis and Antitrust Implications: A Study in the Economics of Internal Organization*. New York: Free Press.

Williamson, Oliver E. 1985. *The Economic Institutions of Capitalism*. New York: Simon and Schuster.

Wolff, Jonathan. 1998. "Fairness, Respect, and the Egalitarian Ethos." *Philosophy & Public Affairs* 27 (2): 97–122. https://doi.org/10.1111/j.1088-4963.1998.tb00063.x.

Wolff, Jonathan. 2003. *Why Read Marx Today?* New York: Oxford University Press.

Wollner, Gabriel. and Matthias Wisse. 2019. *On Trade Justice: A Philosophical Plea for a New Global Deal*. New York: Oxford University Press.

Zwolinski, Matt. 2008. "The Ethics of Price Gouging." *Business Ethics Quarterly* 18 (3): 347–378. https://doi.org/10.5840/beq200818327.

Zwolinski, Matt. 2011. "Classical Liberalism and the Basic Income." *Basic Income Studies* 6 (2): 1–14.

Zwolinski, Matt. 2015. "Property Rights, Coercion, and the Welfare State: The Libertarian Case for a Basic Income for All." *The Independent Review* 19 (4): 515–529.

# Index

Figures are indicated by *f* following the page number

*For the benefit of digital users, indexed terms that span two pages (e.g., 52–53) may, on occasion, appear on only one of those pages.*

Lightning Source UK Ltd.
Milton Keynes UK
UKHW011601120521
383160UK00010B/197